ARYANS, JEWS, BRAHMINS

Theorizing Authority through Myths of Identity

DOROTHY M. FIGUEIRA

STATE UNIVERSITY OF NEW YORK PRESS

Published by
State University of New York Press, Albany

For information, address State University of New York Press,
90 State Street, Suite 700, Albany, NY 12207

Production by Marilyn P. Semerad
Marketing by Michael Campochiaro

Library of Congress Cataloging-in-Publication Data

Figueira, Dorothy Matilda, 1955–
    Aryans, Jews, Brahmins : theorizing authority through myths of identity /
Dorothy M. Figueira.
    p. cm — (SUNY series, the margins of literature)
    Includes bibliographical references and index.
    ISBN 0–7914–5531–9 (HC : alk. paper) — ISBN 0–7914–5532–7
(pbk. : alk. paper)
    1. Indo-Aryans. 2. India—Civilization. 3. Vedic literature–History
and criticism 4. Racism—Europe—History—19th century.
    5. Antisemiticism. I. Title. II. Series

    DS425 .F57 2002
    934—dc21
                                                                2002024176
                    10 9 8 7 6 5 4 3 2 1

I dedicate this volume to my daughter, Lila,
and in loving memory of my mother, Marion Gentile Figueira

Contents

Acknowledgments

I am grateful to several organizations without whose funding this volume would not have been possible. I thank the American Institute for Indian Studies for a Senior Research grant to Poona in 1992–1993. I am also grateful to the Fulbright Foundation as well as the National Endowment for the Humanities. I also thank the Center for Advanced Studies of the University of Illinois for their support. Material adapted from "Aryan Aristocrats and Übermenschen: Nietzsche's Reading of the *Laws of Manu*," which appeared in *The Comparatist* 23 (May 1999): 5-20, is reprinted by permission of John Burt Foster Jr., editor.

The Westerner who returns to India no longer recognizes his cradle. I am well aware that these Hindus are Aryans of our stock, our brothers; but we are brothers who refuse to reach out in one another's direction. We are too different. Too many millennia divide us. We said farewell to one another too long ago.
      —G. Gozzano, *Journey to the Cradle of Mankind*

Anything can be believed if one cites the authority of the Veda, if one takes some passage from the Veda, juggles it, gives it the most impossible meaning and murders everything reasonable in it. If one presents one's own ideas as ideas meant in the Vedas, "all fools will follow me in a crowd."
      —Swami Vivekananda, *The Complete Works of Swami Vivekananda*

Introduction

SHARED MYTHS

The present is fractured; it consists of competing pasts. By positing the past as a special case of the present, one not only remakes the present, but creates a new past and redefines identity (as kin, race, family) through an act of memory. The past thus possesses sociopolitical instrumentality when perceptions of "history" are made relevant to the present. Conflicts concerning the past are, in fact, struggles suggesting the proper shape the present should take. In such instances, history may be elevated to myth, when the needs of the present are read into the past and an image of the past is imposed on the present. History, once transformed into myth, becomes an instrument to construct social forms. It shapes the present through an evocation of the past and specific groups that inhabit it.

In this volume, I will examine how the Aryan past can be studied as a myth or a form of discourse that can be employed in the construction or the deconstruction of society. In particular, this examination focuses on the discourse concerning the Aryan race as a "shared myth" (Thapar 1992: 71) in nineteenth-century India and in Germany and as a reification of ancient textual sources in service of social practice. The Aryan myth has given historical value to ancient Indian history and has contributed to Indian nationalism during the colonial period and after the departure of the British. Myths concerning the Aryan race also served the ideological interests of Europe. The history of India could be appropriated as a means of expressing nineteenth-century European concerns with origins.

THE ARYAN CANON

Since the Aryan arrival in India is associated with the compilation of the *Rig Veda*, we will focus on how the construction of Aryan racial identity developed through a continued rearticulation of the authority vested in "Vedic" texts. For Indians and Westerners alike, the Veda functioned as the touchstone for Hindu orthodoxy as well as for their understanding of the Aryan. It served as a point of reference to be regarded as absolutely authoritative. Yet it provided a rather peculiar canon: open yet unerring, complete yet subject to reinterpretation. It posed multiple problems from a hermeneutical point of view.

In India, while the Vedas are revered and recognized as omniscient, the texts themselves were weakened, altered, or even lost (Renou 1965: 1). Although traditional Hinduism accedes to the infallibility and authority of the Vedas, their importance in practice was textually and historically limited (Llewellyn 1993: 95). Before the nineteenth century, they were not used beyond their ritual status as a practical guide.[1] The Vedas were invoked, rather than laboriously analyzed as communicative texts. In Europe, different hermeneutic issues presented themselves, since the Veda engendered critical discussion in the form of spurious fragments, misattributions, and forgery (Figueira 1994: 201). When we speak of the reception of the Veda in pre-nineteenth-century Europe and India, we are referring to either an absent or a falsely present text. In critical terms, the Veda functioned as an aporia. It also served as a metaphor since the Vedic tradition was often culled from texts that were not strictly "Vedic," but "Vedāntic"[2] or even later.[3] Various Sanskrit texts function therefore as mediators of knowledge between the Aryan and its Other. On the level of history, they recount truth. On the level of the text's own production, the reader mediates this truth through idiosyncratic readings and authoritative definitions of what was considered "Vedic."

As the textual reference in the formation of an ideology regarding the Aryan, the Veda also posed problems on the level of canonicity. In what manner was the Veda used to legitimize assertions of faith or law? What were accepted procedures for interpreting the Veda as a canonical text? How did it change over time and place? Was there ever an accepted interpreter whose exegesis was seen as binding (even before it was read)? To what extent did the Veda's reception characterize the situation where "the Devil can quote Scripture to his need?" A canonical literature arises through the consensus of a group elite and normally serves to stabilize that group. It lends value to the interests and products of that group. A fictive Veda or the fiction of the Veda was used to this effect in both the East and the West. In this manner, the Vedic canon could change to meet one challenge after another.

METHODOLOGY AND PLAN

This study has a twofold aim, as a contribution to the theory and methodology of literary analysis and as an illustration of the historical reconstruction of myth. It attempts to retrieve fictions of the Aryan past through a consideration of rhetorical conventions and an awareness of the interaction between literary texts and other nonliterary and subliterary discourses. Because the Aryan myths described in this study originated in the literary reception of surviving

"Vedic" texts, particular significance is attached to textual exegesis. The modern reader's task consists of restoring both the linguistic and the extralinguistic context.[4] It is necessary to understand the cultural milieu and genre of the work itself as well as those conventions being echoed, since both European and Indian authors attempted to subvert tradition.

This study does not focus on the linguistic, ethnographic, archaeological, and physical anthropological literature dealing with the identity and migrations of the Aryan. Rather, I examine various European and Indian thinkers who built an ideology of the Aryan out of readings of "Aryan" texts. Adopting the general systems thinking of comparative literature,[5] rather than the expertise of the area specialist,[6] I focus on how myths of identity can be tied to textualities. This cross-cultural comparison involves critical choices.[7]

The foundations of my methodology have their roots in anthropology. For my interpretation of myth, I draw from the Mauss/Durkheim legacy wherein society is viewed as constituted from sentiments of affinity (affection, solidarity, mutual attachment) and estrangement (alienation and detachment). I am indebted to Cassirer's analysis of myth as a political tool constructed to confront or abet the overriding influences of the occult or irrationalism. I am also influenced by Malinowski's view of myth as a form of social charter, Eliade's understanding of myth as a true narrative, and Barthes' sense of myth as a second order semiotic system, a metalanguage of preexisting signs that can be appropriated, stripped of their original context, and infused with a new content. Finally, I borrow from Bruce Lincoln, who, drawing upon Geertz, interprets myth as discourse functioning either to preserve social stability or to deconstruct order and reconstruct society according to a novel pattern (Lincoln 1989).

My working definition of myth, therefore, is a composite of several approaches: Myth functions as a narrative which possesses credibility and authority and whose charters are manipulated to elicit sentiments which, in turn, construct social formations or legitimize changed social and political conditions. A myth can be restructured to activate "latent" symbolic meanings that play upon the sentiments of affinity to effect political reform. As Romila Thapar maintains, myth functions as the self-image of a given culture, the medium through which its social assumptions are expressed (Thapar 1992: 140). Following Thapar, I view the Aryan myth as a myth of descent, a narrative that can both serve to integrate diverse groups by providing common origins as well as be used for the reverse process of distinguishing one group from the other (Thapar 1992: 142). By positing an authoritative beginning, a myth of descent uses the past to explain the present.

Inasmuch as this study examines myths of identity, it also deals with the writing of history. History as opposed to myth is shaped by the system in which it is developed. As a combination of a social place, "scientific" practices, and writing, the historical operation takes limited evidence and seeks to unify it into coherence. I am indebted to Michel de Certeau's understanding of history as a staging of the past (Certeau 1988: 9): Historians translate ("carry over") elements of the past embedded in present-day consciousness and repackage them to figure in their own interpretative system. The historian thus creates a heterology or a discourse of the Other, wherein strategies are employed to convert alterity into something assimilable to the prevailing configuration of knowledge.

In any selection of materials, shards or remainders are created. What disappears from the product appears in the production, not so much the personal intentions, but the sociocultural localizations that inspire the foci of research. Historiography then becomes the treatment of absence. Certeau's concept of the heterology structures this investigation. The various myths of the Aryan that we will encounter all address concerns central to the heterological process: assimiliation, authorial control, and absence. The Aryan as a mythic construct only exists in relation to its non-Aryan Other. We will see how in each seductive representation of the Aryan an unassimilable residue escapes interpretive control in order to return and upset organizations of meaning. The Aryan and its Other appear as phantasmal projections, rather than as effectively "real" populations. This volume examines the manner in which the past, or competing pasts, were constructed, changed status, and claimed historical value.

Part I begins with an examination of the Aryan myth's formation and activation in Western Orientalist scholarship through the construction of the Vedic Golden Age. I then juxtapose this initial Western depiction of the Aryan that was grounded in the reception of the Veda with that of the Enlightenment nonspecialist. I next examine the Western myth of the Aryan race and the Vedic Golden Age in the work of European Romantic mythographers. As an extension of the Romantic emplotment, I turn to the work of Friedrich Max Müller, the first Western "reader" for whom the Veda was a present document and the Aryans actual literary subjects. The remaining chapters in part I focus on the myth of the Aryan in European nineteenth-century race theory. The work of Gobineau and Nietzsche and their theories of social evolution provided an important link to the later nationalist emplotment of the Aryan in Chamberlain and Rosenberg.

Part II examines the Indian myths of the Aryan, beginning with Rammohan Roy's rejection of the exclusivity of Sanskrit and his reliance on the vernacular in his interpretation of the Upanishads. Dayānand Saraswatī worked from the authority of the Veda as a present text. In chapter 6, I examine his iconoclastic interpretation of the *Rig Veda* and the fiction of the Aryan that was formulated in his readings, commentaries, and debates. The time frame of part II encompasses the period during the solidification of British colonial rule, when Indian elites became concerned with the threat from above as well as from below. The desire for change, whether along lines of modernization or tradition, was motivated by the desire not to lose one's position in the hierarchy. Thus, the Aryan myth enabled privileged segments of society to revitalize Hindu traditions by positing them as canonically centered and appropriating them in the name of modernization, whether liberal or not. Finally, I examine how low-caste social reformers such as Jotirao Phule and B.D. Ambedkar subverted the nationalist script by overturning the hierarchic relations encoded within Indian society. Through counter-hegemonic/taxonomic inversion, they sought alternative models wherein subordinates and marginals under the present order agitated for the deconstruction of that order and the reconstruction of a novel pattern. Such reform relied upon this disruptive discourse gaining a wide audience and propagation. It also relied upon the domination of sentiments of estrangement over those of affinity. In the contest for political power between caste and non-caste groups, emphasis was thus placed on cultural separateness of the Aryan and the non-Aryan. Such reformers sought to sharpen separation, with each group searching for divergent roots.[8]

Initially, I limit my analysis to the myth of the Aryan as it was constructed from readings of a "Veda." Presented consistently as the central sacred book, the various "Vedas" offer the reader a literary rather than historical construct of a single Hindu community that implies multiple imagined communities based on various identities (Thapar 1992: 84–85). I must stress, again, that this analysis differs from earlier examinations of the Aryan myth in that it is uniquely tied to the textual construction of race. Chapters 1 and 2 deal with the Western discourse on the Aryan predating the appearance of the *Rig Veda* in edited form, when an ideology regarding the Aryan was imposed upon absent or falsely present texts. Of necessity, this reception was not text-specific. Chapters 5 and 6, dealing primarily with the Indian strategies of reading reconstructed "Vedas," are exegetical and address issues of textuality. The remaining chapters examine a curious situation in which the Vedic text, although present and available, recedes from its reader's grasp. These readings are more evocations than models of reception. The "Vedic" text all but disappears or surfaces as an optical illusion. Beyond the mirage of the text, all that remains are the aspirations of readers who feel themselves marginalized under existing social structures. Their evocation of an Aryan canon, their call to the authority of an "Aryan" text, becomes the means whereby they confront their sense of estrangement and assert a reified Self. Whether the text is present, absent, or symbolic, these readings are no less "textual." Each use of a "Veda" to construct an Aryan identity is concerned with key literary issues of reading, canonicity, textual accessibility, hermeneutic strategies of reading, and ideal readers. The reception of the Veda in India and Europe is ultimately grounded in a discourse of readership and, as such, suggests the broader theoretical concerns of textually-bound identities and hegemonic textualities.

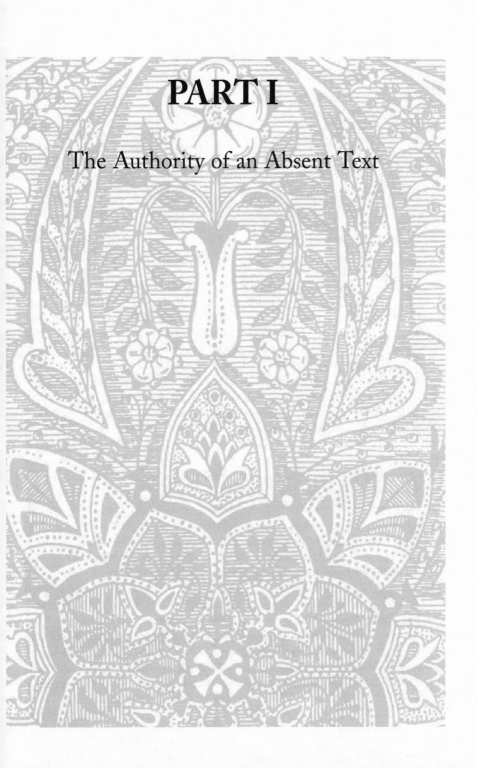

PART I

The Authority of an Absent Text

CHAPTER 1

The Enlightenment and Orientalist
Discourse on the Aryan

THE ENLIGHTENMENT BACKGROUND

Orientalist and postcolonialist criticism has positioned the origin of much that it seeks to critique within the Enlightenment project. Edward Said identified the Enlightenment as a unified trajectory and master sign of both Orientalism and colonialism (Said 1978). Ashis Nandy traced the roots of colonialism's mandate to absolutize the relative differences between cultures to the cultural arrogance of Enlightenment Europe. Partha Chatterjee problematized Enlightenment historiography (Chatterjee 1986). Peter van der Veer has blamed Enlightenment discourse for the erroneous politicization of Hinduism (Van der Veer 1998). Curiously, none of their arguments dwells on specifics—a common methodological flaw of critical schools which measure past texts against contemporary claims of emancipation or fantasies of dissent (Fluck 1996: 228). In these instances, critics assess the Enlightenment in light of the subsequent colonial experience. Their critical canon virtually ignores the fundamental texts of the period. Indeed, the Enlightenment has suffered much at the hands of poststructuralism's vague and atextual treatment. There is clearly a need for a reappraisal of the Enlightenment with reference to its literature.

In satirical works of the eighteenth century, there appeared a general theme, barely hidden under the fiction and in the satire itself: Asia can and should offer lessons. The pittoresque Oriental tale provided an ideal medium through which authors could expose the vices of their own corrupt civil and religious institutions. The satirist's task had been made that much easier, since travel accounts minutely described the religious and secular institutions of Asia and marked analogies to European systems of rule. Somewhat bemused, the voyagers drew comparisons between Christian and Asian mores. They noted in detail the various resemblances and their far-seeing readers were spurred on to draw further comparisons. In Diderot, Raynal, and Helvétius, for example, the strategy consisted of distancing readers from their normal surroundings in order to make them understand dangerous truths. Incessantly, Helvétius protested that his critique was aimed at the Orient and not at France, but the context of his discussion clearly pointed to misery found in a France stifling under the yoke of oppression.

In contradistinction to the voyagers' descriptions, the Jesuits had formulated a portrait of an Asia noteworthy for its enlightened customs and institutions. They represented the Chinese as philosophers of subtle wisdom, a marvelously civilized people who were ruled by a paternal government. They obeyed pious and tolerant magistrates who governed with admirably just laws. These Jesuitical observations were, in turn, appropriated by the *philosophes*, who were not adverse to borrowing their teachers' arguments to attack the Church. The Jesuitical emplotment of an enlightened Asia allowed the *philosophes* to question the principle of revealed religion.

For philosophers lost in the century of Louis XV, where visions of utopia collided daily with the contradictions of reality, the fiction of exotic "pure" religions proved captivating. Hindu or Confucian tolerance could be contrasted to the relentlessness of a Church suppressing liberty and to the sad spectacle of European religious disputes. One discovers, therefore, in the Enlightenment emplotment of the Orient, a subtle rhetorical strategy: Asia is portrayed as the victim of prejudice and superstition as well as the domain of reason and virtue. In its former role, it engendered political discussions and emphasized secularized history. In its latter use, the Enlightenment depiction of Asia helped define the disciplinary parameters of the history of religions. The comparisons of religious dogmas resulted in paradigms for practical analyses, most notably a form of biblical exegesis and a criticism of religious superstitions.

In this manner, Montesquieu's *Esprit des lois* (1748) presented, for the first time in European literature, an examination of India with the purpose of illuminating universal history. Asia offered Montesquieu a vision of diversity which was unavailable in the classics or in European cultural attitudes. In an important respect, Montesquieu's understanding of Asia contributed to the work's originality. He showed that although nature was the same all over, climates differed and affected human behavior. Data culled from Asia enabled Montesquieu to develop this theory in book 17 of the *Esprit des lois*. Montesquieu's provocative conclusions directly inspired Voltaire's *Essai sur les moeurs* (1756–78). Voltaire adopted Montesquieu's theory of climates, which in turn legitimized the objective comparison of different social institutions.

Although Montesquieu and Voltaire herald the beginning of the scientific or philosophical reception of Asia, the didactic model still informed their work.

VOLTAIRE AND THE SEARCH FOR AUTHORITY

The Aryan Rewrites History

For Voltaire, Asia was the ideal. In fact, in the eighteenth century, Voltaire was a principle panegyrist and official defender of Asia's moral rectitude. It held the key to understanding the European present as well as its future. At first, Voltaire directed his enthusiasm toward China. But its radical foreignness and the indecipherability of its literature stymied his efforts. He then turned his attention toward India, consoling himself with the belief that Indian religion was "very possibly" the same as that of the Chinese government, that is, a pure cult of a Supreme Being disengaged from all superstition and fanaticism (Voltaire 1885: 11.190). He maintained that the brahmin religion was even more ancient than that of China (Voltaire 1885: 28.136). The Indians were, perhaps, the most ancient assembled body of people. It appeared that other nations, such as China and Egypt, went to India for instruction (Voltaire 1885: 11.49). The brahmins were the first theologians in the world (Voltaire 1885: 29.488), and Indian religion formed the basis of all other religions (Voltaire 1885: 45.448). Voltaire believed that Indian philosophers had discovered a new universe "en morale et en physique" (Voltaire 1963: 2.318).

With time and with a more complete documentation, Voltaire became better informed and refined his characterization of ancient India. As inventors of art, the Aryans were chaste, temperate, and law-abiding (Voltaire 1963: 1.65). They lived in a state of paradise—naked and without luxury. They subsisted on fruit rather than cadavers. Paragons of morality and specimens of physical perfection, the Aryans embodied prelapsarian innocence and sobriety. Their gentleness, respect for animal life, and deep religiosity incarnated the virtues of "Christianity" far more than anything found in the civilized West. Unlike the Saracens, Tartars, Arabs, and the Jews, who lived by piracy, the Aryans found nourishment in a religion (Voltaire 1963: 1.229, 231; 1.60; 1.234) that was based upon universal reason (Voltaire 1963: 1.237).

While Voltaire had initially based his information on the travel accounts of Chardin, Tavernier, and Bernier (Voltaire 1953–65: D 2698), he later came to rely heavily on the Lettres édifiantes et curieuses . . . par quelques missions de la compagnie de Jésus (Paris: 1706–76), especially the letters from Père Bouchet to Huet. As elsewhere in his oeuvre, even in his most virulent cri-

tiques of the Church, Voltaire was never truly distant from his Jesuit teachers. Jesuitical documentation on India supplied him with a theme he was to
exploit with verve. Although the reverend fathers expressed horror for idolatrous superstition, they were not totally negative in their assessment of
Indian religious potential. Jesuit missionaries judged the Indians eminently
capable and worthy of conversion. After all, one could find in their "ridicu-
lous" religion belief in a single God (Voltaire 1953-65: 11.190; 11.54), suggesting a kind of proto-Christianity. Bouchet's mention of parallels between
Aryan religious thought and Christianity prompted Voltaire to develop the
idea that the West had derived its theology from India.

In short, Voltaire appropriated from the Jesuits data to suit a specific
polemic—that Vedism comprised the oldest religion known to man and represented a pure form of worship whose loftly metaphysics formed the basis of
Christianity. Voltaire found no difficulty in reconciling the sublimity of
Indian religion with its modern superstitions: the Vedic Indian had simply
been made soft by the climate (Voltaire 1963: 1.235–37). The climate's effect
was so pernicious that India's conquerors even became weak under its influence (Voltaire 1885: 13.158). Thus, human frailty (Voltaire 1963: 2.325) and
nature (Voltaire 1963: 1.61) conspired to render man idolatrous.

By disengaging a fictive *Urform* of Hinduism from all superstition and
fanaticism, Voltaire effectively set up an ideal against which all other religions could be measured to their disadvantage. What religion could compete
with that of the initial brahmins, who had established a government and religion based upon universal reason? When you have peaceful prelates, ruling
an innately spiritual people, religion is simple and reasonable. More importantly, India was to supply Voltaire with information to combat the Church
and its role in society. As a culture ignored by the Bible, India allowed
Voltaire to question the accepted biblical chronology. Most significantly,
however, Voltaire's discussion of India enabled him to vent his spleen against
the Jews. In other words, Voltaire's emplotment of India concentrated on
four problems: it allowed him to call into question the chronology of the
sacred book, the chosen status of the Jews, the origin of the Judeo-Christian
tradition, and the diffusion of our mythology, all of which challenged the
historical importance of the Jewish people (Hawley 1974: 139–40).

Voltaire's [H]anskrit Canon

One can almost forgive Voltaire his subjective portrayal of India, given
the quality of the information culled from travel accounts, missionary letters,
"scholarly" works, and "translations." Although he sought out European
accounts that he felt were exempt from sectarian prejudice, he was inexorably
drawn to texts glaringly slanted by Protestant anti-Catholic rhetoric, as in

the case of La Croze and Niecamp. He studied those Europeans who purported to know Sanskrit, yet knew none. He studied authors who, although
they had spent sufficient time in India, were nevertheless woefully ignorant
of the culture. Having literally read everything available concerning India,
edited and unedited, Voltaire realized only too well the necessity of basing
any future discussion of India upon an authentic Sanskrit text. He, therefore,
set out to discover one. After having depended so long on secondary sources,
he tended to ascribe authenticity to any Sanskrit text that fell into his hands.
Time and again, he was deceived by his sources.

As the oldest theologians, Indians were the first people to possess books
(Voltaire 1885: 26.325–6). One such book was the *Shaster Bedang*, a supposedly four-thousand-year-old exposition of the doctrine of the "Bedas" written
by the philosopher Beass Muni. It was found in Alexander Dow's *History of
Hindostan translated from the Persian to which are prefixed two dissertations concerning the Hindoos* (1768, French translation in 1769).[1]Voltaire believed that
the *Bedang* taught Vedic monotheism. Voltaire was also familiar with
another purportedly ancient and sacred book, the *Shasta* or *Shastabad of
Brahma*. Voltaire maintained that the *Shasta* was five thousand years old,
probably the oldest book in the world (Voltaire 1885: 15.326) and the source
for subsequent law books (Voltaire 1885: 28.138).[2]It possessed real wisdom
and the pure original expression of Indian religion. The *Shasta* was actually a
small "theological" treatise of recent date that had been transmitted to John
Zephaniah Holwell, who included it in his *Interesting historical events relative
to the Provinces of Bengal and the Empire of Indostan* (1765–71). However,
Voltaire read its existence to prove that the brahmins had preceeded by several centuries the Chinese, whom Voltaire initially thought had preceeded
the whole world in wisdom. The *Shasta*'s importance for Voltaire, therefore,
was not so much that it was the oldest book but that its style prefigured, in
his estimation, all wisdom, including that of Greece.[3] The *Shasta* proved to
Voltaire that the Indians were monotheists (Voltaire 1885: 29.167). More
importantly, however, it showed that the Chinese and the West borrowed
from India both their vision of God (Voltaire 1885: 29.210–11) and their
myth of the Fall of Man (Voltaire 1885: 26.326; 28.138; 29.472–73).

Voltaire also discovered a manuscript, entitled the *Cormo Vedam*, that
he described as a résumé of opinions and rites contained in the Veda
(Voltaire 1885: 11.52). Voltaire did not believe the *Cormo Vedam* to be a text
worthy of the modern brahmins. He judged it a ludicrous ritual "pile" of
superstitions (Voltaire 1963: 1.242–43). Voltaire cited the *Cormo Vedam* primarily to show how the Veda and brahmins had degenerated. Traces of such
decay were particularly prevalent in Voltaire's primary document of Aryan
religion, the *Ezour Vedam*. In Voltaire's estimation, the *Ezour Vedam* was the

most important Hanskrit [sic] text that he possessed.[4] He claimed that its composition predated Alexander's expedition to India (Voltaire 1885: 41.12, 367, 464; 45.448). Voltaire received the manuscript of the *Ezour Vedam* from the Comte de Maudave (1725–77) who had brought it to France. The count was purportedly a close friend of a francophone brahmin (Voltaire 1885: 45.170; 46.117) who had tried to translate the manuscript from Sanskrit into French (Voltaire 1885: 47.72). Voltaire alternately defined the *Ezour Vedam* as the beginning of the Veda (Voltaire 1885: 26.325–26) or "a copy of the four vedams" (Voltaire 1885: 26.392). In *La Défense de mon oncle*, he characterized it as "the true vedam, the vedam explained, the pure vedam." By 1761, however, he described it as merely a commentary of the Veda.

In reality, it did not matter to Voltaire that this text was not really the Veda; what mattered was that it satisfied the idea of a Veda which, for Voltaire, represented an exemplum of sublimity and the scripture of the world's oldest religion. The *Ezour Vedam* became such a text: it was the authentic text par excellance (Voltaire 1885: 41.464), the real *Urtext*, anterior to Pythagorus and anterior to the *Shasta* (Voltaire 1885: 19.58).[5] Not only did Voltaire value it but, at the Bibliothèque du Roi where he had deposited a copy (Voltaire 1885: 47.72), he claimed that it was regarded as the most precious acquisition of the collection (Voltaire 1885: 45.464). This "Veda" announced a pure cult, disengaged from all superstition and all fanaticism (Voltaire 1963: 1.236). Written by the first brahmins, who also served as kings and pontiffs, it established a religion based upon universal reason.

More importantly, the *Ezour Vedam* provided Voltaire with the ideal text with which to challenge the historical perspective of Judeo-Christianity. Voltaire read the *Ezour Vedam* to show how the vaunted aspects of the Judeo-Christian tradition existed in India centuries before the Old Testament. The general thrust of this argument was to displace the Jews from a favored position in the Christian tradition. Vedic India represented a more distant antiquity than that of the Jews (Voltaire 1885: 17.55–56). Or, as Voltaire allowed his Indian narrator to articulate his message:

We are a great people who settled around the Indus and the Ganges several centuries before the Hebraic horde transported itself to the banks of the Jordan. The Egyptians, Persians and Arabs came to our country in search of wisdom and spices, when the Jews were unknown to the rest of mankind. We could not have taken our Adimo from their Adam. (Voltaire 1885: 17.55)[6]

The *Ezour Vedam* harkens back to a time before brahmins and their cult had degenerated. The religion existing in modern India had obscured sage Vedic theology, marketed superstition, and profited modern brahmins (Voltaire 1963: 2.405–6). The *Ezour Vedam*, however, combated the growth of idolatry and the very superstitions that eventually destroyed Aryan religion (Voltaire 1885: 26.392). For his part, Voltaire hoped to prove how all the principles of Christian theology that had been lost with the Veda could still be found in the *Ezour Vedam* (Voltaire 1963: 1.240–42), thanks to its retrieval and circulation by a French *philosophe*.

The Ezour Vedam

Max Müller characterized the *Ezour Vedam* as a "very coarse forgery" (Müller 1978: 5).[7] It consisted of a poor compilation of Hindu and Christian doctrines mixed up together in the most childish way. While Müller believed that it was probably the work of a "half educated native convert at Pondicherry" (Müller, 1891: 39) and the silliest book that could be read by a student of religion, he did not believe that the original author intended it for the purpose for which it was used by Voltaire (Müller, 1872: 20).

In *La Renaissance orientale*, Raymond Schwab characterized the *Ezour Vedam* as an insidious piece of propaganda consisting of certain "Vedic" materials translated by Jesuits with the intention of isolating elements most in harmony with Christianity (Schwab 1950: 166–68). With this fraud, Schwab maintained, the Jesuits sought to refute idolatry and polytheism in the name of the purer doctrine of the Vedas, and, ultimately, to convert Indians. As the Indologist Willem Caland noted, the fraud was clever: The *Ezour Vedam* did not reject all Hinduism, but granted those tenets not in contradiction with Christiam dogma. Its author tried to make readers think that the *Vedam* differed entirely from what they might have believed it to be (Rocher 1983: 24).

The editor of the *Ezour Vedam*, the Baron de Sainte Croix, did not present it as one of the four Vedas (*Ezour Vedam* 1778: 116),[8] but offered it as the first original Sanskrit text published on religious and philosophical dogma. He did believe, however, that the *Ezour Vedam*'s scriptural citations were authentic.[9] This point was important, since the editor also maintained that the four Vedas were lost (*Ezour Vedam* 1778:130). Sainte Croix felt that, given the mendacity of the brahmins and the large fees offered by the West for the Veda's retrieval, the texts would have long since fallen into missionary hands had they still existed (*Ezour Vedam* 1778: 109–10).

It was upon its arrival in Europe that the confusion concerning the *Ezour Vedam*'s identity occurred. Ludo Rocher has suggested that error arose due to the work's title. The *Ezour Vedam*'s reference to itself as a "veda" should have been understood in a generic sense, as the term "veda" is used in India by both missionaries and Indians alike. In fact, Rocher suggests that the *Ezour Vedam* did not pretend to be one of the four Vedas, but rather a "veda" in the general sense of the term, a holy book or, as the text defined itself, a "corps de science" (*Ezour Vedam* 1778: 203). It made no attempt to rank itself among the Vedas. In fact, the text clearly presents itself as a commentary.[10] By resolving the *samdhi*[11] of the *Ezour Vedam*'s original title (*Zozur Bedo*), Rocher translated the title as the "Gospel of Jesus." It seems likely that the *Ezour Vedam* was, indeed, a syncretistic pastiche compiled in the hopes of converting Hindus to an amenable Christianity. What the *Ezour Vedam* actually was is less significant than the use to which it and the mythic Aryan society it described were put during the Enlightenment. The Veda (in the form of the *Ezour Vedam*) allowed Voltaire and Sainte Croix to draw a distinction between what was Vedic and post-Vedic, the latter being a degenerated form of the former. Just as scripture had degenerated, so too had its interpreters.

A considerable portion of this early discourse surrounding the "Veda" consisted in mourning the loss of a rational religion that had suffered corruption (Voltaire 1963: 1.238) and blaming the brahmin elite, who neither instructed their people properly nor desired knowledge themselves (Voltaire 1963: 1.243–44). In this diatribe, Voltaire always presented the brahmin clergy as mendacious and generally corrupt (Voltaire 1963: 1.61).[12] Voltaire blamed the brahmin priests for having led the Aryans astray, just as he blamed the Jesuits for the state of French Catholicism. In both instances, priestly machinations had entrapped the faithful in the snares of superstition and intolerance. Aryan India mirrored the Human (that is, French) Condition: Rational religion had degenerated into superstitions and abominable cultic practices. The prime actors in both instances were the priests. Brahmins offered Voltaire a most pregnant symbol: Where in the world could he have directed his anticlerical polemics so successfully? The brahmin priests allowed him to "écraser l'infâme" and, for once, the objects of his critique were not Catholic, Jesuits, or French.

The polemic directed against the brahmin clergy was seen inscribed within the narrative structure of the *Ezour Vedam* itself rather than as an intentional product of it. Biache, the caricature of a degenerate brahmin, preaches superstition in the form of popular theology to the philosopher Chumontou. By challenging Biache with refutations culled from the "Veda," Chumontou imparts "pure" Aryan wisdom concerning the unity of God, creation, the nature of the soul, and the doctrines of suffering and reward. By enumerating the proper forms of worship (*Ezour Vedam* 1778: 150), the text itself is seen to exhibit the extent to which original Aryan theism had degenerated into Hindu polytheism (*Ezour Vedam* 1778: 13). With a brahmin priest spouting foolish superstition ably refuted by a philosopher championing reason, the *Ezour Vedam* was tailor-made to voice

Voltaire's critique of organized religion and faith in rationalism. But, Voltaire's exoticism did not limit itself to a simple Deist idealization of the Aryan past. India was to provide Voltaire with a forceful weapon for a more significant battle in historical revisionism.

India, What Can It Teach Us?

This question, adopted by Max Müller as the title of a collection of essays, addresses a fundamental concern of this study, namely, that a fictive India and fictional Aryan ancestors were constructed in the West to provide answers for questions regarding European identity. India enabled Europe to discover its "true" past. Nowhere is this more true than in Voltaire's attempt to rewrite the history of religions. It was in his efforts to compare world mythologies, especially the myth of the Fall of Man, that Voltaire's true need to construct an Indian alibi (Latin: elsewhere) surfaced.

Voltaire compared the "Indian" version of the Fall with the classical myth relating the revolt of the Titans and the apocryphal account of Lucifer's rebellion found in the Book of Enoch (Voltaire 1885: 18.34). The common use of this myth in three traditions suggested to Voltaire that the Greeks and the Jews had knowledge of brahmin mysteries. Voltaire placed additional significance on this myth, attributing all subsequent religious thought to it. It provided the foundation for the entire Christian religion (Voltaire 1885: 11.184), since it set the stage for Original Sin, which in turn set the stage for everything that followed. Voltaire also claimed that the Aryans originated the concept of the Devil, who, as the agent of sin, animated all Judeo-Christian theology (Voltaire 1885: 29.482). If this was indeed true, why, Voltaire asked, did Christianity bother to use a source as tenuous as a Jewish apocryphal book to explain the existence of evil (Voltaire 1885: 29.172–73)? Why did Christianity seek to base itself solely on a myth that did not even appear in the Old Testament (Voltaire 1885: 28.139)?

Voltaire posed these questions with a clear response in mind. By inserting this fundamental myth into an apocryphal book, the Jews contrived to claim authorship and displace the true founders of our faith. It was the Aryans, the Vedic brahmins, who had first developed these truths. The Jews subsequently repeated this mythology, after stealing it from its ancient Indian source. Just as the Jews stole the source of religions, so too did they steal the idea of Adam as the progenitor.

> Did they get this from the Jews? Did the Jews copy the Indians, were both original? The Jews are not allowed to think that their writers took (*ont puisé*) anything from the brahmins, of whom they have never heard. It is not permitted to think about Adam in

another way than do the Jews. I will be quiet and I will not think.
(Voltaire 1885: 19.59)

Such is Voltaire's polemic: The Jews stole what was of worth in their religion
from the Aryans, people whom they called Gog and Magog (Voltaire 1885:
29.471). They then conspired to keep their fraud a secret. We, as Christians,
have not dared to reveal this fraud, as our own beliefs are implicated
(Voltaire 1885: 29.481). We have to believe the Jews, although we detest
them, because they are regarded as our precursors and masters (Voltaire
1885: 11.47).

Ironically, Voltaire's strategy to reveal this fraud involved those very
individuals who, had the Jews not been his scapegoats, would have been his
natural enemies—the Jesuits. Voltaire felt that the Jesuits alone were capable
of proving whether "the vast Indies or a part of Palestine" comprises the most
ancient society. They alone possessed the scholarly means to determine
whether brahmins had plagarized the Pentateuch or the Jews had appropriated the wisdom of the Aryans (Voltaire 1885: 29.184).

The Veda was never more than a symbolic text for Voltaire.
Nevertheless, it supplied him with an effective tool to launch a considerable
attack: it combated idolatry, introduced Adam to the world, and provided an
alternative scenario for the Fall of Man. In short, the Veda provided "all the
principles of theology" (Voltaire 1885: 11.192) that Voltaire needed or
desired: baptism, the immortality of the soul, metempsychosis, the identification of Abraham with Brahm (*sic*), and of Adam and Eve with Adimo and
Procriti. The description of the revolt of the angels found in Holwell's *Shasta*
prefigured the biblical account of Lucifer's fall.

The political repercussions of this reconstruction of Aryan religion were
signficant. We have seen how the *Ezour Vedam*'s creation myth enabled
Voltaire to attack the originality of the Hebrews and their religion. It
allowed him to claim the anteriority of the Indians and, in doing so, effectively challenge the authority of the Bible. India provided another basis for
religion unencumbered by the Judaic tradition. Indian "scripture" also
allowed Voltaire to make the argument that the Jews were the great plagia-
rists of history:

> Some very intelligent thinkers say that the brahmin sect is incon-
> testably older that that of the Jews . . . they say that the Indians
> were always inventors and the Jews always imitators, the Indians
> always clever and the Jews always coarse. (Cited in Hawley 1974:
> 151)

In sections appended at a later date (1769) to the *Essai sur les moeurs*, Voltaire
accuses the Jews of stealing from the Indians both the myths of Creation and

the Fall. The Jews did not set the stage for Christianity; rather it was the Aryans who bequethed to us a religion based on universal reason that the Jews subsequently distorted. In a late letter to Frederick the Great (December 1775), Voltaire reiterated that Christianity was founded solely on the ancient religion of "Brama" [*sic*].

Voltaire's reading of the "Veda" is, indeed, as ironic as it is inventive. He was able to imbue a clever piece of propaganda (or a clumsy attempt at ecumenicism) with characteristics that suited his polemical needs. Vedic India became a privileged site of Deist rationalism. He enlisted the Aryans in an attack on the pretensions of the Catholic Church and invoked their originality in order to displace the Jews from their privileged position in history. Less spectacular yet not less noteworthy is the simple fact that hidden behind Voltaire's polemic lie the seeds of modern historiography, the study of comparative mythology, and the history of religions. It was with such faulty source material and prejudice that Voltaire initiated the comparative study of religion by comparing our myths to those of the Aryans.

LOCUS OF POETIC INSPIRATION OR SITE OF CULTURAL DECAY?

Herder: Poetry versus Metaphysics

Kant proclaimed that the modern state resulted from man's progressive development. How was one to reconcile this theory with the perception that many "primitive" peoples were happier and better off than inhabitants of the civilized world? In accordance with popular Enlightenment propaganda, one could render these "primitives" more sophisticated than the modern Western man. Thus, Kant could declare that Indian religious thought was free of dogmatism and intolerance: "It is a principle of the Indians (i.e. the Hindus), that every nation has its own religion. For this reason, they do not force anyone to accept theirs" (cited in Halbfass 1988:61).

We have seen how in the French Enlightenment discourse, India provided an alibi: by satisfying, through spacial displacement, the need for a new social and religious geography. Moreover, Indian religion also illustrated how "natural light" had been eclipsed through superstition, fanaticism, and idolatry. As Wilhelm Halbfass has noted, this theme of the suppression of natural light through superstition enjoyed great popularity among thinkers of the Enlightenment. Finally, the discourse on India also gives expression to the motif of religious decay (Halbfass 1988: 60–61). It was in the writings of Johann Gottfried von Herder that this strategy, linking self-reflection to an exotic, was first used to indulge politically charged fantasies of structural collapse and decay.

The *philosophes* and their followers believed in the unity of mankind and held that all men subsisted under the same natural law of right and reason. They supposed that all would participate alike in progress and that the outcome of history would be one of uniform civilization in which all peoples and races would share equally. As Herder maintained in the *Ideen*, man has the potential of ascending to the ideal of infinite perfection even without the benefits of Western culture. The study of peoples such as Indians (Herder 1877–1913: 4.357, 425; 5.214; 8.208; 11.247; 16.13) contributed to the development of *Humanität*, defined by Herder as the sum of the virtue and talents peculiar to human beings or the divine in man (Herder 1877–1913: 13.350; 14.230). However, the Enlightenment's belief in the potential similarity of all human beings and in freedom from intolerance and ignorance would not be so easily realized. Herder's discussions of India brings to the foreground this very dilemma.

Contrary to the account found in Genesis, Voltaire had placed the origin of mankind in the East on the banks of the Ganges. Herder followed Voltaire in that he too discovered the cradle of humanity in India (Herder 1877–1913: 13.38, 399, 403, 406).[13] Since all men were descended from the same race (Herder 1877-1913: 5.447; 13.252, 405), Herder attributed the development of different cultures and languages to environmental forces (Herder 1877–1913: 5.539). Language, the purest expression of the spiritual character of a national group (Herder 1877–1913: 17.58–59), like man himself, descended from a unique source (Herder 1877–1913: 30.8). By positioning the childhood of humanity in India, Herder referred not only to the ancestors of Europeans, but also to progenitors of all humankind.

In the *Ideen*, Herder described India as the birthplace of all languages, sciences, and art (Herder 1877–1913: 13.411). He characterized the Hindus as the gentlest race of man (Herder 1877–1913: 13.222, 225–26). The Indian has respect for all sentient beings. His nourishment is sound and his demeanor as graceful as his spirit (Herder 1877-1913: 13.222). Indians are endowed with supernatural physical and spiritual qualities (Herder 1877–1913: 14.32, 73–74). No people exceeds the Indian in calmness and gentle obedience. Herder attributed the Indians' tranquility to the climate as well as their innate character (Herder 1877–1913: 14.28). Their gestures and speech are unconstrainedly charming, their intercourse free, their bodies pure, and their mode of life simple and harmless. Children are brought up with indulgence and are not lacking in sensitivity, knowledge, or diligence. Even the lowest strata of society learn to read, write, and add (Herder 1877–1913: 14.28–29). Their vision of God is great and beautiful.

However, Herder did not give India the least importance in the comparative history of primitive revelation. It was as though Indian religion,
since the supposed loss of the *Rig Veda*, had been cut off from primitive revelation and reduced to human speculation. Indian religion was interesting in
and of itself, but inappropriate to illuminate the authenticity of pure
Christianity or Judaism, which, after all, were the objects of legitimate exegesis. Herder found much to respect about India. Like his friend Goethe, he
admired the graceful simplicity of Kālidāsa's *Śakuntalā*. He even felt that it
must be more valuable than all "the Vedas, Upavedas and Upangas" put
together. Its poetry, undistorted by tendentious religious speculation, provided greater beauty and truth than was thought possible in Sanskrit literature. Herder judged the Vedas, "Upavedas" and "Upangas," although absent
to his gaze, as interminable, less useful, and far less agreeable than the poetry
of Kālidāsa. He even surmised that it was the Veda that had blunted the
spirit and character of the Indian people. Compared to the poetry, all those
"Upnekats" and "Bagavedams" must have presented faint notions of the
Indian mentality (Herder 1786–92: 91).

In Herder's mind, India and the primitive world, the primitive world
and nature, nature and poetry become synonymous and interchangeable. He
joined the eighteenth-century belief in the anteriority of poetry to his own
variation of the *bon sauvage* theme and posited an equivalence of India and
poetry (Herder 1877–1913: 5.50; 1.32). The compiler of the *Stimmen der
Völker in Liedern* also encouraged Germans to seek new inspirational models
and question the absolute value of Greek classical norms. The *philosophes* and
their German disciples believed that reality and, by extension, the arts were
ordered in terms of universal, timeless, objective, and unalterable laws which
rational investigation could discover. Their detractors believed that logic was
incompatible with the force of inspiration necessary for poetic creation.
Herder sought a middle ground between these diametrically opposed alterna-
tives. He rejected the particular concept of reason propounded by
Enlightenment rationalism and endeavored, rather, to interpret rationality in
such a way that it was not inimical to spontaneity and vitality.

The *Fragmente, Über die neuere deutsche Literatur*, and *Abhandlung über
den Ursprung der Sprache* reveal Herder's struggle with the possibility of dis-
covering a native German literature. The movement of German authors to
found a German national literature developed along two distinct lines: the
first consisting of a need to establish a clear criterion for assessing a work's
national characteristics, the second, to create a literature unique in itself. As a
corollary, this movement stimulated speculation on the nature of artistic
inspiration in general. To proclaim the poetic origin of language, to situate
the land of poetry in India, to present popular songs against the classics, to
underline the sacred character of inspiration—in other words, to found a

Weltliteratur—already entailed the assertion of the artistic equivalence between the *Nibelungenlied* and the Vedas (Gérard 1963: 65).

With man's origin in India, it followed that Sanskrit poetry should provide the source from which all poetry descended. Sanskrit poetry thus played a pivotal role in Herder's thought. Its beauty and sublimity provided an excellent argument in favor of Herder's humanistic aesthetic. The study of songs, fables, and myths of nationalities such as that of India (Herder 1877–1913: 16.13; 4.357; 5.214; 8.208; 11.247) contributed to the development of one's national culture, which, in turn, contributed to the development of humanity (Herder 1877–1913: 13.356; 14.230).

Due to the West's necessarily incomplete knowledge of Sanskrit literature, Herder could cut it to measure out of the poetic presuppositions of an unpoetic age. As a result of Herder's theories and instigations, Sanskrit poetry became required reading for anyone who desired to experience "real" poetry. In Herder's thought, the *Śakuntalā* possessed everything the absent Veda lacked. In fact, for Herder, Kālidāsa's *nāṭaka* assumed a significance which subsequent writers attributed to the Veda in their depiction of an Aryan humanity. Herder chose to emphasize the *Śakuntalā* for two reasons. Kālidāsa's play existed and could be read in support of Romantic claims which found their germ in Herder's writings. The Veda did not exist. But, even as an absent text, it was never absent as a counterpoint to Sanskrit poetry and was a negative authority in his discourse to be rejected because of its degeneracy and superstitious beliefs.

According to Herder, Aryan religion was destroyed long ago by Vaiṣṇavite and Shivaite sectarians. Its legends came down to us only in the form of more recent interpretations. While some residue of the initial purity of primitive Aryan religion remains in these legends, they have been grossly distorted by myth. While quasi-biblical and quasi-Christian, Indian religion suffered from a particular evil, metempsychosis, that destroyed Aryan spirituality and morality, leaving Hindu quietism, indifference, and social disaster in its wake. Herder suspected what modern Indologists can prove from the *Rig Veda*—that the Aryans did not believe in metempsychosis. Herder believed that metempsychosis betokened the regression of Aryan spirituality from contact with aboriginal tribes given to totemism (Herder 1877–1913: 16.78). For Herder, metempsychosis signified the illusion of sensual men who envied the fate of animals. Populations that are more evolved and happier invent a locus where their terrestrial life can be prolonged in idealized form. The Aryans had done this. But the later Indians had degenerated. Their belief in metempsychosis encouraged compassion for plants and animals, rather than for people (Herder 1877–1913: 14.31).

In actuality, Herder distinguished three Indias: the primitive kingdom of poetry and natural religion provided by the presence of the *Śakuntalā*, the

mystico-metaphysical worldview represented by the Aryans of the absent
Veda, and the degenerate present. For Herder's subjective reasoning, the first
alone was of interest, the second inaccessable, and the third a monstrous
product of the human spirit. All three Indias—the locus of true poetry, the
lost Aryan hierophany, and the degenerate present—would, however, reappear in subsequent discussions. It would be the task of the Romantic
mythographers to incorporate these fictive Indias within an interpretation of
the Semitic-Christian religious cycle. India was still too distant, however, in
Herder's time.

Nevertheless, many of the Romantic theses regarding India begin to
coalesce in Herder. Already, in Voltaire, we saw the Aryans inhabiting a
golden age and their religion offering a tradition older than the Bible. Aryan
India saw primitive revelation degenerate under the influence of a corrupt
priesthood and monotheism reduced to polytheism. Upon this script, Herder
and the Romantics projected their own aesthetic need: the desire to discover
a true national poetry. Once the Veda appeared on the literary scene,
Herder's notions concerning the poetic origin of language and poetry as a
spontaneous expression of the folk spirit and Sanskrit poetry as natural
national poetry would be applied to it. Herder's depiction of India as an
ancient poetic utopia and modern site of cultural decay would also reappear
in subsequent discussions.

Jones and Colebrooke: Myth versus Text

Sir William Jones was Europe's foremost Orientalist scholar. He mas-
tered twenty-eight languages, translated the *Śakuntalā* and the *Mānava
Dharmashāstra* (*Laws of Manu*), and served in India as a judge. Nevertheless,
he depicted the ancient Aryan in terms not dissimilar to those of the nonspecialists of his time. The Aryans were a superior people. All that was considered valuable in the Ancients found an initial expression among the Aryans.
They possessed a highly evolved moral wisdom and a fertile imaginative
genius (Jones 1788: 728-29). They originated the study of astronomy (Jones
1788: 430) and developed metaphysical theories that the Greeks later appropriated (Jones 1788: 425). The Aryans also supplied the Ancients with their
gods (Jones 1788: 724). They were somewhat related to the great cultures of
mankind, including our own. Aryan society was so magnificent that, even
after so many revolutions and conquests, they still surpassed the world in
wealth. However, Aryan culture degenerated and only vestiges of its former
glory appear in modern India.

> Today they appear degenerate and abased . . . in some early age,
> they were splendid in arts and arms, happy in government, wise in
> legislation, and eminent in various knowledges. (Jones 1788: 421)

Before the Aryans disappeared, however, they left a textual trace of their genius behind in the Veda and its "compendium, the Upanishads." According to Jones, these texts provided source material for information regarding the Aryans and their noble metaphysics (Jones 1788: 429). To this script, Jones added several key points that would provide valuable information for an ideological portrait of ancient India that subsequent thinkers in India and the West would exploit.

Jones is credited with the discovery of the affinity between Sanskrit and the Classical, Persian, Celtic, and Gothic languages. His speculation regarding the importance of Sanskrit not only initiated the scientific study of India, but proved revolutionary to the then barely nascent study of linguistics. For, in addition to noting the similarity between Sanskrit and the classical languages, Jones informed his readers that Sanskrit was "more perfect" than Greek, more copious than Latin and, more exquisitely refined than either (Jones 1788: 422). If Sanskrit so far surpassed those languages previously held as the highest forms of expression, then the Indians who spoke it were truly a race to be admired. We have seen how others had made similar assertions. Jones, however, was the first to be able to back his claim with "scientific" data. The belief in a linguistic affinity of the Aryans with Persians, Ethiopians, Egyptians, Phoenicians, Greeks, Tuscans, Goths, Celts, Chinese, Japanese, and Peruvians implied that these peoples all proceeded from some central site of origin (Jones 1788: 431). That they all possessed languages structurally similar to our own became politically significant. Scholarship could now be enlisted in the service of empire. By rediscovering India's Aryan past, England could subsequently presume that it was helping India help itself. This motive, explicit in Jones's translation efforts (Figueira 1991: 25), also informed the portrayal of the Aryan in the scholarship of Henry Thomas Colebrooke (Müller 1837: 1.2). Colebrooke's assessment of the Vedic materials was, however, more directly instrumental in defining the British colonial mission.

Jones, along with other scholars (Halhed, Marine, and Chambers) had collected numerous Vedic fragments and deposited them in the library of the College of Fort William in Calcutta (Kopf 1969:40). In 1800, Colebrooke was assigned by Governor-General Wellesley to teach Sanskrit at Fort William. During his tenure there, he found an ideal opportunity to collate the Vedic fragments residing in the college library. In the *Asiatick Researches* of 1805, Colebrooke offered an approximate idea of the contents of the Veda (Colebrooke 1805: 377–497). His readings of this material offered Westerners for the first time the textual evidence to chart the decline of Indian civilization from Vedic to modern times (Müller 1837: 1.3).

Colebrooke had initially doubted whether the Vedas were extant or whether their obsolete dialect could be read by anyone.[14] He had thought that even if brahmins possessed the Veda, they would not have shared them. Although the Upanishads had already been translated into Persian, the brahmins still jealously guarded their scripture (Colebrooke 1805: 377). Colonel Polier's discovery of a purportedly complete copy dispelled Colebrooke's doubts. The Veda did, in fact, exist and it became Colebrooke's task to introduce it in general terms to the West.[15]

The bulk of Colebrooke's article, however, dealt with proving the authenticity of his manuscripts. Although the Veda's date and authorship could not be determined "with accuracy and confidence" (Colebrooke 1805: 489), Colebrooke confirmed its authenticity by cross-referencing it to other works. He also compared fragments of numerous commentaries whose authenticity had been secured by interpretations of their annotations in other works.[16] He further verified Vedic quotations with the testimony of grammars, collections of aphorisms, law digests, astronomy, medical texts, profane poetry, and even the writings of heretical sects (Colebrooke 1805: 481–84). This corroboration offered sufficient grounds to prove that no forger's skill was equal to the task of fabricating large works in all branches of Sanskrit literature to agree with the numerous citations pervading thousands of volumes in every branch of that literature (Colebrooke 1805: 484). The "superstitious" manner in which the Veda was read, its explanatory table of contents, and indices as well as glosses of every passage and every word made interpolations impracticable (Colebrooke 1805: 480). Colebrooke assured his readers that the Veda, as he presented it, not only was genuine but had survived in an unadulterated form. After authenticating the texts in question, however, Colebrooke showed little interest in analyzing their message or the civilization out of which they arose.

He did, however, corroborate Jones's more significant assertions. Colebrooke read the Veda as a negative authority. It did not so much relate what the Aryans were like as what they were not like: modern Hindus. All the abuses of modern Hinduism were absent from Vedic religion. There were no blood sacrifices (Colebrooke 1805: 437–78). The numerous gods of modern cultic practice could be reduced to the three major Vedic deities and these were ultimately manifestations of one supreme god (Colebrooke 1805: 395). Just as Aryan religious rituals differed dramatically from those of modern India, so did its social practices (Colebrooke 1795: 209–19; Colebrooke 1798: 33–67).

Colebrooke's thesis, while evidently more informed and expert than that of the nonspecialist commentary, was remarkably similar to the Enlightenment discourse on the Aryans. It emphasized an ideal Vedic age whose religion had degenerated through superstition and clerical abuse. The monotheistic religion that Colebrooke discovered in the Vedas was no longer in use and had been superseded by polytheism and decadent ceremonies, founded on the Purāṇas or, even worse, the Tantras. Bloody sacrifices to Kālī had taken the place of the less sanguinary *yajña*, just as adoration of Krishna and Rāma had succeeded the worship of elements and plants (Colebrooke 1805: 495-96). As Colebrooke would note in his essay "On the Religious Ceremonies of the Hindus," modern Hinduism functioned as a misunder-standing of ancient texts (Colebrooke 1802: 229–31). Rituals such as *satī* were not part of the authentic scriptural tradition (Colebrooke 1785: 109–19). Colebrooke also found discrepancies between the ancient texts and contemporary practice with reference to caste exclusionary practices. David Kopf has characterized the Jones-Colebrooke depiction of the Aryans in the following terms: they "were thought to have been outgoing and non-mystical. They were pictured as a robust, beef-eating, socially egalitarian society" (Kopf 1969: 41). These Aryans believed in one God, did not practice *satī* or idolatry, and did not adhere to caste regulations. They were in no way similar to modern Hindus.

Despite the length of Colebrooke's article, his specific conclusions were scant and uninspiring. He limited his discussion to providing a *soupçon* of the Vedas, citing passages to show the "seeming absurdity" of the text under analysis (Colebrooke 1805: 434). They were too voluminous for a complete translation, their language was obscure, and they presented too little reward to the reader and the translator.[17] Colebrooke concluded that the Vedas deserved to be consulted occasionally by the Oriental scholar for those few remarkable and important things found in them, however difficult it was to extract such pearls. On this negative note, Colebrooke concluded his 120-page analysis introducing the Veda to Europe. His article had the effect of dampening interest in the Vedas and discouraging scholars from delving deeper into them for profitable information. However, Colebrooke's analysis had a significant political effect upon the colonial administration's assessment of the worth of Sanskrit literature and modern Hindu religion, as Thomas B. Macauley's oft-cited *Minute* will attest. It took another half-century to amend Colebrooke's dismissive judgment and shift the focus of scholarly interest away from the classical period of Sanskrit literature back to the *Urtext*.[18]

CONCLUSION

The discourse on the Aryan during this period, culled from fraudulent or largely absent textual material, expressed concerns that were crucial to the Enlightenment vision of historical progress and knowing subjects acting within history. The Veda's discovery, "scientific" analysis, and presence in the West as a text would not significantly alter the nonspecialist portrait of the

Aryan. In fact, Orientalist scholarship is seen to have provided the documentation necessary to support the Enlightenment conceptual apparatus. Such validation may, indeed, explain critical interpretations of the Enlightenment's influence on Orientalism and colonialism. As we have noted, postcolonial critiques of the Enlightenment tend to avoid actually engaging Enlightenment texts. This failure should not be attributed to critical laziness, the theorists' restrictive canon, or the fact that Foucault has exhausted the possibilities of interpreting the Enlightenment. By evoking the Enlightenment without allowing its literature to inform any analysis and projecting onto Enlightenment anthropology the discursive source of colonialism without engaging texts, critics can neatly avoid having to confront what the literature reveals: the Enlightenment's ambiguous representation of the Other. Poststructuralism's limited canon normally protects certain ideological presuppositions, the first and foremost of which is Deconstruction's critique of Western rationalism. Actual engagement with Enlightenment texts might very well call such presuppositions into question. Therefore, postcolonial theory, spawned as it is from Deconstruction's confrontation with logocentrism, must present the Enlightenment as a unified trajectory. It must be seen as a period that uniformly absolutized differences. The Enlightenment must be made to fit the master narrative of Orientalism and colonial discourse analysis.

Moreover, any actual confrontation with Enlightenment literature would highlight the extent to which poststructural criticism embraces its presentism, equates politics with oppositionalism and power with rationalism. If poststructuralist theory's universalization of power defines itself as a systemic limitation to individual choice (Fluck 1996: 227), then postcolonial criticism has a vested interest in dismissing the Enlightenment. If a key concern of this criticism involves the rejection of ideals that were fundamental to the Enlightenment project, then the Enlightenment as the perpetrator of rationalism, empiricism, and historicism must be suspect. The Enlightenment belief in the idea of historical agents and/or knowing subjects must also be ignored, since the edifice of poststructuralist criticism has been erected upon the impossibility of self-reflection and intersubjective validation (Fluck 1990: 17). Thus, criticism's own agenda must be projected onto texts from the past. A valuable lesson can be learned from this critical reading of the Enlightenment. As readers, we should look beyond critical gestures of empowerment and assess the larger politics of identity that not only informed historical and literary analysis, but continue to be played out with Indian props.

CHAPTER 2

The Romantic Aryans

ROMANTIC MYTH THEORY

The development of myth theory in the seventeenth and eighteenth centuries primarily contributed two factors to general intellectual and scientific history. It initiated a gradual change in understanding aesthetics from objective and rational imitation to a more subjective and emotional principle of expression. Secondly, it contributed to the development of historiographical, philological, and theological hermeneutics, in other words, to the beginning of historical biblical criticism. During the Enlightenment, the source of myth was believed to reside in humanity's subjective inwardness, imagination, and fantasy. Myths were seen as intentionally and arbitrarily invented by the individual. Created out of an arbitrary freedom of consciousness, myths were viewed as trans-empirical.

The Romantics (beginning with Schelling and culminating with Bachofen) shifted the origin of myth from the individual sphere into the collective, from the conscious into the unconscious. Under the influence of the historical school and its founder and leader Karl von Savigny, myth was thought to emanate from unconscious necessity and the regulation of natural instinct, out of a general human need or within specific national *Volksgeister* (Grimm and Bachofen). Historically real and concrete myth traditions mediated the unconscious nature of humanity. Through myth, the greatest nations put their stamp upon all history.

Although situated in geographical and time-specific points of empirical history, myth expressed itself as renewing repetitions of divine revelation. Just as Romantic *Naturphilosophie* valued nature as the emanation and objectification of the Divine, so too did Romantic myth theory represent myth as *Naturpoesie*, developing out of nature and returning to the Divine. By placing the source of myth in the collective unconscious, Romantic myth theorists such as Görres, Kanne, Grimm, and Bachofen presupposed a unified mythical *Weltanschauung* among all peoples, epochs, and generations that evidenced

27

objectively knowable and legitimate Truth. This mythological *sensus communis* developed unmistakably from the Enlightenment construction of natural religion and vision of common beliefs in a common humanity.

For the Romantics, therefore, myth was viewed in the ethical sense as an internal embodiment of the *summum bonum*: uncontrived, original, and natural. This idealized conception of myth owed much to Rousseau and *Sturm und Drang*. It read myth as an index of internal and external life, a medium whereby modern society and culture could be analyzed. The child-like, pure, and innocent virtues found in myth appeared as a positive *Gegenbild* to the rotten and degenerative affectedness of modern civilization. The past was better than the present; the mythical past functioned as a model for an ideal form of present and future society. Romantic mythography presented a flight before worldly, artistic, and political difficulties and duties of the modern world into a sentimental romanticized and idealized past. Grounded as it was in historical traditions, the valorization of myth necessarily entailed the valorization (and mythologization) of national cultures as a favored worldly site of the Divine. In nineteenth- and twentieth-century Germany, myth theorists, especially proponents of the *Lebensgefühl* ideology and their rationalist opponents, set the stage for the German myth of the *Volk*. This myth of the *Volk*, that contributed so significantly to the growth of nineteenth- and twentieth-century nationalism, can thus be traced to Romantic mythography.

FRIEDRICH SCHLEGEL AND THE FOUNDATIONS OF ROMANTIC LINGUISTICS

In offering a vision of India in which myth triumphed over reason, chaos stood in place of Olympian calm, and the primitive impulse left system and structure scattered in its wake, Herder (at least in his *Sturm und Drang* period) instigated the cult of the primitive and the symbolic and, as such, was a precursor of Romantic mythographers. Since Herder's time, however, the source material on India had changed. Many more Sanskrit texts had been translated, and the Asiatic Society of Bengal had published a number of groundbreaking articles. Friedrich Schlegel, a pioneer in the study of the Sanskrit language and author of the first direct translation from Sanskrit into German, maintained that mythology had been revitalized (Schlegel 1906: 1.136) and was now generally recognized as a largely untapped reservoir of poetic inspiration (Schlegel 1846: 4.174). Since the modern Occident had no mythology of its own, he noted that "one would have to be invented" (Schlegel 1846: 4.197). The inspiration for this new mythology and hence the new Romantic poetry was to be found in the Orient (Schlegel 1906: 2.362). By Orient, Schlegel meant India (Schlegel 1906: 2.357 ff).

What the West recognized as religion, mythology, and poetry originated in the Orient. Classical Indian culture exhibited in a pure, undiluted form what, in the West, was a mere vestige of the union of philosophy and poetry. Just as one would go to Italy to learn about art, one should now go to India to learn about beginnings (Schlegel 1966: 7.261, 263), God, and poetry (Schlegel 1966: 7.74). Schlegel clearly saw himself as the guide for this aesthetic and religious pilgrimage. The unique fruit of his metaphorical journey, *Über die Sprache und Weisheit der Indier* (1808), comprised, as it were, the Romantic manifesto on India. However, *Über die Sprache* also disclosed the difficulties that made Schlegel's dream of a philosophical and aesthetic revolution via India (Schlegel 1846: 7.39–40) an impossibility.

Über die Sprache charts the degeneration of the land of primitive revelation into the atomistic and materialistic India that Schlegel came to discover. Although traces of divine truth could still be found in Indian philosophical systems, Schlegel came to the conclusion that they had been inextricably mixed with error. Schlegel's devaluation of Indian speculative thought in the initial chapter of the book allowed him, in the remaining chapters, to focus on the divine nature of the Sanskrit language. In fact, Schlegel maintained that the only valid inquiry into the past consisted in the science of language. Traditional methods sought to demonstrate the superiority of one language over another, that is, to distinguish languages from each other by superficial differences and to view such differences as manifestations of the diverse national genius of individual populations. Not relying upon noting the superficial similarities among Greek, Latin, German, Persian, and Sanskrit roots as the standard methodology would have dictated, Schlegel sought, by analyzing grammatical structures, conjugations, and declensions, a critique for the relationship between languages in morphological comparison.

However, Schlegel met with problems when he tried to resolve the question of the origin of language by basing his arguments on historical research. His insistence on linguistic polygenesis led him to group languages either as inflected or agglutinative. The former possessed divine origin; the latter, animal. Using the then popular analogy of botany, Schlegel saw inflected languages as linguistic vegetation. Just as a stem, branches, and leaves develop from a plant's root, so nominal and verbal forms come from the linguistic root (Schlegel 1977: 41–59, 65–70). Schlegel postulated that German and other languages developed from Sanskrit because they possessed inflection (Schlegel 1977: 3.35–36, 71, 62, 66). He believed that other languages, such as Chinese and Hebrew, lacked this inflection and were agglutinative by means of affixes joined to the roots (Schlegel 1977: 33, 44ff, 48, 50ff). Because of inflection, Sanskrit and its derivative languages were seen as living organisms, capable of penetrating intelligence (Schlegel 1977: 68–69).

Agglutinative languages were labeled mere agglomerations of atoms (Schlegel 1977: 51).

This erroneous linguistic theorizing served Schlegel as a metaphorical edifice constructed to isolate Sanskrit from other languages and support his belief in its perfection and divine origin. The larger plan was to salvage palatable aspects of the Divine from his abortive Indic studies. He projected onto Sanskrit what he could not find in Indian philosophy and religion. Unfortunately, the divine status he accorded to inflected Sanskrit necessitated a less than divine origin for what he perceived as the agglutinative languages. This was clearly a negative by-product, rather than a motivating factor. Although Schlegel presented India as a problematic locus of the Divine in the philosophical, religious, and translation sections of *Über die Sprache*, in the linguistic chapters India emerges as the cradle of humanity and Sanskrit appears as the mother tongue of Indo-European languages.

Language itself provides source material for the comprehension of history (Schlegel 1966: 257). Through the study of the language of the ancient Indians, the most talented and wisest *Volk* of antiquity, we find the "traces of divine Truth" (Schlegel 1966: 209). It had been Schlegel's intention to show that just as in language, so too with mythology, there exists an inner structure and a fundamental texture whose similarity signifies a related origin. However, the absence of the Veda prevented Schlegel from completing the comparative analysis of mythology (Schlegel 1966: 172–73, 199, 235). Moreover, had the Veda been available, Schlegel judged that its value would have been minimal. Of necessity, the Veda would have long since been falsified (Schlegel 1966: 251). Original revelation, long lost to the Indians with the loss of the Veda, had completely degenerated (Schlegel 1966: 207).

What resulted from its distortion and loss? Detoured from the path of truth, Indians fell prey to wild fiction and coarse error ("System der Seelenwanderung und Emanation"). The Veda, in its imagined pure form, represented lost truth and thus had authority as an irretrievable artifact. With the absence of this source of revelation, myth, and poetry, Schlegel made the argument that a comparison of languages provided the only alternative to historical research ("Von den ältesten Wanderung der Völker"). In the final book of the volume, he connected the seemingly disparate strands of his argument to conclude that history, religion, and mythology can best be understood by their relationship to speech. Thus, Schlegel offered to use philological research, rather than the mythology lost with the Veda, or the religion he found distasteful, to argue his thesis that India and Europe formed an indivisible whole.

In Über die Sprache, Schlegel placed language in the foreground and developed a "scientific" method to be able to promote comparative linguistics and *Urgeschichte*. Having approached India in search of unity and revelation,

Schlegel came away only with faulty linguistic theories that allowed him to transform Herder's depiction of India as the cradle of humanity into the *Urheimat* of his own language and *Volk* family. Although the Veda functioned for both thinkers as an absent text, Herder and Schlegel developed a hermeneutic structure for viewing India and its scriptural canon that would resonate in subsequent discussions.

ROMANTIC MYTHOGRAPHERS AND THE *UPNEKHATA*

Up to this point, European knowledge of the Veda has centered upon its significance as an essential aporia in the emplotment of the Aryan. Voltaire, Herder, and Schlegel established this interpretive model, and it was the task of Romantic mythographers to incorporate a "Veda" into the previously established ideological edifice. With the Romantic mythographers, we are still talking about an absent text. They differed from their predecessors only in the increased availability of possible "Vedas." The message of the Veda and the Aryan worldview depicted therein had been sufficiently delineated that it was merely an issue of grafting them onto texts as they appeared.

The Heidelberg philologist Friedrich Creuzer identified the essence of the Veda with Anquetil Duperron's Latin translation from a Persian rendition of the Upanishads, the *Oupnek 'hat* or *Upnekhata* (Creuzer 1819–23: 1.551, 554). In his autobiography, Creuzer remarked that one of the reasons he delved into the history of religions was Anquetil's seeming proof of the thesis that polytheism developed from primitive monotheism (Creuzer 1840: 65). In his magisterial opus, *Symbolik und Mythologie der alten Völker, besonders der Griechen*, Creuzer sought arguments in favor of Anquetil's thesis and, toward this end, India proved more fruitful than the yet undeciphered Egypt. India revealed a marvelous humanity, different in all respects from other nations (Creuzer 1819–23: 1.539). Anquetil's "translation" of the "Veda" taught the most ancient religious system of the world as well as an instance of authentic monotheism (Creuzer 1819–23: 1.546-47).

At several reprises, Creuzer emphasized that primitive monotheism existed in India (Creuzer 1819–23: 1.569, 586, 642). The "Veda" posited Brahma as God the Father. Its religion was older than those of Greece and Egypt. Indeed, it presented the oldest religion known to man, and its language was the most organic and alive (Creuzer 1819–23: 1.569, 544, 548, 570). Creuzer held that this religion had degenerated into polytheism under the influence of orgiastic cults to Shiva that had themselves been reformed by Vaiṣṇavism (Creuzer 1819–23: 1.576). The belief that initial

Vedic wisdom had degenerated would become a common theme among Romantic mythographers.

The real innovation that Creuzer effected upon previous emplotments of the Veda in the West consisted in the role he ascribed to Aryan religion. While others touted the sublimity, purity, and antiquity of Indian speculative thought relative to the Judeo-Christian perspective, Creuzer specifically assigned it an equal position to that of the Hebrews. Creuzer claimed that "Brahmaism," the primitive worship of Brahma as articulated in the "Veda," might well have formed the basis of the Hebrews' religion. The purest cult of Jehovah, as practiced by Abraham, would then represent nothing more than an isolated branch of old "Brahmaism" (Creuzer 1819–23: 1.570). With such assertions, Creuzer went further than other polemicists in deemphasizing the role of Judaism in the history of religions. The Jews were not the only recipients of the true doctrine (Creuzer 1819–23: 2.375–76). This logic called into question the authority, even for someone like Schlegel, of the Old Testament. For Creuzer, Israel became an equal partner with Aryan India (Creuzer 1819–23: 1.575).

A decade earlier, Joseph Görres had also sought primitive religion beyond Judea. Christianity constituted the penultimate stage in religious evolution, with the final stage consisting in a return to primitive monism (Görres 1810: 1.13–14). Görres believed that the oldest prophet, law, and cult on earth were to be found in India, the cradle of humanity (Görres 1810: 1.37–40). Görres ranked other religions as mere imitations of this lost *Urreligion* (Görres 1810: 2.611). The closer a religion was to India, the more it retained a rich, pure, and living form (Görres 1810: 1.54). As others of his generation, Görres identified the Veda with the *Oupnek' hat*, which he took to be the oldest document known to humanity (Görres 1810: 1.117–19) and its religion, *Brahmaismus*, the oldest religion (Görres 1810: 1.569). Görres identified this "Veda" as the source from which all other myths derived (Görres 1810: 1.xiii). The hermetic books of Egypt, a land once colonized by the Hindus, derived from it as did all vestige of what was positive in Greek thought. Görres also reduced the religion of Judea to primitive "Brahmaism" imparted by Brahma-Abraham (Görres 1810: 2.329, 435–36, 556). The Jews owe their entire religion to the Vedic Indians, and Christians worship the Aryan Brahma as Christ (Görres 1810: 571). According to Görres's schema, the center of gravity has once again shifted from Judea to India (Görres 1810: 1.xxxiv–xxxvi), and the Hebrews have become a subgroup of the elected people. Görres characterized Aryan religion by its innocence. This golden age lasted but a short time manifested primarily in its custom of bloodless sacrifices of fruit offerings. Its adherents suffered persecution. This pure and simple faith was eventually replaced by wild orgiastic phallic worship (Görres 1810: 1.570–71, 576). On the textual level, Aryan religion became extinct, when the naive nature myths of the "Veda" degenerated into their present lamentable form (Görres 1810: 1.590, 593).

While Herder tried to incorporate India within his exegesis of the Old Testament and Creuzer posited the equivalence of India and Judea, Görres elevated Indian religion above Judaism. He associated other prophets (Toth, Zoroaster, Fohi, Theut, and Othin) with Brahma (Abraham) only to the degree that their doctrines reflected those of the *Oupnek 'hat*. Creuzer and Görres (as well as other Romantic mythographers such as Majer and Kanne) attributed the universality of myth to divine revelation. They all situated this revelation in India. But, the idea of the existence of a purely Indo-European religious community did not enter their formulations. It was Karl Ritter who developed the first features of Indo-European primitive religion.

Ritter characterized India as the vestibule (*Vorhalle*) of Western history. It represented the world's stage (*Völkerbühne*); since the oldest and most important documents of humanity came to us from India, Ritter derived a religious and cultural community from the linguistic community of European peoples grouped around ancient India (Ritter 1820: i–xix). Within this community, Ritter made important distinctions. The ancient Indians represented a breed apart from their successors. The European stands certainly far closer to the ancient Aryan than the modern Oriental. Most important, however, Germans are closer to the ancient Indians than to their modern neighbors (Ritter 1820: 23). Germans have far more affinity with Indians than with Greece (Ritter 1820: 33–34). In fact, there existed a direct lineage between the Aryans and the Teutons.

Ritter grounded the religious, linguistic, and racial community of Indo-Europeans in a vision of monotheistic religion originating in India. He identified the *Buddhakult* (his term for Vedic religion) with the cults to Apollo, Odin, Woden, and the like. Priestly teachings concerning metempsychosis and salvation had eroded the primitive belief in a single god, resulting in polytheism. Religion originated in India with the Veda (Ritter 1820: 24-25, 27, 30–33) and, as it moved into new areas, became individualized and localized. Ritter discovered in ancient India exactly what Schlegel had found: emanatist monotheism and metempsychosis. Whereas this discovery led Schlegel to reject Indian philosophical thought, these dogmas formed for Ritter the bridge between Sanskrit and Old German (Ritter 1820: 23–24, 26). In other words, Ritter revealed a civilization, religion, and language irreducible to that of the Hebrews. Judeo-Christianity became the intruder in his as well as other Romantic mythographers' schema. Indeed, it appeared to have turned Europe from its historic path and subverted its true mission.

The historical school emphasized the national aspect of myth as popular phenomenon. This conception of myth developed throughout the nineteenth century. When the Veda finally permitted the mythographer to compare Indo-European national mythologies, the Romantic thesis, especially that of Ritter, received renewed prominence (Gérard 1963: 196). India proved the existence of primitive monotheism and laid to rest any illusions regarding the primacy of the Jews. Speculations regarding the imagined Indo-European community that these Romantics developed would resurface with the appearance of the Veda in print and, in fact, would find their substantiation in the scientific research of its editor. Friedrich Max Müller would popularize the important Romantic thesis that by the mid-nineteenth century was far from moribund—the idea of an Indo-European religious community inferred from the concept of the Indo-European linguistic community. With his edition of the *Rig Veda*, the West finally discovered the chronicle of its past.

ROMANTIC INDOLOGY: THE CASE OF MAX MÜLLER

Our Veda, Our Ancestors

Early European scholarship on India consisted of an internal conversation. Nowhere was this dialogue more forceful than in the Vedic scholarship of Max Müller. For Müller, as for others we have examined in these pages, the quest for the Aryan exhibited a cultural attempt to restore one's own tradition.

I wished that the Veda and its religion and philosophy should not only seem to you curious or strange, but that you should feel that there was in them something that concerns ourselves, something of our own intellectual growth, some recollections, as it were, of our own childhood, or at least of the childhood of our own race. (Müller 1892: 254)

More importantly, it offered "solutions to some of the greatest problems of life, and the needed corrective for the inner life of Europe" (Müller 1892: 6). The Aryans

were the true ancestors of our race; and the Veda is the oldest book we have in which to study the first beginnings of our language, and of all that is embodied in language. (Müller 1895: 1.4)

Müller's task, as he envisioned it, was to discover the first germs of the language, religion, and mythology of "our" Aryan forefathers (Müller 1978: 3). The Veda was the most important document of "Aryan humanity" (Müller 1891: 148–49) and the first book of the "Aryan nations" (Müller 1895: 167). It presented the "sharp edges of primitive thought, the delicate features of a young language, the fresh hue of unconscious poetry" (Müller 1849–74: 3.xliii). Until Müller's edition, "our own" history was only gleaned through guesswork and endless, baseless speculations. Now, answers could be found in the Veda (Müller 1895: 1.4, 25, 62). With the tools of Indology, an

> ancient city has been laid bare before our eyes which, in the history of all other religions, is filled up with rubbish, and built over by new architects. Some of the earliest and most instructive scenes of our distant childhood have risen once more above the horizon of our memory which, until thirty or forty years ago, seemed to have vanished forever. (Müller 1892: 244)

Few Westerners would be capable of reading Müller's *editio princeps* of the *Rig Veda* (1849–74). Many, however, came into contact with Müller's vision of Aryan India through his numerous public lectures and books on India directed toward a general audience. Müller's edition is noteworthy for many reasons, not the least of which was his inclusion of Sāyaṇa's commentary. The inclusion of this medieval commentary generated a debate concerning the feasibility of reading the Veda and speculation regarding the Veda's ideal or target audience. Could the Veda as a "text" be read? If so, by whom? Specifically, the appearance of the Veda in print raised the issue of the European's real relation to this work. Rudolf von Roth, who in 1846 produced the first important European scholarly treatment of the Veda after Colebrooke's essay, disparaged the need for the use of native commentaries. He noted that a "conscientious European interpreter" of the Veda may understand it far better "being in a position to search out the sense which the poets themselves have put into their hymns and utterances" (quoted in Tull 1991: 30). Such a statement suggests just to what extent the use or rejection of Sāyaṇa's commentary reflected not only issues of translation technique, but, more interestingly, ideological concerns of readership. As we have seen throughout our examination of the Veda's reception in the West, even when it was not an issue of translation conventions, the Veda always engendered discussions on race and ethnicity and exhibited a European attempt both to appropriate the Aryan worldview and to dissociate it from anything Indian. The claim, championed particularly by Roth, that the conscientious European understood the Veda and its Aryan *Weltanschauung* better than Sāyaṇa presupposed a common cultural heritage with the Vedic people (Tull 1991: 40). It was an opinion shared by the American Sanskritist W.D. Whitney, when he noted that "The conditions and manners depicted in (the *Rig Veda*) are . . . of a character which seems almost more Indo-European than Indian" (Whitney 1987: 1.112). Whitney went on to add that European Indologists commanded the Sanskrit idiom more thoroughly than brahmins who had been trained in it since boyhood. The crux of the matter was as follows: The

Aryan tradition was lost to the Indians in the post-Vedic period, but not to the European who, no matter how far removed from the tradition, was never far removed from its vision (Tull 1991: 40). The German Romantics had adequately set the stage for European readers to believe that, through the science of language, they could access an identity that was theirs alone and foreign to modern Indians.

As we have seen, the traits of the representative groups who comprised "Aryan humanity" had long captivated the European imagination. Max Müller merely continued this tradition. He identified the Aryans as "our nearest intellectual relatives" (Müller 1892: 15; see also 1895: 1.63). They were the "ancestors of the whole Aryan race, the first framers of our words, the first poets of our thoughts, the first givers of our laws, the first prophets of our gods, and of Him who is God above all gods" (Müller 1892: 117).

According to Müller, the Aryans originated in the northern regions,[1] living together within the same precincts as the ancestors of the Greeks, Italians, Slavonians, Germans, Persians, Hindus, and Celts (Müller 1978: 14; see also 1895: 1.63–64, 66, 2.20). The actual site of the Aryan paradise, the "cradle of our race" (Müller 1888: 91), was not known (Müller 1888: 127). However, Müller was sure that it was in the East, since the earliest centers of civilized life are found in Asia (Müller 1888: 117).

The Aryans were men of strong individuality and great independence. Early on, they separated into two branches (Müller 1978: 12). The northern branch roamed northwestward (Müller 1895: 1.61; see also 1978: 14)[2] and civilized the whole of Europe, completing the "one act allotted to them on the stage of history." As the "prominent actors in the great drama of history, they carried to their fullest growth all the elements of active life with which our nature is endowed" (Müller 1978: 14). These Aryans perfected society and morals and taught us the elements of science, the laws of art, and the principles of philosophy; they embodied man's historic character (Müller 1895: 1.63–64). In this respect, they fundamentally differed from the southern branch of the Aryan race, who represented the flip side of the human character, the passive and meditative who were "absorbed in struggles of thought" (Müller 1895: 1.65–66). This persona reached its fullest growth in India (Müller 1892: 95).

Whitney, not one to ignore Müller's flights of poetic fancy, mocked Müller when he seemed to depict the Aryans as "perched for a couple of thousand years upon some exalted post of observation, watching thence the successive departure from their ancient home of the various European tribes" (Whitney 1987 1.95–96):

> . . .the fathers of the Aryan race, the fathers of our own race, gathered together in the great temple of nature, like brothers of the

same house, and looking up in adoration to the sky as the emblem of what they yearned for, a father and a god. (Müller 1895: 4.210)

Whitney then questioned whether Müller wrote such descriptions under the influence of paintings such as the Kaulbach murals in Berlin, depicting people at the foot of the ruined tower of Babel. While not a kind assessment, Whitney touched upon our very argument: Müller's entire discussion of the Veda elaborated Romantic rhetorical and ideological concerns.

The Aryan World: A Romantic Utopia

It is to be remembered that the Romantics held that the simplicity of religious dogmas defined the original state of man and its corollaries that monotheism was anterior to polytheism and primitive revelation had progressively degenerated. Once a people has unfolded its spirit to its fullest expression—from the Romantic point of view—it has fulfilled its role in history and only "repetition" (revivals), stagnation, and decay could follow. Müller's conclusions concerning the Veda recapitulated this central Romantic thesis.

What we see growing in the Veda, we have only encountered full grown or fast decaying in Persia, Greece, and Rome (Müller 1895: 1.26), where mythology had become a "disease" because "its poetical intention has been forgotten" (Müller 1895: 2.12; 5.90), "washed away by the successive waves of what we call tradition, whether we look upon it as a principle of growth or decay" (Müller 1849–74: 3.xliii). Homer showed but a view of outward life, not the inward thoughts regarding gods and men that one finds in the Veda (Müller 1891: 20). Hesiod presents a distorted caricature of the original image whereas, in the Veda, we find a real theogony (Müller 1895: 2.76). As the source of all other religions, the Veda could show us how the Persians came to worship Ormuzd and the Buddhists came to protest against temples and sacrifices. It explains how Zeus and the Olympian gods came to be what they were in the mind of Homer and how Jupiter and Mars came to be worshipped by Italian peasants (Müller 1895: 1.25). "What to the Greek scholar seems wild and fanciful is simply a matter of fact before the eyes of the student of Vedic hymns" (Müller 1897: 429).

Müller confirmed the Romantics' idealization of the Veda (Müller 1978: 12–15). The Veda was so important, it "impressed itself on all branches of literature, all religious and moral ideas, every public act" (Müller 1978: 9). It formed the background for the whole Indian world. No matter how fragmented (Müller 1978: 10) or corrupted, the *Rig Veda* was still a monument without equal (Müller 1909: 287); its point of origin a utopia and its Aryan authors the best and the brightest.

> If I were to look over the whole world to find out the country most richly endowed with all the wealth, power, and beauty that nature can bestow—in some parts a very paradise on earth—I should point to India. If I were asked under what sky the human mind has most fully developed some of its choicest gifts, has most deeply pondered on the greatest problems of life, and has found solutions to some of them which well deserve the attention even of those who have studied Plato and Kant—I should point to India. And if I were to ask myself from what literature we, here in Europe, who have been nurtured almost exclusively on the thoughts of Greeks and Romans, and one Semitic race, the Jewish, may draw that corrective which is most wanted in order to make our inner life more perfect, more comprehensive, more universal, in fact, more truly human, a life not for this life only, but a transfigured and eternal life—again I should point to India . . . I am thinking chiefly of India, such as it was a thousand, two thousand, it may be three thousand years ago—not of towns today but village communities. (Müller 1892: 6–7)

The hymns of the ancient Aryan seers were spontaneous expressions of a pure race (Müller 1978: 526); the Veda, spontaneous poetry (Müller 1895: 1.16) created by simple hearts (Müller 1895: 1.71).

There exists no literary relic that carries us back to a more primitive time than the Veda (Müller 1895: 1.34). However, its poetry was "neither beautiful, in our sense of the word, nor very profound" (Müller 1892: 163). Many of the hymns sound "childish and absurd" (Müller 1909: 282), "vulgar and obscure" (Müller 1849–74: 3.xliii), or "utterly unmeaning and insipid" (Müller 1895: 1.37). Its "simplicity and naturalness" (Müller 1909: 188; 1892: 118) is what transports us back to our origins in religious thought and language (Müller 1909: 212). It was precisely what was "childish" (Müller 1895: 1.34, 37, 101),[3] what harkened back to the childhood of humanity, that made the Veda particularly instructive (Müller 1892: 87). This was a period when childish thoughts presumably stood side by side with modern ideas. The fatal divorce between religion and philosophy had not yet occurred (Müller 1919: 33). The Veda gives us the very words of a generation of men, of whom otherwise we could form but the vaguest estimate by means of conjectures and inferences (Müller 1978: 63). It offers one of the few relics of humanity's childhood that had been preserved (Müller 1895: 1.3). In it, ancient thought is expressed in ancient language (Müller 1895: 1.67).

> There is more real antiquity in the Veda than in all the inscriptions of Egypt or Ninevah . . . old thoughts, old hopes, old faith, and old errors, the old Man altogether. (Müller 1895: 1.75–76)

Müller was careful to distinguish the *Rig Veda* from the other Vedas, which he viewed as solely liturgical (Müller 1895: 1.72)[4] and dating from a period of complete brahmin ascendancy (Müller 1978: 461). The other Vedas, like the subsequent literature, contained exactly what Müller found absent from the *Rig Veda*: the unfortunate religious and cultic apparatus of Hinduism, under whose influence Aryan spontaneity and truth had become misunderstood and perverted (Müller 1909: 282). The Veda itself was not immune to the process of decay (Müller 1909: 281; 1895: 1.54; 1978: 456). In places, it too bears witness to the ruins of faded grandeur and the memories of noble aspirations (Müller 1978: 389). Signs of degeneration could be seen as early as the mantra period of the late hymns, when a spirit was at work in the literature of India that was no longer creative, free, and original but living only on the heritage of a former age: collecting, classifying, and imitative. On the whole, however, the Veda was strong, original, pure, and natural: the later creations were modern and artificial.[5]

The Veda chronicled a period when the Aryans had not yet become "completely enslaved by a system of mere formalities." Vedic poems were collected with great zeal and accuracy (Müller 1978: 477) at a time when the Aryans were still creative and impulsive and still had the power to uphold the tradition of a past. Müller compared this poetry to the later lyric, lamenting that Europe had first been introduced to India through the prettiness of Kālidāsa. He judged Sanskrit *kāvya* to be a mere literary curiosity, a pleasant occupation for a Jones or Colebrooke during leisure hours, not the object of life study (Müller 1879: 38). Aryan Indian differed from classical India. The natural and spontaneous (Müller 1978: 498) "half-naked Hindu" repeating under an Indian sky the sacred hymns that had been handed down for three or four thousand years by oral tradition (Müller 1879: 152) differed from the courtly lyricist. The Aryans differed from their antithesis, the modern practitioners of the "hideous" religion of Shiva and Vishnu (Müller 1879: 140).

Müller's constant concern was to distinguish between the Vedic Aryan and the degenerate Hindu who was ineffectual as an historical being (Müller 1895: 1.65).[6] Toward this end, he read the Veda with a view toward rediscovering the purity of Aryan religion and promoting it as an antidote to corrupt Hindu practices. The primitive worship of ideal gods sanctioned in the Veda had degenerated into Hindu idolatry (Müller 1895: 1.37). There had been no worship of idols among the Aryans. The Aryans were actually monotheists of a sort. They believed in Kathenotheism (Henotheism, for short), the worship of single gods (Müller 1892: 147), where all deities are but different names of one and the same Godhead.[7] Like the Romantics, the Aryans recognized God's presence in the bright and sunny aspects of nature. Belief in metempsychosis did not exist in Vedic times. Rather, we find the concept of immortality, the *sine qua non* of all "real" religions. Moreover, there were no caste distinctions among the Aryans. What is mistaken for caste in the Veda differs radically from the draconian regulations found in the *Laws of Manu* or in modern usage (Müller 1879: 330; 1895: 4.306). In short, the Aryan faith was a "real" religion and Hinduism appears as its distortion (Müller 1895: 2.76). The Aryans did not practice any of the "abuses" prevalent in Hinduism:

> [t]here is no trace in the Veda of the atrocities of Shiva and Kali, nor the licentiousness of Krishna, nor of most of the miraculous adventures of Vishnu. We find in it no law to sanction the blasphemous pretentions of a priesthood to divine honors, or the degradations of any human being to a state below the animal. There is no text to countenance laws which allow the marriage of children and prohibit the remarriage of child-widows, and the unhallowed rite of burning the widow with the corpse of her husband is both against the spirit and the letter of the Veda. (Müller 1895: 4.307)

The Aryans' religion not only differed radically from Hinduism, it resembled our own beliefs in several respects (Müller 1895: 4.307). We even share their word for God.

> The same word, Deva, in Sanskrit, Deus in Latin, remained unchanged in all their prayers, their rites, their superstitions, their philosophies, and even today it rises up to heaven from thousands of churches and cathedrals—a word which, before there were Brahmans or Germans, had been framed in the dark workshop of the Aryan world. (Müller 1895: 4.221)

As the above quote makes perfectly clear, it was to be through the medium of language that Müller was able to identify with the Aryan. The study of language (comparative philology) would provide him with the only true data (Müller 1897: 1.3–12, 18–19).

Language in the Service of Myth

In a manner similar to that of Friedrich Schlegel, Müller applied linguistic systems of classification to interpret Aryan mythology and religion (Müller 1978: 1.178–80). Whitney was particularly critical of this methodology, noting that Müller did not employ a very good form of science (Whitney 1987: 1.258) and that comparative mythology could not be viewed as a branch of linguistics (Whitney 1987: 1.261). Müller, however, was not to be dissuaded.

From recognition of the connectedness of English, German, Greek, Latin, Slavonic, and Celtic with the languages of Armenia, Persia, and India, Müller set out to discover the roots these languages held in common. It is through an analysis of these common roots that Müller reconstructed the original Aryan home through a mosaic picture of their fauna, flora, agriculture, food, drink, family life, political organizations, arts, morality, and mythology (Müller 1888: 126–27). Since there had been no exchange between the Aryans who went toward Persia and India and those who went to Europe, all the common words, especially those of mythology and religion, could be claimed as common property of the whole Aryan race before the initial dispersion (Müller 1889: 295).

First, we can see that the Aryans of India separated from the Iranians before they reached the mouth of the Indus, because the names for sea in Sanskrit and Persian are totally different (Müller 1888: 152). The testimony of language also shows that before the separation, the Aryans led an agricultural and nomadic life, similar to that described by Tacitus for the ancient Germans (Müller 1899: 356). Müller concludes that the Aryans were agricultural from the existence of the root "*ar*" ("to stir"). Although Müller admitted that this root was not used in Sanskrit in the sense "to plough," it nevertheless bears witness to the Aryans' agrarian nature, since very old derivatives with this meaning can be found in other languages (Müller 1888: 134, see also 1895: 1.161). Following the same baroque logic and analyzing the Sanskrit term for daughter (*duhitṛ*) back to its "Vedic" significance as "little milkmaid," Müller proved that the Aryans were nomadic (Müller 1895: 2.24). Similar linguistic legerdemain allowed Müller to claim that the Aryans also knew the arts of making roads, building ships, weaving, sewing, and erecting houses. The science of language also suggests that they had domesticated the most important animals (cow, horse, sheep), were acquainted with the most useful metals, carried arms, recognized the bonds of blood and laws of marriage, and distinguished between right and wrong by law (Müller 1899: 356). All this data was "written in the archive of language, stretching back to times far beyond the reach of any documentary history" (Müller 1899: 357).

Since all Aryan languages have peaceful words in common and "differ so strangely in warlike expressions" (Müller 1895: 2.41), Müller concluded that all the Aryan nations led a long life of peace before they separated. Only as each colony searched for new homes and new generations formed new words reflecting their new warlike and adventurous lives, did their language acquire individuality and nationality. Aryan language preserved no traces of brutality, savagery or barbarism and "there is no evidence . . . more ancient and more trustworthy than language" (Müller 1888: xvii). It enables us to describe the Aryan utopia and acknowledge our relationship to it or the place that it holds in our study of our true selves (Müller 1892: 14).

> We are all essentially Aryans. Since Sanskrit is the most ancient
> type of English of the present day, being but varieties of one and
> the same language . . . its thoughts and feelings contain in reality
> the first roots and germs of that intellectual growth which by an
> unbroken chain connects our own generation with the ancestors of
> the Aryan race. (Müller 1895: 1.4)

Sanskrit, the ancient language of the Veda, is no more distinct from the
Greek of Homer, from the Gothic of Ulfilas, or from the Anglo-Saxon of
Alfred than French is from Italian. All these languages together form one
family, one whole, in which every member shares certain features in common
with all the rest (Müller 1895: 1.21). We are, quite simply, "the descendants
of those Vedic poets, their language is essentially our language, their
thoughts are essentially our thoughts, the world we live in is much the same
as their Aryan home" (Müller 1889: 240), and we can read the annals of our
own race, the Aryan race, among dark-skinned people (Müller 1891: 17).

> The language of the Sepoy and that of the English soldier are, in
> one sense, one and the same language. Both are built up of materi-
> als which were definitely shaped before the Teutonic and Indic
> branches separated. (Müller 1899: 385)

In the Veda, we are going to our "old home, full of memories, if only we can
read them" (Müller 1892: 31). Now, with the advantages of "special Oriental
training . . . a liberal truly historical education," we can read these memories
(Müller 1892: 31).

> Whatever the blood may be that runs through our veins, the blood
> that runs through our thoughts, I mean our language, is the same
> as that of the Aryas of India, and that language has more to do
> with ourselves than the blood that feeds our body and keeps us
> alive for a time". (Müller 1903: 71)

Within the fold of the Aryan race, Müller included the Hindus, the
Persians, the Greeks and Romans, the Slavs, the Celts, and "last, not least,
the Teutons" (Müller 1892: 116; see also 1891: 21). Certain groups, however, did not belong to his schema. For example, Müller excluded from the
Aryan family the "really barbarian races" such as Africans and American
Indians (Müller 1978: 558) as well as the Turanian and Semitic races, over
all of whom the Aryans historically ruled (Müller 1978: 15). Even before the
initial dispersion, the Aryans lived separately from the Semites and
Turanians (Müller 1978: 14, also 1895: 1.63–66). Therefore, Europeans
need claim no parenty with these races.

We are by nature Aryan, Indo-European, not Semitic: our spiritual kith and kin are to be found in India, Persia, Greece, Italy,
Germany; not in Mesopotamia, Egypt, or Palestine. (Müller
1895: 1.4)

Until the deciphering of the Veda, there had been "but one oasis in that vast
desert of ancient Asiatic history, the history of the Jews." The Veda now
offers another such oasis (Müller 1895: 1.5–6) as well as another instance of
revelation (Müller 1895: 1.17), "the wisdom of Him who is not the God of
the Jews alone" (Müller 1978: 3). Our knowledge of universal history is
imperfect if we narrow our horizon to history of Greeks and Romans, Saxons
and Celts, with a dim background of Palestine, Egypt, and Babylon, and
leave out of sight our nearest intellectual relatives, the Aryas of India, the
framers of the most wonderful language, Sanskrit, the fellow-workers in the
construction of our fundamental concepts, the fathers of the most transparent of mythologies, the inventors of the most subtle philosophy, and the
givers of the most elaborate laws (Müller 1892: 15).[8]

In the contest between Sanskrit and Hebrew, it was necessary for
Sanskrit to prevail. To do so, Müller first demoted Hebrew from its position
as the *Ursprache* (Müller 1879: 246–67).[9] Next, he sought to isolate Sanskrit
from any filiation with Hebrew. The linguistic similarities between Sanskrit
and Semitic, he noted, were coincidences, as were any parallelisms between
Aryan and Semitic religions (Müller 1891: 274). They were just too dissimilar; it was simply impossible to imagine that a Semitic language could ever
have sprung from an Aryan or an Aryan language from a Semitic tongue
(Müller 1899: 324).

Similarly, in the contest between the *Rig Veda* and the Old Testament,
it was clear which text Müller preferred. Since he could not fix the date of
individual books of the Old Testament, Müller just dismissed them as the
basis of our ideas on ancient history or religion (Müller 1891: 214). The Old
Testament merely revealed the extent to which decay was prevalent in the
religion of the Jews. Although Old Testament writers had tried to hide the
traces of degeneration, by placing the religion of the Jews before us as ready-
made from the beginning, perfect, revealed, and incapable of improvement,
they only succeeded in highlighting its pervasive decay (Müller 1879: 125).

Müller judged the Jews also to be deficient in poetry, scientific inquiry,
political thought, and philosophical originality. The Jews were mired in their
own subjectivity.

We look in vain among their poets for excellence in epic and dramatic composition. Painting and plastic arts never more than at the
decorative stage. Politics patriarchal and despotic, and their inabil-

ity to organize on a large scale has deprived them of the means of military success. Perhaps the most general feature of their character is a negative one,—their inability to perceive the general and abstract whether in thought, language, poetry or politics; and, on the other hand, a strong attraction towards the individual and personal, which makes them monotheistic in religion, lyrical in poetry, monarchical in politics, abrupt in style and useless for speculation. (Müller 1895: 1.339)

Müller thus sought to dismantle any Jewish pretensions of superiority. As we have seen elsewhere, the displacement of the Jews served as a prerequisite to the valorization of the Aryan.

Race was truly a metaphor for Müller. He spoke of the Aryan as a means of describing the ideal Self. To create a Self entailed distinguishing an Other, lacking those qualities one attributed to the Self. The Jew, of course, became that Other. In this manner, the mythologization of the Aryan completed the process of mythologizing the Jew. But we are still in the realm of the imagination. Müller might say anything he wanted about Jews and Aryans, but he resisted the appropriation of his catagorizations in the realm of the real.

On several occasions, he sought to distance himself from the misuse of his formulations by contemporary racial theorists (Müller 1869–76: 4.103–27), by distinguishing between linguistic and racial classification.

I have declared again and again that if I say Aryas, I mean neither blood nor bones, nor hair nor skull; I mean simply those who speak an Aryan language. The same applies to Hindus, Greeks, Romans, Germans, Celts and Slaves [*sic*]. When I speak of them I commit myself to no anatomical characteristics. The blue-eyed and fair-haired Scandinavians may have been conquerors or conquered, they may have adopted the language of their darker lords or their subjects, or vice versa. I assert nothing beyond their language when I call them Hindus, Greeks, Romans, Germans, Celts and Slaves [sic]; and in that sense and in that sense only, do I say that even the blackest Hindus represent an earlier stage of Aryan speech and thought than the fairest Scandinavians. This may seem strong language, but in matters of such importance, we cannot be too decided in our language. To me an ethnologist who speaks of Aryan race, Aryan blood, Aryan eyes and hair, is as great a sinner as a linguist who speaks of a dolichocephalic dictionary or a brachycephalic grammar. (Müller 1888: 120)

Blood has nothing to do with language (Müller 1888: 108). Aryanness becomes the sign of culture.

> There is no Aryan race in blood, but who ever, through the impo-
> sition of hands, whether of his parents or his foreign masters, has
> received the Aryan blessing, belongs to that unbroken spiritual suc-
> cession which began with the first apostles of that noble speech,
> and continues to the present day in every part of the globe. Aryan,
> in scientific language, is utterly inapplicable to race. It means lan-
> guage and nothing but language; and if we speak of Aryan race at
> all, we should know that it means no more than X + Aryan speech.
> (Müller 1888: 89–90)

In other words, he firmly stated that you cannot base ethnological classification on linguistic and anthropological terms (Müller 1872: 17).

The science of language and the science of ethnology should not be mixed up. Races can change languages. Different languages can be spoken by our race and the same language by different races (Müller 1899: 450). Of course, Müller spoke too little and too late. Myths take on lives of their own, when they support the political interests of those in power or those seeking power.

In a long letter to Risley commenting on his *Ethnological Survey of India*, Müller tried to exonerate himself from the mischief produced by employing the terminology of comparative philology in an ethnological sense.

> My warnings have been of little effect; and such is the influence of
> evil communications, that I myself cannot help pleading guilty of
> having occasionally used linguistic terms in an ethnological sense.
> Still it is an evil that ought to be resisted with all our might.
> Ethnologists persist in writing of Aryas, Shemites and Turanians,
> Ugrians, Dravidians, Kolarians, Bantu races and c., forgetting that
> these terms have nothing to do with blood, or bones, or hair, or
> facial angles, but simply and solely with language. Aryas are those
> who speak Aryan languages, whatever their color, whatever their
> blood. In calling them Aryas we predicate nothing of them except
> that the grammar of their language is Aryan. The classification of
> Aryas and Shemites is based on linguistic grounds and on nothing
> else; and it is only because languages must be spoken by somebody
> that we may allow ourselves to speak of language as synonymous
> with peoples. (Müller 1888: 244–45) [10]

Müller's most public statement of position appeared in his *Antrittsrede* at the University of Strassburg in 1872, when he reiterated that there existed only

Aryan and Semitic linguistic families, but no Aryan race, blood, or skulls. In later instances, Müller was clearly defensive. Eventually he did not speak of races and *Völkern*, rather "the Aryan family," "Aryan humanity," and "the civilization of the Aryan race, that race to which we and all the greatest nations of the world . . . belong" (Müller 1892: 116).

However, Müller's myth of the Aryan throughout the thirty-odd years of editing the *Rig Veda* entailed the very type of categorical mixing that he condemned in the Strassburg lecture. How do we explain this paradox? I have tried to show how it was far less an issue of Müller's blindness toward his methodology (though that too was at issue) than his adherance to a Romantic emplotment of India. His need to construct the Vedic Aryan from the text and identify with this Aryan stemmed from religious and aesthetic concerns far more akin to the aims of Romanticism than nineteenth-century race theory.

Müller would be shocked at an assessment of his work in light of Romanticism. He maintained that his Aryans were merely an earlier stage of our own race (Müller 1891: 385–86), not a "race of savages, of mere nomads and hunters" (Müller 1895: 2.40) as he felt they had been presented by his academic rivals. It was, he disclaimed, scholars like Pischel and Geldner, who were under the influence of Rousseau regarding the simplicity and innocence of primitive man versus the "modern" Aryans who had reached the summit of civilization. Müller did not recognize his penchant for lyricism, even when he speaks of Aryan "home-grown poetry" (Müller 1892: 140) as "natural growth" (Müller 1892: 97) that has been "carried down the stream of time, and washed up on the shores of so many nations" (Müller 1895: 2.40), or their "home-grown religion" that history has preserved for us "in order to teach us what the human mind can achieve if left to itself, surrounded by a scenery and by conditions of life that might have made man's life on earth a paradise if man did not possess the strange art of turning even a paradise into a place of misery" (Müller 1892: 140). But a Romantic he was and not just in a rhetorical sense.

One can see a pattern in Müller's classifications of language, gods, and mythology. His analyses move from the material to the immaterial, the concrete to the abstract, the simple to the complex, and the single to the general. Just as language began as monosyllabic and developed agglutination and inflection, so then did Müller conclude that monotheism preceeded polytheism (Müller 1978: 510–12, 528, 559; see also 1892: 1.91–92; 2.132). By placing mythology and polytheism at the door of language, he continued a tradition begun by Friedrich Schlegel. He retooled the methodology of Romantic linguistics into his science of language. Müller's reading of the Veda verified the Romantic claim that India was the original seat of true poetry and primitive revelation, and the site of its degeneration. Max Müller was a worthy heir to his father, the German Romantic poet Wilhelm Müller.

This Indologist, a final avatar of Romanticism in service of linguistics, popularized an ideal vision of the Aryan that would bear fruit. Although he himself tried to resist the "patriotic" impulses, Müller had to admit that he would be as proud as anyone to look upon "Germany as the cradle of all Aryan life" (Müller 1888: 127) and "Teutonic speech as the fountain of all Aryan thought" (Müller 1888: 154). So, indeed, did the nonspecialists who expanded upon his theories.

CONCLUSION

The Western quest for origins received an initial formulation in the recognition of philological relationships among Sanskrit, Greek, Latin, and other languages of Europe. Already, in the Enlightenment, there was much speculation regarding India, its culture, language, and peoples. Many of the uninformed assessments of this time would resurface in subsequent Orientalist scholarship, Romantic mythography, nineteenth-century linguistic science, and race theory. Excited by the linguistic affinity between Sanskrit and other languages, Orientalist scholars fostered the comparative science of religion and mythology that developed a vision of an Aryan race as the originator of Indian and European culture. The belief in the Indo-European origins of Europe and India further spurred European interest in Vedic Aryan sources. Enlightenment thinkers idealized the Vedic past in an attempt to find a utopia outside Europe and as an alternative to the biblical tradition. Romantic mythographers not only accepted Aryan genius, but prioritized it. Speculation regarding the Aryan provided a means whereby Indian history could be used to create a "fresh historical tradition" that expressed specifically European political and ideological interests (Thapar 1992: 2). While Evangelicals, Utilitarians, and colonial administrators could only envision India's salvation through a rejection of its irrational culture, conversion to Christianity, and embrace of British rule, scholars sympathetic to Indian culture, epitomized by the figure of F. Max Müller, effectively promulgated an idealized portrait of the Aryan in order to counter those who championed this backward view of the Indian past. By focusing on the common descent and the legitimate relationship between the Hindu and the Anglo-Saxon, however, Müller adopted a strategy that would have serious repercussions.

Let us remember the dates of Müller's Veda (1849–74). Rather than have it begin our examination of the reception of the Veda in the West, we have allowed it to mark the turning point of our inquiry. The Veda as a "real" text was either unknown or little known to Western authors before Müller. Nevertheless, we have shown how the Veda played a significant role in Enlightenment, pre-Romantic, and Romantic literary and philosophical speculation. As an absent text, it wielded great authority. Although neither

discovered nor fully translated, the Veda served as an important tool in formulating European discourse concerning poetry, race, and religion. The possibility of the existence of the Veda effected a renewed interest in the
Romantic theses of a revealed and primitive monotheism and the degeneration of Greek culture. What Europeans sought in India was not Indo-
European religion, but a reassessment of Judeo-Christianity. The
development of the concept of an Aryan religion proved to be a consequence,
rather than the goal of these metaphorical journeys to the East.

The Romantics, whose origins can be traced to pre-Romanticism and
Herder, sought in the Veda a religious and national poetry. By "national,"
they meant indigenous and popular. The Veda, in particular, permitted comparison with an ultimately diverse national mythology. As the publication of
the Veda marks the birth of Indology (the philological, historical, and religious studies of ancient India), its appearance in print should have
announced the death of Romantic Indomania. However, one is surprised by
the similarity between Max Müller's exegesis and the critical discussion that
preceded his work. When juxtaposed to the Enlightenment, Storm and
Stress, and Romantic emplotment of the Aryan, Müller's commentary on the
Rig Veda and its medieval native gloss revivified (with the aid of "science")
those very Romantic yearnings believed dormant. The Romantic concepts of
the degeneration of primitive monotheism into polytheism and the view of
history as a development of the unique character of a people would reach
complete articulation in time. Once the pinnacle was reached, the subsequent
history was an inevitable falling off, punctuated by attempts and revitaliza-
tion. Stagnation comes to define India in Western consciousness, appearing
ultimately in the philosophy of Hegel, Marx, and Spengler.

History was in a state of motion, a living organism. Universal history
was structured organically and could be reduced to certain recurring elemen-
tary phenomena with the birth, development, and death of the individual or
group organism as eternal. Decadent cultures distinguished themselves from
cultured populations. Decadent peoples consisted of those cut off from the
soil, hovering between peace and war, the national and international. The
cultured were those bound by a common destiny. Culture was Faustian, constantly in progress. The *Rig Veda*'s "appearance" in Max Müller's abundant
commentary merely confirmed these Romantic hypotheses.

The discovery that there existed in India a tradition older or at least as
old as the biblical tradition was regarded as an event of the first magnitude,
only to be compared in its consequences to the rediscovery of classical
antiquity in the Renaissance. Through the study of India's past, it was
hoped that scholars could reconstruct the history of mankind's origin and
past, the development of religions and philosophies. By giving Vedic
Aryans a place in universal history, a crucial displacement of the Jews was

effected. Much of the discourse concerning the Veda effectively resulted in assigning the Jews a subaltern role in history. In Voltaire's case, we saw how the valorization of the Aryans, who had been ignored by the Bible and universal histories, necessarily entailed a devaluation of the Judeo-Christian tradition. Voltaire was always motivated by his need to challenge the primacy of the Church. For others, the motivations for this displacement were less clear.

Testimony from Vedic India also allowed Europe to refute and/or denounce the Greek miracle. In India, one could discover an old civilization whose cultural riches had been passed down to Greece. However, India could also be cited to prove that ancient Greece represented a real catastrophe, a mutilation that had detoured humanity from its true mission by replacing the cult of god with the cult of man. Finally, the Veda provided essential information concerning the European past. Thought to be the oldest available text of an "Indo-Germanic" language, the *Rig Veda* promised to reveal the state of civilization that was closest to the supposed common ancestors of all Indo-Germanic peoples.

One can distinguish, therefore, two motives for the beginnings of Vedic scholarship in the West. First, there entailed the search for the oldest forms of religion and language. Second, it set the stage for the inquiry into the origin and past of the European people through information drawn from old Indian sources. With the twentieth-century legacy of Aryanism fresh in our memory, it is difficult not to overstate the argument. We can acknowledge, however, that the European discourse on the absent Veda created a portrait of pure and cultivated Aryan ancestors which wielded such authority that the subsequent discovery of the text could not alter the welter of assumptions and fantasies that formed its initial interpretation. This ideology of the Aryan participated in the formation of a new mythology of the past. This mythology was fueled by irrational impulses growing out of anxiety regarding questions of national identity and mission. Themes which resonate in the works of the authors we investigated found their way into the new mythology: the displacement of the Jews from a central position on the stage of history; theories regarding the degeneration of peoples and religions from unity and purity to multiplicity and polytheism; and the idealization of imaginary ancestors and their fictitious descendants. Thus, the myth of the Aryan was employed not only to construct the origins of society, but also to foster nationalism. In its latter configuration, it could eventually be used to disarticulate existing society and rearticulate an alternative noteworthy for its identification of a mythic scapegoat.

CHAPTER 3

Nietzsche's Aryan *Übermensch*

Mastery over nature, the Idée fixe of the 20th
century, is Brahmanism, Indo-German.
—Friedrich Nietzsche, *Nachgelassene Fragmente*

INTRODUCTION

Much has been written on Nietzsche's reconstruction of Indian thought.[1] Indologists and historians of religion have placed great importance on Nietzsche's appropriation of Indian themes; and, indeed, the philosopher's evocation of India is varied and often tantalizing. These evocations range from use of terminology and concepts to Nietzsche's penchant for "quoting" Sanskrit sources.[2] One critic has, however, recently discounted the role that Indian thought played for Nietzsche, viewing such references as late and insignificant. This position views Nietzsche's evocation of India as specious and accuses him of the very trivialization that he accused Schopenhauer of committing (Nietzsche, *Untimely Meditations* iii, 7).[3] To my mind, this is a harsh judgment. While the traces of India's influence in Nietzsche's work are elusive, and the philosopher did not view India with the "trans-European eye" that he claimed (cited in Sprung 1991: 83), India did, in fact, play a significant role in Nietzsche's final work.

Any discussion of Nietzsche's reception of India must begin with the *Genealogy of Morals* (I.5), where he develops his myth of the Aryan. In the first part to this section in the *Genealogy*, Nietzsche claims that the term *ārya* denotes "the wealthy" or the "owners" rather than its conventional meaning of "honorable" or "noble" (Monier Williams 1990: 152).[4] According to Nietzsche, this connotation of the term *ārya* points to the Aryans' true nature as masters. However, the Aryans must have undergone some tremendous psychological and physical defeat, if their descendants offer any valid testimony. The blond Aryan, a conqueror and master, was eclipsed by the dark-skinned common man. Races that the Aryans once subjugated, such as the pre-Aryan inhabitants of Italian soil, clearly prevailed in modern times. Their color, size of skull, and perhaps even intellectual and social instincts have neutralized Aryan traits, and a miscegenated population now predominates in Europe.

Aryan blood has thus racially and morally degenerated. Although Nietzsche believed that the Western Aryan had all but disappeared, he felt that the Indian Aryan had largely avoided his distant cousins' fate. The Indian Aryan escaped moral and physical degradation due to his adherance to dictates promulgated in the *Laws of Manu*.

In a letter to Peter Gast (May 31, 1888), Nietzsche describes *Manu* as the primeval (*uralte*) "absolute Aryan product," that presented a code of morality based on the Veda (Nietzsche 1984: 3.324ff.). As "a summary of the Veda" (Nietzsche 1986: 6.426), *Manu* was *the* text of Aryan religion (Nietzsche 1986: 13.380–81), the racially purest Aryan law book (*Will to Power* 143) and the only source from which one should develop an understanding of the Aryan worldview. In the following discussion, we will discuss how and why Nietzsche chose *Manu* as source material for his reconstruction of Indian thought. Before we tackle this issue, however, a short digression into *Manu*'s place in Nietzsche reception may prove fruitful.

Although Nietzsche makes numerous references to *Manu* throughout his work, and his editor Giorgio Colli referred to its excessive influence on him (Nietzsche 1986: 13.667), traditional Nietzsche scholars have tended to ignore the philosopher's references to the Hindu law book. Walter Kaufmann's post–World War II rehabilitation of Nietzsche began this trend. Kaufmann underplayed the philosopher's comments on the Indian lawgiver (Kaufmann 1974: 304–15) for the simple reason that they dealt primarily with breeding, a topic that would ill-serve Kaufmann's desire to distance Nietzsche from the Nazis. In fact, Kaufmann even denied that Nietzsche ever dealt at length with the topic of breeding. Though here is not the place to categorize or assess the Nietzsche-Nazi relationship, I might note, in passing, that beginning in the 1940s, Kaufmann (along with other champions of Nietzsche such as the Mann brothers, Camus, and Bataille) sought to exonerate the philosopher from any inspirational role he may have played for the Nazis.[5] Their position ran counter to that of Lukács and the historian Crane Brinton, who claimed that Nietzsche served the Nazi cause. In the last fifty years of Nietzsche reception, a middle ground has prevailed, wherein Nietzsche is seen to have provided elements in his philosophy that were attractive to the Nazis (Santaniello 1994: 149).[6]

Another logic of a less political nature might also account for the critics' refusal to question Nietzsche's references to *Manu*. While literary-minded scholars approach Nietzsche with a view to honoring the philosopher's resistance to systematization,[7] the same care cannot be said of theoretically or philosophically oriented scholars. Nietzsche's evocation of as exotic a reference as *Manu* could, indeed, trouble a conceptual reading, prompting a desire to ignore anything that does not fit a systematic approach. As respected a Nietzsche scholar as Richard Schacht, for example, encourages readers to look beyond the ephemeral noise that clutters Nietzsche's prose and filter out the static. One must pass over those frequent "rhetorical excesses" that obscure the philosopher's message.[8] If this critical approach is accepted in the field of Nietzsche scholarship, it is no wonder that traditional Nietzsche scholars generally ignore the philosopher's references to the Hindu law treatise.

Readers faced with Nietzsche's fragmentary *Nachlass* might sympathize with the critic who simply ignores Nietzsche's arcane discussions of *Manu*. Those same readers, however, might also pause at the implications of such an approach. In broad historical terms, we know that Nietzsche has suffered far too much from the impositions and selectivity of his readers, whether they be sinister (like his sister and the Nazis) or systematic (like academic analyses that have come to dominate the institutional reception of Nietzsche). In theoretical terms, if poststructuralism and deconstruction have taught us anything, we must be leery of any "filtering" process. Nietzsche's indebtedness to Indian thought is an excellent case in point. His references to India can be read in two ways. Either Nietzsche constructed his works so that nothing was superfluous and everything rendered as content, or Nietzsche's numerous yet incohesive references to India should be viewed as rhetorical excesses that distract us from his larger message. I tend to believe that Nietzsche's literary economy exhibits a propensity to develop a wide variety of themes. Among those themes we should include the breeding mechanism of caste. It is my belief that caste, or as Nietzsche termed it, "order of rank," played a far more important role in the philosopher's thought than many critics would allow. In fact, it is my contention that Nietzsche constructed a myth of the Aryan from the discussion of caste found in *Manu* that would play a significant role in his philosophy of the *Übermensch*. In this chapter, we will investigate how he used the Hindu law treatise to develop an ideology of the Aryan. We will begin, however, by explaining how *Manu* came to represent for Nietzsche the Aryan text par excellence, equal in authority to Hindu scripture. Nietzsche's assessment of *Manu*'s authority was only partially correct and, as we shall see, his *Manu* had little in common with the Sanskrit original.

READING NIETZSCHE READING INDIA

An examination of Nietzsche's references to the Hindu lawgiver points out a rather significant issue—the quotations from *Manu* do not correspond to the Sanskrit text itself or to any translations that were available in Nietzsche's time.[9] Annemarie Etter has shown the extent to which Nietzsche based his discusssion on material not found in *Manu* (Etter 1987: 342–45). The question then becomes, where did Nietzsche cull his citations? In his own footnotes, Nietzsche identified Louis Jacolliot's *Les législateurs religieux:*

Manou-Moïse-Mahomet as a source reference for his understanding of *Manu*.[10]
Jacolliot claimed to offer excerpts from a southern recension that he identified as the basis for the manuscripts found throughout India and, as a consequence, the recension used in the European language translations.

Jacolliot had been stationed as a French colonial offical near Calcutta.
His publications were of a nonspecialist nature. He was a populizer of the
"fantastic" school who believed that all intellectual and spiritual thought
could be traced back to India (Etter 1987: 345–46). Jacolliot's *Manu* is a
product of the India that had been codified in the Enlightenment. Jacolliot's
anti-Semitism and anti-Christianity (directed primarily against Rome) have
their precedent in Voltaire's fulminations, as does his notion that
Christianity is a pale copy of brahminism. That Jacolliot continued a tradition of idealizing ancient India as the source of all subsequent culture is less
significant than the new fantasies he brought to this script and transmitted to
Nietzsche. Jacolliot supplied Nietzsche with the significant and erroneous
notion that *Manu* was the oldest sourcebook of the Aryan world, dating its
compilation at 13,000 B.C. It was, therefore, thanks to Jacolliot that
Nietzsche's entire understanding of *Manu* was flawed. Although Nietzsche
possessed a fraudulent *Manu* and a false chronology, his understanding of
Manu's significance was not entirely misplaced.

Manu is indeed a standing authority in the orthodox Hindu tradition
(Manu 1992: xviii).[11] As a compendium of religious law, custom, and politics, *Manu* makes ample references to Vedic literature and refers extensively
to earlier law codes. Its eponymous author, a mythological figure believed to
be the original man and the son of the god Brahma, gives the text authority.
As a fundamental text in the literature of *dharma*,[12] *Manu* deals with the customs governing the development of the individual and proper relations of
different groups in society. It codifies belief in the fourfold caste system as a
means of social cooperation for the common good, even though the system
does not promote social coherence (Radhakrishnan and Moore 1957: 172).
Manu stresses that individuals must perform the function for which they are
suited as well as that for which they are born.

In theory, Indians place a tremendous emphasis on *Manu*.[13] It serves as
an absolute authority of both Hindu knowledge and practice, competing
with the Veda itself. As a text, *Manu* is cited more frequently than any other
dharmashāstra. It has always been brokered by the priestly class who borrowed from the prestige of its "Aryan" origin (Manu 1992: xli–xlii). *Manu*,
however, could neither claim the authority or the antiquity of the Vedas or
the Upanishads, which are thought by Hindus to be a continuation of the
Vedas (*vedānta*, that is, "end of the Veda"). Although the Vedas and the
Upanishads were available in Nietzsche's time in translation and commentary, Nietzsche chose *Manu* as a "synthesis of the Veda" and ignored all

other Sanskrit canonical texts. In order to accept the Hindu law book as an alternative to scripture, Nietzsche first established the priority of human law in relation to God's word.

In the *Antichrist*, written shortly before his breakdown in early 1889, Nietzsche claimed that a population at some point in its evolution declares that the values by which it lives are fixed and are no longer subject to experimentation. The stabilization of core values is achieved either by declaring them revealed or sanctioned by tradition. As revelation, these values appear as laws created not from human experimentation but from divine intervention. As such, they are perfect and outside history, a gift from God. Tradition claims its own authority. It too exists from the beginning. Since it was created by our ancestors, it would be impious to call it into question. Thus, for Nietzsche, both scripture and tradition lay claim to equal textual authority (*Antichrist* 57). Either God has given us our values or our ancestors have lived them and codified them as law. Nietzsche maintained that the Aryan philosophers of the Vedānta took this notion one step further when they usurped all power, authority, and credibility. By judging the whole course of nature as conditioned by their laws, the Aryans equated truth with the teaching of priests and reduced reason to a mechanism of conformity with law itself as the highest end. According to Nietzsche, law became their highest reference. The exemplum of Aryan lawbooks, *Manu*, thus became for Nietzsche *the* authoritative Aryan reference. The priority that others assigned to the Veda, Nietzsche gave to *Manu*.

Nietzsche made human law supersede divine revelation for the very reason that *Manu* complemented his ideas on religion in a noteworthy manner and provided him with a revolutionary system of human morality.[14] Indeed, Nietzsche came to believe that all the moral teachings of nations such as Egypt or Greece were only caricatures of Aryan moral laws first articulated in *Manu* (*Will to Power* 143). An examination of Nietzsche's references to *Manu* quickly reveals what he found so captivating. Nietzsche's reading of *Manu* focused exclusively on caste and its relationship to breeding (*Züchtung*). In fact, the breeding of caste was the only thing that Nietzsche found appealing in India at all (*Twilight of the Idols* 7.3).

MANU AS A "SEMITIZED" ARYAN SOURCEBOOK

According to Nietzsche, *Manu* was founded upon a "holy lie" consisting of the priests' belief that they represented the supreme expression of the type "man." Priests derive their concept of "improvement from themselves." Believing in their own superiority, they will themselves to *be* superior. The origin of their holy lie (or new concept of truth) resides in this will to power.

In order to establish their rule, they needed to place power in the priesthood. This was a radically new concept, since priests did not physically or militarily possess power. In fact, they were powerless (*Genealogy* I.7),[15] the direct antithesis of the knightly aristocrat and, as such, the most evil creatures. There was even something unhealthy about them. Priests turned away from action and combined brooding with emotional volatility, as seen in the anti-sensual and enervating metaphysics of the brahmins.

> With priests, everything becomes more dangerous: not only cures and therapies, but also arrogance, revenge, perspicacity, extravagance, love, desire to dominate, virtue, illness. (*Genealogy* I.6)

Priestly claims to power did not stem from naivete or self-deception. "Fanatics" do not invent such carefully thought-out systems of oppression. The most cold-blooded reflection was at work. *Manu* provides the classic model in a specifically Aryan form of priestly ambition. It presents the most fundamental lie ever formulated, a lie that, copied almost everywhere, has corrupted the whole world (*Will to Power* 142).

In particular, this Aryan spirit of the priest corrupted the Jews and Christians. The ideal of a state run by priests ("Semitism") consists of reviving the Aryan order of caste (*Will to Power* 143). Nietzsche felt that caste should be reinstated, since modern society had been overrun by scum, criminals, and the mentally ill. Because of Christianity, modern society is no longer a society at all, but a "sick conglomerate of *caṇḍālas*"[16] without the strength to excrete (*Will to Power* 50).[17] The establishment of equal rights had created a social hodge-podge, where the *canaille* of all the castes had mingled their blood. After two or three generations of mixing, race was no longer recognizable and everything had become a mob (*Will to Power* 864).

The brahmin priest and the *caṇḍāla* outcaste became pregnant symbols for Nietzsche.[18] He equated the *caṇḍāla* with all that was wrong with society.[19] However, Nietzsche also identified the *caṇḍāla* with the figure of the philosopher (*Antichrist* 13) and, by extension, with himself. Finally, he established the *caṇḍāla* as the antithesis to the *Übermensch* and identified the brahmin with the Aryan. Thus, the philosopher's fascination with caste regulations had wide-ranging significance for his moral system.

THE ARYAN AS *ÜBERMENSCH*

In a late fragment, Nietzsche wrote: "What is noble? Thoughts on the order of rank" (Nietzsche 1986: 12.45). He viewed the order of rank as an order of power (*Will to Power* 856). When Nietzsche called for a "new aristocracy" or a "new ruling caste" he advocated, in actuality, an order of rank between classes modeled on the caste regulations he found in *Manu*. Nietzsche felt impelled to reestablish an order of rank, since universal suffrage had eroded the "pathos of distance" necessary for the aristocratic values upon which society depended.[20] A doctrine was needed that was powerful enough to work as a breeding agent that would strengthen the strong and paralyze or destroy the world-weary (*Will to Power* 862). Since no social grouping had the courage to claim master rights and society continued to suffer (*Antichrist*, 43), Nietzsche demanded a return to an order that would sanction master privilege and engender a pathos of distance between classes. He found this order in the Indian caste system, but also, it should be noted, in medieval Europe and ancient Rome.

The pathos of distance grew out of the ingrained difference between strata. Nietzsche believed that when a ruling caste can look down upon its subjects, it easily suppresses them. In doing so, "that other, more mysterious pathos" can grow up, that

> craving for an ever new widening of distances with the soul itself, the development of ever higher, rarer, more remote, further-stretching, more comprehensive states—in brief simply the enhancement of the type "man," the continual "self-overcoming of man" to use a moral formula in a supra-moral sense. (*Beyond Good and Evil*, sec. 257)

Thus, the pathos of distance that engendered caste separation also served as the origin of higher aspiration.

Moreover, order of rank was essential to any genuine culture (*Will to Power* 184) and a precondition for every elevation in culture (*Antichrist* 43). It provided the catalyst and an arrangement for breeding (*Beyond Good and Evil* 262) human beings who would carry the seeds of the future (*The Gay Science* 23).[21] The reestablishment of an order of rank would make possible the creation of the *Übermensch*, whom Nietzsche envisioned as the goal of human striving (*Will to Power* 1001), upon whose arrival the destiny of humanity depended (*Will to Power* 987). It was this very order of rank that was lacking in European culture and lacking in Christianity (*Will to Power* 195).[22] Europe needed a new order lest Christian values of mercy and compassion destroy it.[23] Without an order of rank, the sick and the weak flourish, and culture becomes "the sum of zeroes, with every zero having equal rights" (*Will to Power* 53). Nietzsche found a propitious model for such a highly stratified social and political system in the aristocratic "Aryan" society that he discovered in *Manu*.

Nietzsche clearly equated morality with the improvement of man as a species. He viewed such improvement taking two possible forms: through taming (as in the case of an animal in a zoo or a human in the Church) or through breeding of a definite race.[24] Judging the latter option preferable, he viewed its most grandiose example revealed in *Manu*. Nietzsche understood *Manu* as a text primarily dealing with the task of breeding four races.[25] He found the Aryans who developed *Manu*'s "breeding" morality a hundred times more gentle and rational than the Christians who had devised a taming morality (*Twilight of the Idols* 7.3). To enter the Aryan utopia described in *Manu* was akin to escaping the fetid air of the Christian sick house and dungeon (*Kranken-und Kerkerluft*). Quite literally, the New Testament "stinks" when compared to *Manu*. Juxtaposed to the law book of the ruling class of Aryan India, it represented a paltry (*armselig*) tradition.

CHRISTIANITY, AN ANTI-ARYAN OUTCASTE RELIGION

In Nietzsche's view, Aryan religion deified the feeling of power (*Will to Power* 145), while Christianity represented a rejection of the Aryan moral imperative of breeding race and privilege.

> The problem I thus pose is not what shall succeed mankind in the sequence of living beings (man is an end), but what type of man shall be *bred*, shall be *willed*, for being higher in value . . . Even in the past this higher type has appeared often—but as a fortunate accident, as an exception, never as something *willed* . . . From dread the opposite type was willed, bred and *attained*: the domestic animal, the herd animal, the sick human animal—the Christian. (*Antichrist* 3.4)

In Christianity, the individual had become so important that he could no longer be sacrificed. According to Nietzsche, nothing was more dangerous than when all types became equal before God (*Will to Power* 246). Christianity, as a counterprinciple to selection, represented the anti-Aryan religion par excellence: a total subversion (*Umwerthung*) of Aryan values and a victory of *caṇḍāla* values (*Twilight of the Idols* 7, 4). With Christianity, the masters had been defeated by common men. Their victory entailed blood poisoning (*Genealogy* I.9). As the religion for the poor and downtrodden, the wretched, ill-constituted and underprivileged, plebeian Jewish Christianity defeated race (*Genealogy* I.9). Although it passed itself off as a religion of love, Christianity represents nothing but the revenge of the *caṇḍāla* (*Twilight of the Idols* 7.4). It denies the enslavement necessary to bring about the emergence of a higher type (*Will to Power* 259).

In order for Christianity to function as a *caṇḍāla* religion, it had to have originated among a *caṇḍāla* people. And indeed, Nietzsche speculated that the Jews were once *caṇḍālas* under the servitude of Hindus.[26] It was during this time that "their type" as an enslaved and despised group took root. As a *caṇḍāla* race, the Jews gradually ennobled themselves by taking control of lands and creating gods (Nietzsche 1986: 13.377–78). They learned from their Indian rulers how to make a priesthood their master and how to organize a people (*Will to Power* 143).[27] In fact, it was in the figure of the Jew that *caṇḍāla* hatred first became flesh (*Antichrist* 58). In other words, the Jews recognized their *caṇḍāla* status, embraced it, and turned it to their advantage. They incorporated animosity against the aristocratic, noble, and proud into their religion.[28] They institutionalized their hatred against power and the ruling classes (*Will to Power* 184). Their revolt ultimately resulted in the creation of the true *caṇḍāla* religion, Christianity (*Will to Power* 145), when the Jewish priestly caste itself became a privileged aristocracy and was overthrown. Christ was the ultimate *caṇḍāla*, a figure who rejected the Jewish priests in order to be redeemed (Nietzsche 1986: 13.396). Nietzsche's argument, however novel its contours, points to the familiar strategy that has informed much of the discussion regarding the Aryan in European thought. Its message dates from the Enlightenment; the displacement of the Jewish faith from its position of religious prominence.

THE JEW AND THE ARYAN

While Nietzsche's Aryan brahmins functioned both literally and symbolically, it is important to note that he did not identify them with Germans or contrast them to the Jews. In fact, his future master race was to be reared from international racial unions (*Will to Power* 960).[29] Nietzsche had long since repudiated the anti-Semitism he flirted with in his Wagner days (Kaufmann 1974: 42–47); the argument is primarily theological and secondarily racial. He reviled German anti-Semites and felt they should be expelled (*Beyond Good and Evil* 251). Closer to home, he mocked the anti-Semitic colonial venture of his sister and brother-in-law in Paraguay and their attempt to form a racially pure new Germany. Indeed, contrary to anti-Semitic and Germanophile groups, Nietzsche viewed the Jews racially as the strongest and purest race in Europe.[30] He maintained that when Semitic stock bred with Aryans, a particularly fruitful mixture arose (Nietzsche 1986: 12:45). He claimed, in fact, that the much vaunted purity of the German soul was a blend of Slav, Celt, and Jew (Nietzsche 1986: 11.702). Nietzsche felt that, had it been their predeliction, the Jews could have conquered Europe. Their priority lay elsewhere—in finding a homeland—and Nietzsche called upon Europe to accommodate the Jew in this legitimate quest (*Beyond Good and Evil* 261). He feared the increasing violence directed against Jews (*Human, All Too Human* 1.475). In other words, Nietzsche admired both the contemporary Jew and the prophets of the Old Testament. It was the priestly, prophetic strand of Judaism that he despised.[31]

In other words, Nietzsche's sympathy with the modern Jew as a self-sufficient and incorruptible threatened minority did not influence his negative judgment of Judaism in its priestly manifestation and the Christianity that it had spawned. It was this line of descent that posed the problem. Prophetic Judaism was condemned for its role in producing Christianity (Duffy and Mittleman 1988: 301–17). The important point of this reasoning was to expose the Jews as imitators of the Aryans. They should not appear as the true authors of Europe's origins.

We have seen how Nietzsche was not unique in this line of thinking. Just as Voltaire tried to show with his discovery of the lost Veda, so Nietzsche attempted to prove with his reading of *Manu*: the Jews are only agents, intermediaries, and mediators (*Vermittler*): they "discover" *nothing* (*Will to Power* 143). Unlike the Aryans, Jews were not creative.[32] The *philosophes*, the Romantics, and Nietzsche all called upon the authority of "Aryan" texts to support their polemics. Voltaire et al. had called upon "Vedic" revelation to debunk Hebrew revelation. Nietzsche, however, called upon the authority of Aryan law, since his philosophy had rendered any kerygmatic authority meaningless. It is only logical that, with the death of God, tradition should carry more weight than scripture.

Nietzsche found it significant that the Aryans had sought to regulate morality through human law rather than through divine scripture. He felt that by creating a law book like *Manu* and imbuing it with superordinate authority, the Aryans were willing to concede for themselves the right to become masterful and perfect. Nietzsche, in fact, viewed them as a master race (*Will to Power* 145). Through experimentation, they had perfected their way of life. The caste system, the supreme dominating Aryan law, was made to appear as a natural law sanctioning a natural order, exempt from arbitrary caprice and "modern ideas" (*Antichrist* 57). The highest caste represented this nobility.

> The most spiritual human men, as the *strongest*, find their happiness where others would find destruction: in the labyrinth, in hardness against themselves and others, experiments; their joy is self-conquest; asceticism becomes in them nature, need, and instinct. Difficult tasks are a privilege to them; to play with burdens which crush others, a recreation. Knowledge—a form of asceticism. They are the most venerable kind of man; this does not preclude their being the most cheerful and kindliest. They rule not because they want to but because they *are*; they are not free to be second. . . . The order of castes, *order of rank*, merely formulates

the highest law of life; the separation of the three types is necessary
for the preservation of society, to make possible higher and highest
types. The *inequality* of rights is the condition for the existence of
any rights at all. . . . As one climbs *higher* life becomes even harder:
the coldness increases, responsibility increases. A high culture is a
pyramid; it can stand only on a broad base, its first presupposition
is a strong and soundly consolidated mediocrity. (*Antichrist* 57)

Compared with this Aryan order of rank, the modern moral order was bank-
rupt. The mixture of classes and races had leveled out and mediocritized all
humanity. Man was on his own and needed a new nobility with a will for the
future (*Zarathustra* 3.11). *Manu* provided Nietzsche with the "conscious
breeding process" that he envisioned as the foundation for the development
of the master race (*Will to Power* 954; *Beyond Good and Evil* 251).[33]

Although in the above quote Nietzsche specifically described the highest among three castes, he clearly envisioned the brahmin as a partial model
for his man of the future, shaped through breeding (*Gay Science* 577). He
considered the brahmin as the highest type of man, the complete antithesis
of the *caṇḍāla* (*Will to Power* 139). Brahmins incarnated for Nietzsche the
abstract Aryan virtues of strength, duty, power, and order (Nietzsche 1986:
13.381). Their asceticism consisted of moderation in diet and sexual activity.
Their disdain for wealth and worldly power enabled them to rule over
others.[34] Nietzsche even endowed his ideal brahmins with a will to power.[35]
Nietzsche claimed that the brahmins were emancipated from the senses and
dignified, as opposed to the savage, who was an unclean and incalculable
beast (*Will to Power* 237). The brahmin was a terror-inspiring animal-tamer
toward his beasts.[36]

Nietzsche thus accepted the reality that the breeding organization of
Manu had to be fearsome (*furchtbar*) in order to work. It necessitated con-
fronting the non-bred *caṇḍāla*.[37] Simple hygienic measures had not been suf-
ficient, necessitating more draconian sanctions in order to better separate the
"virtuous" and the "people of race" from the *caṇḍāla* breed (*Twilight of the
Idols* 7.3). It was precisely *Manu's* variation of the *jus talionis* that allowed the
Aryan to "atone" and become religiously free again (Nietzsche 1986: 13.380).
Nietzsche claimed that by reinstating the breeding regulations of caste,
Aryan humanity could exist again for modern man in its pure and primordial
form. He willingly acknowledged that the consequences of this eugenic ideal
were severe. *Manu*, in fact, exemplified just how the notion of pure blood
was not a harmless concept, but rather, the immortalization of hatred as a
religion and as a form of genius.

Nietzsche not only incorporated *Manu* in his work, but even embraced
the harshness with which *Manu* ordered the Aryan world. Given the attention and praise Nietzsche extended to the Hindu lawgiver, it is difficult to

accept Kaufmann's assertion that Nietzsche denounced the way in which *Manu* dealt with outcastes.[38] I believe that this assessment reflects Kaufmann's rehabilitating mission far more than any confusion or misreading of Nietzsche's intent. It seems evident that Nietzsche embraced the brutality of the concept of breeding as an integral attribute of the *Übermensch* and an historical necessity for his development. Kaufmann was clearly distancing his subject from the recent past when he stated that Nietzsche was "against the concept of pure blood that could be invoked again someday to justify the oppression of non-Aryans" (Kaufmann 1974: 225–27). Historically, Kaufmann had to deny Nietzsche's ideology of breeding. He first minimized the philosopher's treatment of the theme. He then overemphasized Elisabeth Förster-Nietzsche's heavy-handed emendation. Finally, after initially discounting any thematic of breeding in Nietzsche, Kaufmann claimed that the philosopher's "strong concern with breeding derived from Plato" (Kaufmann 1974: 305).[39]

Two strategies appear to be at work here. First, Nietzsche must not be held in any way accountable for Nazi eugenics. Second, and more obscurely, Kaufmann had to reject the possibility of any non-Western influence upon Nietzsche in order to elevate him to the first rank of continental philosophers. As Wilhelm Halbfass has shown, an historical refusal to engage Indian philosophy has contributed to the Eurocentrism of the institutional discourse of philosophy. India was excluded both from the genetic context of the European history of philosophy and from the domain to which the concept of philosophy is applicable (Halbfass 1988: 155). Traditionally, and thanks to the added impetus of Hegel, "caretakers of a specialized scholarly discipline" were unwilling to concede to India a real philosophy (Halbfass 1988: 146). The traditional view of doxography and the history of philosophy have obscured a significant aspect of Nietzsche's thought, namely, how India, or more precisely, *Manu* informed his idea of the *Übermensch*.

CONCLUSION

Until the mid-nineteenth century, the Aryans' presence in the West was limited to the scholarly domain of philosophy and the "scientific" fields of ethnography, botany, craniology, and so forth. Max Müller's enthusiastic public relations work on behalf of the Vedic Aryans effected their entree into the public domain, where a new generation of "philosophers" working outside an institutional framework developed popular theories regarding the Aryans. The discourse regarding the Aryan based itself on loose attribution of Vedic sources, Indological scholarship, and translations of other canonical Sanskrit materials, regardless of their status or antiquity. Nietzsche's reception of Indian thought must be viewed in this context.

Nietzsche's commentary on *Manu* is found primarily in his late works. Nevertheless, his interest in India was lifelong. Like Goethe, who wrote his two Indian poems after a lifetime of reflection on Indian lyric (Figueira 1994: 40), and Wagner, who on his deathbed lamented the unwritten Buddhist opera that had occupied him for forty years (Figueira 1994: 106–9), Nietzsche's thoughts on India also matured before he tried to articulate them. Like Wagner, there was not sufficient time. In passing, we might note that a large part of exoticism's lure is to be found precisely in its indigestibility. Either Nietzsche suffered his breakdown before he fully developed his thoughts on India, or what we have is really the only aspect of India that mattered to him. The interesting point is that Nietzsche chose to emphasize *Manu* as the sourcebook for his fiction of the Aryan race. Rather than Müller's voluminous commentary on the *Rig Veda* or other Sanskrit canonical sources that were available to him, Nietzsche prioritized *Manu*. It alone offered him the necessary corrective to cultural degeneration.[40] In establishing *Manu* as the sourcebook for the Aryan *Weltanschauung*, Nietzsche identified the "Vedic" canon that would be adopted by subsequent German racial theorists. How ironic that his sourcebook was not what he envisioned it to be.

Nietzsche posited a lost Aryan Golden Age and attributed its loss to the deleterious effects of religious compassion. Christianity destroys race by making populations soft. Nietzsche's metaphors were complex: The Jews appear as anti-Aryans or *caṇḍāla* outcastes; Jesus is the ultimate *caṇḍāla*. The *Übermensch* possesses values that Nietzsche attributed to the virtual Aryan. In each instance, Jews have been managed: either displaced from their primary position in religious history or bracketed in a role of existential insignificance.

Nietzsche's discourse on the Aryan fixated on the issue of caste and its role in maintaining blood purity. He focused on the manner in which Aryan blood was diluted in various populations. Nietzsche held Aryan brahmins to be a group that, thanks to *Manu*, had largely escaped blood degeneration. For Nietzsche, the brahmin assumed the characteristics of this idealized Aryan. In fact, Nietzsche's portrait of the Aryan is ineluctably bound to an ideological assessment of modern brahmin behavior. In Nietzsche, the Aryan coalesces with the brahmin (Hulin 1991: 70).

The critical reception of Nietzsche's exoticism is particularly instructive. We have seen to what degree Kaufmann was disingenuous in his assessment of Nietzsche's use of *Manu*. The only cross-cultural link acknowledged is Nietzsche's indebtedness to Greek thought. I have noted some of the factors that might have contributed to the dismissal of the philosopher's debt to Indian thought: the need to distance Nietzsche from Nazi eugenics and the unwillingness to take Indian philosophy seriously. Elisabeth Förster-Nietzsche, in her desire to make the *Will to Power* her brother's ultimate statement, initially confused the issue by arbitrarily raising the theme of breeding to a structural principle in the edition she compiled. As I hope this discussion has shown, beyond his sister's kind ministrations, Nietzsche himself had presented a coherent vision of caste and breeding at various junctures in his final versions of his work.[41]

The time has long passed for protecting Nietzsche from any Nazi association or legitimizing his place in the pantheon of philosophers. The time has also past for denying Indian thought its rightful place in the development of Western philosophical thought. Critically speaking, the need to manage Nietzsche cannot be completed by the construction of an expurgated Nietzsche, but only by a willingness to look squarely at and accept all aspects of his work, however exotic and distasteful they may be. A crucial lesson to be learned is how politics direct our (mis)readings. There are great dangers in reading literature in the service of ideological rewritings of history. Literary works should not be dissected and mined for what they can offer by way of a specific thesis, nor should they be made to fit dogmatic institutional scripts. When this occurs, criticism becomes brahmanical: it hierarchizes a caste of readers wielding priestly power in the temples of academe.

CHAPTER 4

Loose Can[n]ons

RACIAL THEORY: AN OVERVIEW

Beginning with the Enlightenment, racial myths of origin sought their justification in science. There was widespread speculation in the research of Cuvier, Linnaeus, and Buffon regarding the fixity of the species and the role of environment in causing human difference. There was but one variety of mankind, with humans differing from each other only by degrees. Writers such as Montesquieu (*L'Esprit des lois*, 1748) and Blumenbach (*De Generis humani varitate*, 1775) attributed the differences among nations to climatic variations. Populations were rooted in the land and soil. European barbarians, it appeared, had not wandered the earth aimlessly. The ordinary people of history were seen to function as rational beings.

With the development of comparative linguistics, the European quest for origins found a new scientific basis. The thought that there might be two distinct linguistic families, the Semitic and the Indo-European, and that there was an affinity between Sanskrit, Greek, Latin, Persian, and Germanic languages, contributed to the growing significance of India for Europe. Theories regarding the nature of language and the origin of man contributed to the belief that the Aryan Indians had initially migrated westward and were the direct ancestors of modern Europeans. Such speculation encouraged an even greater interest in India. An equally significant factor was the desire on the part of Europeans to escape their Judeo-Christian roots. The European quest for origins and desire to minimize their indebtedness to the Hebrews motivated the initial modern theories of race.

A second wave of racial ideas found expression in Herder, who focused on the collective personality of a people stemming from a common language. Ordinary types comprised the ethnic culture of a *Volk*. The various *Völker* could be differentiated by their temperament, character and inward sensations as expressed in cultural products. The relation of the individual to the *Volk* was viewed not so much in political terms as spiritually—through literature, religion, folk songs, and ritual. In the *Fragmente über die neuere deutsche Literatur* (1767), Herder drew the analogy between human history and organic growth. Like all living bodies, states, languages, literatures, and institutions experience a youth, prime, and decline. History was thus envisioned in terms of evolution and degeneration. Each *Volk* embodied a self-contained entity with a character of its own, growing and developing in time and space and under specific geographical circumstances. Although Herder himself rejected racial classifications, the mystical notion of the *Volk* that he initiated influenced subsequent racial theories.

The idea that a people's character was inexorably tied to blood found particular resonance in the work of Kant and Fichte. While Kant reasoned that there existed a national physiognomy that characterized entire societies, Fichte relied on a state's ability to compel people toward civilization. Fichte's *Reden an die deutsche Nation* (1807–8), delivered just after the defeat at Jena, inaugurated a major development in racial thinking. The disinterested cosmopolitanism of Herder or Goethe in the name of *Weltliteratur* was replaced by ardent nationalism. Geography and climate still played a role. But now they were credited with having given Germans their incomparable superiority. The German race was a nation in the making, realizing itself in its language and in the purity of its blood. Culture expressed itself as a form of moral order stemming from race, language, and nation. For Fichte (and Schopenhauer), the *Volk* possessed a will. In fact, Germany was the only nation possessing such a will. As opposed to the decadence of the Jews and the Latins, Fichte's Germans alone had the spirit of regeneration. Enlightenment cosmopolitanism, born in an era of political fragmentation, had thus degenerated into national egocentricity. The German Romantic vision of nature and living forms providing the key to the secrets of the universe discouraged moral equality and universality. Fichte's belief in Germany's unprecedented greatness (that so misrepresented political reality) epitomized this shift toward parochialism.

The theoretical debates of nineteenth-century anthropology contributed significantly to the growth of racial speculation. From the 1860s onward, one believed either in monogenesis or polygenesis. Monogenesists accepted the biblical unity of mankind. However, this theory did not prevent its proponents from maintaining the significance of race and its irreversibility, nor did it inhibit belief that Negroes were degenerate. Polygenesists viewed the action of environment as insufficient cause for human diversity. They postulated separate acts of creation as responsible for the human races. Although belief in polygenesis had existed since the seventeenth century, it gained popularity as biologists and anthropologists accumulated more data on human

diversity. By the time Darwin arrived on the scene, polygenesis was the predominant theory. Darwin's work was adopted by racial anthropologists to
corroborate the inequality existing between diverse groups and as proof of
racial upgrading. To determine the physical and moral qualities of races,
there now existed the possibility of placing races on firm "scientific" grounds,
by measuring human anatomy with calipers, craniometers, and spirometers
and by classifying differences. With the development of this pseudoscience of
race, scientists had the illusion of a broader base of material upon which to
construct their theories and substantiate their prejudices. After Darwin, race
was understood to be in flux. Human society had become the site of a
tremendous biological struggle.

The new historiography also contributed to racial speculation. Through
the writing of history, positive conclusions could be drawn from the past
upon which faith could be established. For example, Fichte's fiction that
Germany knew the secret of greatness and that it was her mission to synthesize the experiences of other nations found expression among historians.
Once again, it was through the will that hope was restored to the Germans.
In *Deutsche Geschichte* (1879 onward), Treitschke presented the nation as a
person prevailing against foreign will. Under the aegis of the state, individuals of Kantian character were lifted toward higher civilization. In accordance
with the Romantic belief in the organic interrelatedness of all things, Taine
(*Histoire de la littérature anglaise*, 1863) proposed that character was transmitted by blood. In order to change racial character, it was necessary to change
blood, whether by migration or invasion. According to Max Müller, the
racial will was determined by the imposition of hands, whether they be one's
parents or foreign masters (*Biographies of Words*, 1888). Race, milieu, and
moment persist in the blood and "will out," whatever the environment.

The perception that national identity was bound to an organic will found
its most forceful expression in Renan's "Qu'est-ce qu'une nation?" (1882). In
this seminal essay, Renan defined the nation as a living soul, possessing a unified will or a collective desire as a group to live together and continue living
together. By reducing nationhood to will, Renan rejected the criteria of race,
language, geography, religion, and community of interest. Other key themes
found validation in Renan's work. In the *Histoire générale et système comparé
des langues sémitiques* (1855), Renan set forth the linguistic rationale for the
opposition between Semite and Aryan. Reminiscent of F. Schlegel, Renan
designated Semitic languages as ossified, sterile, and incapable of self-regener-
ation and thus devalued the Hebrew tradition considerably. In the *Vie de Jésus*
(1863), Renan went further when he purged Jesus of his Jewishness. The
Semite was set in direct opposition (in terms of language and race) to the
Aryan. The Jew embodied all that was lacking in the idealized Aryan.

Two predominant attitudes with respect to race and nationality fueled
nineteenth-century racial theory. One attitude, epitomized by Herder and

resonating in scholarship for another fifty years,[1] viewed race as a variety of different anthropological qualities under a common rational humanity. It repudiated the assumption of superior and inferior races with the corollary that no human had the right to enslave another. The other attitude, first articulated by Kant, grounded nationality in the inner constitution of a race, regardless of environment and government. Evolutionary theories, of which Darwin's work was the capstone, introduced the notion of biological degeneration into the discussion of race.

Theories regarding the Aryans' language, physical characteristics, and site of origin were noteworthy for their lack of ethical neutrality.[2] Before 1850, many placed the original home of the Aryan in India. However, when racial anthropologists applied their various sciences to the problem of origins, they found linguistic, archaeological, and anatomical reasons for situating the Aryan homeland in their own backyards, whether that be north or central Germany, Scandinavia, or the Baltic region. They also invariably claimed pure descent. The myth of the Aryan was fundamentally Manichaean. Borrowing from the social Darwinists the vision of humanity in a constant struggle for survival, the Aryan myth explained the world in terms of a relentless combat between the forces of good and evil. The Aryan was solidly identified with everything good.[3] Goodness was defined in terms of its necessary correlative, evil, which increasingly became identified with the Jew. What was needed to complete this vicious equation were theorists who would amalgamate the myths of Aryan superiority and cultural decay with anti-Semitism.

The theme of racial degeneration became important in the works of Gobineau, Chamberlain, and Rosenberg. Their discussion of the Aryan is particularly important in that it opened to a much broader audience what had previously resided in the domain of the specialist. Their racial arguments, couched in the jargon of "serious" scholarship, popularized the Aryan. Their work superficially resembled earlier scholarship by also presuming to ground theories of origin and identity in textual exegesis. These cultural critics favored readings from *Manu*, since the *dharmashāstra* ideally suited a racialist script. The issue, as always, was one of canonicity, as Nietzsche was prescient enough to note (*Antichrist* 57), or rather, the manipulation of canonical authority. Whatever the textual basis for constructing an ideology of the Aryan, the sources evoked became increasingly elusive, disappearing under the weight of a myth that had taken a life of its own, eclipsing those very authorities that were called upon to justify its existence.

GOBINEAU AND THE ARYAN ARISTOCRAT

Arthur de Gobineau wrote the four-volume *Essai sur l'inégalité des races humaines* (1853–55) as an explication of the superiority of his own ancestry and that of the white race over all others. Among whites, a group he called the *Ariens* represented the summit of civilization. These Aryans colonized ancient India, Egypt, and Greece. Civilization originated with them and declined when Aryan blood became diluted. Gobineau held that the Germans represented the purest type of Aryan, an assessment that contributed significantly to his early and warm reception in Germany.[4]

Through an analysis of a society's organic growth, death, and effect on the lives of other nations, Gobineau developed the theme of Aryan supremacy. Unlike other philosophers who spoke of degeneration, Gobineau did not attribute the cause of decadence to climate, luxury, or weakness. In fact, he viewed race as basically static. Since they were created by God, the races were pure. Over centuries of interbreeding, however, they all became contaminated. By relying on documentation supplied by histology, anatomy, and physiology, he charted the course of a nation's decay. A society degenerates when its veins are no longer filled with the same blood as that of its ancestors (Gobineau 1983: 162–63). When a society's essence or primordial ethnic element is drowned out, race becomes irretrievably lost. Aryan history offered a prime example of a once-great civilization's inexorable decay, and such degeneration could even be witnessed in the disaster of the European present. With glaring pessimism, Gobineau refuted any theory of human progress.

Gobineau broke nations down according to male and female tendencies,[5] under three rubrics: the yellow, white, and black, each with their own physical and psychical traits. The yellow race tends towards mediocrity, love of the practical, and respect for custom. Whites comprise the superior race, holding honor as the fundamental rule for conduct (Gobineau 1983: 342). The white race causes the heavens and stars to rejoice (Gobineau 1983: 485). It functions as the *race civilisatrice*. Whites possess powerful intelligence, a sense of order, strength, majesty, and a desire for freedom (Gobineau 1983: 347). Gobineau characterized Blacks by their blind appetites, the predominance of the senses, and the instability of their desires. Blacks are apathetic and unable to rise above the lowest level. In thrall of their sensual and passionate nature, they possess no intellectual aptitudes and are inarticulate. Although dance and music exert an irresistible force over them, Blacks are incapable of giving these faculties any value. However, by disarming reason and diminishing the intensity of the practical faculties (Gobineau 1983: 507), black blood can gradually develop intelligence, imagination, and artistic temperament. By mixing with other races, Blacks can channel their passions into creative form (Gobineau 1983: 474–76). In fact, culture as a whole can only develop from the mixing of blood. Although the white race is the sole culture-creating race, high culture can only exist where Whites have mixed with Blacks. In short, black blood mixed with white blood engenders art. White blood, the source of ponderation and equilibrium, raises the violent passions of black blood, carries it to the summits of the ideal, ennobles it, and creates art. However, too much mixing dilutes blood and leads to racial degeneration.

Gobineau followed the biblical division of the races. He called upon the history of the Aryans as told in the *Rig Veda* to verify the chronology in Genesis, where the three distinct peoples are created from the sons of Ham, Shem, and Japheth (Gobineau 1983: 490).[6] It is to be remembered that biblical genaeology relates how, of Noah's sons, Ham alone gazed upon his drunken father's nakedness and was dispatched to Africa. By relegating Ham to Africa, the Old Testament associated sin with racial difference. Noah's curse of perpetual servitude on the offspring of Canaan, the son of Ham (Genesis ix, 25), condemned the Africans who were supposedly his descendants. Sin was thus embodied racially. Gobineau accepted this geneaology and its consequences. He described how the sons of Ham disappeared early, absorbed by the black nations of Africa in "an ethnic shipwreck." The sons of Shem, who were also originally white, gradually became decadent through the intermixture of blood. Like the sons of Ham, they were overwhelmed by blackness, becoming a negroid race.

Due to racial absorption, the Chamite and the Semites ceased forever to be ranked among the first of nations. They were replaced in their exemplary role by the Japhets, or as Gobineau calls them, the Aryans. Gobineau specifically ranked the Aryans as the chosen race, displacing the Jews from their position of prominence. One branch of the Aryans settled in Iran[7] and another branch settled in southeast Europe as the Greeks and the Romans. There, they intermarried with decadent Mediterranean Semites and were corrupted by the yellow races through Alexander's exploits. Mixed with black blood from the West and South and yellow blood from the East and North, they too degenerated. Their corruption signaled the death of Greek and Roman civilization.

The other Aryan branch, those who had migrated to India, lives on in the Germanic peoples. Among these Aryans, decadence through racial mixing was negligible. With this point, Gobineau solidified his reputation among German imperialists and ensured their cooptation of his "historical" Aryanism (Seillière 1903: xli). It should be noted, in passing, that Gobineau was capricious. He shifted the designation of the purest Aryan to suit his needs. At times, he found its purest strain in English blood. On other occasions, he discovered it in Scandinavia. In other words, when Gobineau spoke of purity, he did not mean it in any absolute sense. The deadly germ of race mixture, "le fond corrompteur," pursued all peoples. The Germanic Aryans, like all other peoples, would also eventually succumb. This key principle of Gobineau's thought was curiously ignored by his German nationalist disciples.

For Gobineau, the Aryans were *Göttersöhne*; they incarnated all that was great, noble, and fruitful (Gobineau 1983: 479). They originated on the great plateau of Central Asia, appearing on the stage of history around 4,000 B.C. Although various peoples descended from the Indian and Iranian branches of the Aryan race (such as the Ethiopians, Egyptians, Jews, Carthaginians, Phoenicians, Greeks, Italics, Germanics, Mexicans, and Peruvians) (Gobineau 1983: 347), Gobineau focused mainly on the Indian Aryans, the Iranians, Homeric Greeks, and Sarmates (the fathers of the Germans). His vision of the Aryans was "Indo-Germanic," rather than Indo-European. Instead of welcoming and embracing all the non-Semitic West into the Aryan fold, Gobineau wished to reserve for the Germans alone the precious heritage of the Veda and sought to exclude neighbors (such as Romans and Slavs) from its philosophical and moral sphere (Seillière 1903: xxxv). Gobineau maintained that these groups, although nominally "Aryans," had nothing in common with their Indian or Iranian *confrères* who had long since "detached" themselves from the moral values of those nations who would eventually become Celts or Slavs (Gobineau 1983: 481).

Basing his analysis largely upon interpretations of Sanskrit source material found in Christian Lassen's *Indische Alterthumskunde* (1844), Gobineau held that the Hindus, Greeks, Iranians, and Sarmates were distinct from all other branches (Gobineau 1983: 484). Gobineau, however, elaborated considerably upon this portrait of the Aryan prepared by the Indologist. While Lassen wrote that the Aryans possessed primordial beauty as is found today among the Kashmiri brahmins (Lassen 1847–61: 1.404), it was Gobineau who, comparing their physicality to the sculpture of the Pythian Apollo and the Venus de Milo, claimed that they possessed the most noble traits, vigor, majesty, tall stature, and muscular force (Gobineau 1983: 407, 854). Similarly, it was Gobineau who held that the Aryans were white, even pink-complected, blond, and blue-eyed (Gobineau 1983: 485).[8] Gobineau also maintained that the Aryans possessed supreme corporal beauty and superior souls (Gobineau 1983: 486). Gobineau, not Lassen, claimed that the Aryans were the most noble, most intelligent, and most energetic of the species because of their racial purity (Gobineau 1983: 552).

Through the institution of caste regulations, these Aryans distinguished themselves from their Egyptian and Iranian brethern. In fact, it was on the point of caste restrictions that the Indian Aryans broke with the future Zoroastrians who, not fearing the Blacks, rejected caste, split with their brethern, and migrated to Iran. The Egyptians, it appeared, had taken to caste too late and were not strict enough in its enforcement. Indian caste isolation, however, had maintained the relative purity of Indian Aryan blood. Nevertheless, even with prophylactic measures in place, the Indian Aryans also degenerated.

Gobineau attributed several factors to the destruction of the Indian Aryan race. The onslaught of aboriginal blacks on the relatively pure Aryan strain through Aryan migrations into areas inhabited by a preponderance of blacks diluted their racial integrity (Gobineau 1983: 554). After long contact with the aborigines, the Aryans even lost their purity, physical beauty, and moral essence (Gobineau 1983: 495). To this somatology, Gobineau cited the literary evidence. The Sanskrit epics taught Gobineau how the "race métissée" and "le teint foncé des mûlatres" overwhelmed the sovereign families. The *Mahābhārata* bore witness to the manner in which Indian society had been invaded by foreign elements.[9] Savage vices, absent from the *Rāmāyaṇa*, appear full-blown in the history of the Pāṇḍavas, who had been raised to divine status in order to veil the blood sins of their mothers. In other words, Gobineau read the epics as chronicles of non-Aryan promiscuity and Aryan battles to avoid the dilution of their blood lines.

In addition to racial miscegenation, metaphysics sapped Aryan strength. As a people, the Aryans had fully developed their high philosophical faculties, heightened sense of morality, and the gentleness of their institutions (Gobineau 1983: 552–53). In doing so, they depleted their ancient energy, their rectitude of judgment, and coldness of reason (Gobineau 1983: 506). Religious superstition further enervated the Aryan soul (Gobineau 1983: 555).[10] Although racial miscegenation and rampant philosophizing had gradually worn away at Indian Aryan purity, it was religious excess that ultimately caused its destruction. Here Gobineau based his argument on Christian Lassen's portrait of the disadvantages of Hindu social organization (Lassen 1847–61: 1.795) and religious structures (Lassen 1847–61: 1.807). Gobineau refashioned Lassen's descriptions of ceremonial minutia into exaggerated descriptions of religious degradation in the form of revolting mortifications of the flesh (Gobineau 1983: 496–97). Lassen's etymological analyses of Vedic Sanskrit terms for secular and priestly power (Lassen 1847–61: 1.812) served as a basis for Gobineau's diatribe against clerical abuse.

It is important to note that Gobineau appropriated Lassen's analysis of Indian religious and social practices (Lassen 1847–61: 1.771), distorted them, and ultimately explicated them in terms of race. In fact, Gobineau made an impassioned plea for us not to view ancient Indian society (or for that matter, any non-White population) solely in terms of metaphysical abstraction (Gobineau 1983: 494). Rather, the Aryan defeat by Indian religion was ultimately reducible to a destruction brought on by Black sensual tastes (Gobineau 1983: 532–34). Lassen's portrait of the Aryan, however faulty it may appear to modern scholars in terms of presentation of material or analysis, approximates in no way the racial fiction contrived by Gobineau.

Gobineau also extensively cited *Manu*, a text he viewed as the most ancient Aryan law source and narrative of their "purest chivalric spirit"

(Gobineau 1983: 500–1). From *Manu*, Gobineau confirmed that black blood had slowly eaten away at the Aryan fiber despite all precautions (Gobineau 1983: 507). Blacks were simply too sensual and too inferior not to overwhelm the Aryan. While the brahmins sought to maintain their purity (and succeeded for a time), they eventually became a mere echo of their former glory (Gobineau 1983: 508). Gobineau's use of this "ancient Aryan" source resembled his selective reading of the Veda (via Lassen). Although Gobineau acknowledged *Manu* in footnotes, he developed a racial argument that was in no way supported by his citations. The point of Gobineau's exegesis of *Manu* was to show how, despite all injunctions,[11] the high castes nevertheless fell prey to bastardization (Gobineau 1983: 512) and the outcaste *caṇḍālas* exploited this racial disintegration and thrived (Gobineau 1983: 529). For Gobineau, *Manu* represents Aryan social theory at its harshest. *Manu's* severity notwithstanding, Hindu (post-Aryan) tolerance negated any salutary effects it might have provided. Nothing could stem the degeneration of blood. In the post-Aryan era, the *caṇḍālas* prospered, while destroying all that was Aryan (Gobineau 1983: 528–29).[12]

Gobineau blamed the final degeneration of the Indian Aryan on Buddhism, which turned the white race away from its correct path by religiously sanctioning racial mixing. The destructive influence of Buddhism's "rationalism" was long-lasting, dating from the fifth to the fourteenth centuries. By the time Buddhism had taken its toll, foreign elements (the Moslems, Turks, Mongols, Tartars, Afghans, Arabs, Portuguese, English, and French) stepped in to finish the job. Brahmin Aryanism had degenerated completely. The great men had disappeared. Absurd superstition had taken over. Theological idiocies originating in black segments of society wiped out antique philosophy. One could no longer distinguish the Aryan from low-caste Negro and yellow types. Confronted with the superior force of white nations coming from Western Europe, this degenerated race did not stand a chance (Gobineau 1983: 551). Gobineau presented India's racial situation as a tremendous object lesson. Its devotion to religious, social, and political ideals, even after being beaten by pillage, massacre, and misery, elicited his praise. Nevertheless, he acknowledged that its total racial debasement was inevitable and should serve as a warning to all nations (Gobineau 1983: 557).

Gobineau's Aryan ideology, while ostensibly based on Vedic scripture and "Aryan" law, used such source material more as a point of departure for creating a racial fiction regarding the European present. This fiction corresponded to Gobineau's notions of monarchy and aristocracy, a world wherein there existed two social strata: the nobles (*les fils de roi*) and the dreck of society (*la boue*).[13] Aryan India thus offered Gobineau a propitious model: a philosophy of the good old times, when the social classes were sharply divided. The nobles played the role of the creators, the bearers of the sacred fire of spiritual progress that separated Amadis from Caliban. They opposed the defilers of culture, the quintessential forces of decadence. Lassen's Aryans who tussled among themselves (Lassen 1847–61: 617) became Gobineau's valiant and audacious Aryans who withstood the assault upon their way of life that was waged by the indigenous tribes they encountered. Their virtue was the heroism of the combatant, a *bravoure* that Gobineau only recognized in his day among the French aristocracy (Gobineau 1983: 488).

The poison of racial mixing, however, degraded the Indian Aryan, just as it will eventually kill humanity as a whole. Gobineau related his version of the Aryan saga as a warning to the Germans, whom he viewed as the last Whites, those who had most evolved and whose duty it had become to save humanity. If the Germans fail, no other nation would be available. They provided the last possibility for culture. When the Germans fell, so would the world. Gobineau concluded his essay with the warning that destiny's greedy hands were already upon us in the form of Asian, Mongolian, and Slavic hordes. By charting the *Arierdämmerung*, Gobineau heralded not only the end of the world (Gobineau 1983: 1161–66), but also the twilight of the gods.

HOUSTON STEWART CHAMBERLAIN: ARYAN PUBLICIST

Chamberlain's "Scientific" Portrait of the Aryan

We have seen how racial history was a well-established genre, especially in Germany, where the race tradition was rooted in the eighteenth century and gained popularity in the early decades of the nineteenth century. We have also examined how racial theorizing was integrated within legitimate scholarship,[14] alongside the work of academic historians, who focused on traditional historical concerns such as diplomatic or military history. Race history found its audience among general readers. It was accessible and appeared profound, especially since it seemed to participate in the broad theoretical debates rampant in the fields of philology, anthropology, and history. In the tradition of anti-traditional scholarship, a trend initiated by Nietzsche in his attack on David Strauss, popular synthesizers and cultural critics sought to fill the gap between dry scholarship and lived experience, trading on the popular belief that the universities had not sufficiently fostered the dominant values of society. Gobineau had set the standard for the popular historical genre subsequently adopted by cultural critics to prognosticate the decline of civilization. Masked by a veneer of scholarly respectibility, a literature of degeneration fed on society's fears of cultural decay. The first generation of racial prophets were not particularly crude nor did they exhibit the occult tendencies of their successor Houston Stewart Chamberlain, the Germanophile son of a British admiral, son-in-law of Richard Wagner, co-founder of the *Revue wagnérienne* (1885), and influential member of the Gobineau Society. In *Die Grundlagen des neunzehnten Jahrhunderts* (1899), Chamberlain sought to offer a physical anthropological basis for racial theorizing. His biological theories on race made him so famous in his adopted country that he was popularly known as the Kaiser's anthropologist.

In Chamberlain's masterpiece, humanity was divided into two distinct races of differing physical structure and mental or moral capacities, the Aryans and the Semites. Chamberlain viewed the struggle between these two races as the driving force of history. Their growth and disintegration in each epoch defined a dominant human type. The larger theme of the *Grundlagen* was to show how the Germanic people functioned as the main architects of civilization. Chamberlain began his analysis by identifying Greek art and philosophy, Roman law, and the personality of Christ as the triple heritage of antiquity. He then proceeded to chart their development up to the nineteenth century. The heritage of antiquity, while operant in the modern period, did not come down to us in pristine form. It had been fundamentally distorted by the singularly most important event in Western history: the fall of Rome. Like Gobineau, Chamberlain was fascinated by the saga of Rome's demise. It represented the pivotal moment in history when the Aryan race and its creative mission began to unravel. Racial miscegenation and the destructive powers of the Jews ultimately brought about Aryan destruction.

Since the heritage of antiquity was transmitted by a decadent and racially mixed body, our vision of Hellenic art, philosophy, and Roman law is, of necessity, distorted. Since the Catholic Church has consistently catered to the papacy and the needs of a degenerate population under the sway of Semitic influences, true Christianity does not even exist. Modern Europeans carry in them the results of cultural decay as well as the seeds of their mongrel origins in the form of present-day *Völkerchaos*. In Chamberlain's estimation, it was the Teutonic mission to undo this chaos by rescuing Christianity, expunging it of Semitic elements, and sifting out the original revelation of Christ.

Chamberlain, whose interest in India was whetted by the study of Sanskrit and contact with Schopenhauer's thought, recognized the important philosophical and religious influence of the Vedas and the Upanishads on world civilization. In and of itself, India provided an important model of a civilized society. As a point of comparison, Vedic mythology supplied German philology with evidence that the ancient Teutons (the Aryans) possessed holy books that were finer and nobler than the Old Testament

(Chamberlain 1968: 1.32, see also 1.lv). It was merely a question of recognizing the divine understanding of the Aryans and acknowledging Germany's racial and spiritual affinity with them. Chamberlain felt that recognition of this parenty should be achieved without resorting to the "pseudo-Buddhistical sport of half-educated idlers" (Chamberlain 1968: 1.liv).[15] Similarly, he felt that Gobineau's analysis was inadequate in drawing the connection between the Germans and their Aryan ancestors. Chamberlain believed that he personally could bring greater scientific precision to the investigation. His analysis, moreover, was necessary since the very existence of the Aryans had been recently called into question (Chamberlain 1968: 1.94).[16]

Chamberlain sought to "construct" a notion of the Aryan based on fact,[17] but acknowledged that this process could entail creating an Aryan endowed with whatever gifts suited its interpreter. In his own analysis, he sought to avoid the errors he ascribed to Gobineau's analysis.[18] Chamberlain faulted Gobineau for basing his work on the dogmatic suppositions of biblical chronology. Gobineau's reliance on the notion that the world was actually peopled by Ham, Shem, and Japhet transformed his otherwise fully documented work into a "scientific phantasmagoria." Gobineau's other mistake, in Chamberlain's estimation, was the fantastic idea that noble races had become irrevocably less pure. Chamberlain held that Gobineau's error rested on his total ignorance of the physiological importance of race. Races, he noted, did not simply fall from the sky. They developed, rather like fruit trees, gradually becoming more majestic and possessing the capacity to renew themselves. Although Chamberlain rejected Gobineau's pessimism (Chamberlain 1968: 1.263), he fully accepted the Frenchman's attribution of cultural decline to racial miscegenation.[19] He supplemented Gobineau's analysis by placing blame for racial decline on the Jew.

The Virtual Aryan

Trusting in science more than the "official simplifiers and levellers and the professional anti-Aryan confusion makers" (Chamberlain 1968: 1.266), Chamberlain rejected the chaotic results of philological research. Speaking German and living in Germany did not the Aryan make. Rather the data provided by physical characteristics determined race. Chamberlain discovered that Aryans did, indeed, possess certain physical traits of skin color, musculature, skull shape (Chamberlain 1968: 1.580), color of hair (Chamberlain 1968: 1.437, 577) and eye color (Chamberlain 1968: 1.575). However, they also significantly differed physically from each other according to these physical criteria, due to breeding with unrelated types. Chamberlain surmised, therefore, that anatomical and somatic anthropology were as problematic as tools in judging Aryanhood as was language. Both the linguistic argument and the community of blood theory offered no conclusive proof of Aryan identity. He concluded, therefore, that the term Aryan could never apply to a whole people, but only to single individuals (Chamberlain 1968: 1.264–65).

Chamberlain was less interested in establishing the location of the cradle of civilization (as were the ethnologists and racial anthropologists) than in revealing the spiritual characteristics of this superior race. Physical indicators had to be complemented by spiritual traits. Inner depth, loyalty to a master that one has freely chosen, and intellectual freedom were characteristics he discovered in the Teuton/Aryan. What was unverifiable by measuring skulls or analyzing philological subtleties could be proved by moral indicators (Chamberlain 1968: 1.592), such as religion, ideology, popular poetry, and legal usage (Chamberlain 1968: 1.320).[20] Other moral criteria that Chamberlain used to determine Aryanhood included the "depth of the soul as defined by a sense of freedom," and idealism combined with practical sense (Chamberlain 1968: 1.604–5). No matter how varied the elements of populations, Chamberlain recognized the existence of a moral Aryanism and moral non-Aryanism. The latter, in particular, was exemplified by Semitic law (Chamberlain 1968: 1.94). Curiously, he did not specifically identify those who historically embodied the former. Their reality in the past and present did not interest Chamberlain as much as their function as a prototype for the future.

> Though it were proved that there never was an Aryan race in the past, yet we desire that in the future there may be one. That is the decisive standpoint for men of action. (Chamberlain 1968: 1.206)

In other words, Chamberlain shifted the criteria for Aryanhood from the linguistic and physical to the moral plane. For all his touted scientism, he ultimately relied on that old Romantic staple, intuition. When a putative Aryan did not conform to type, his identity could always be confirmed by spiritual divination. It was precisely this desire to define Aryans so that they might be (re)created that distinguishes Chamberlain from other theorists we have examined in this study. Chamberlain was willing to acknowledge that the Aryans revealed in his readings of the Vedas and the Upanishads might be a myth. But he was also willing to accept and embrace their mythic value for ideological purposes.

Mythic or not, the Aryans represented values that could be found in modern times among the Germans (Chamberlain 1968: 1.866). The Germans possessed the Aryans' ability to balance between individual and public freedom (Chamberlain 1968: 1.543). Germans combined the Aryan capacity of free creative power with the peculiar Teutonic trait of loyalty (Chamberlain 1968: 1.544). They created all the great minds of Europe. Just as Paul and Jesus were Aryans, so too was the Italian Renaissance a Teutonic Aryan event. Aryan superiority gave Germans the right to be masters of the world. The future salvation of the world, in fact, rested on the Germanic Aryans (Chamberlain 1928: 2.138).

In his portrait of the Germans, Chamberlain was influenced by Tacitus (*Germania* 4). However, unlike the Germans of Tacitus, tribes that are basically unpolluted by marriages with alien peoples, Chamberlain's Germans were polluted. They had been infiltrated by alien elements. The heritage of German Aryans had been destroyed by mongrel races and Jews (Chamberlain 1968: 1.494). Germanic Aryan religion had also been ruined by the Roman Church that itself had succumbed to Semitic materialism and its preoccupation with sin and punishment. In its distorted form, Christianity imposed a literal interpretation upon Aryan myths and symbolism. The Teutons had tried to protect Aryan faith by establishing "Germanic Christianity" through the Reformation. They had also tried to rid themselves of Jewish and Latinizing elements. In fact, from the sixth century onward, Teutonic Aryans had waged a continuous battle against the forces of Rome and *Judentum*. They had, however, not been sufficiently successful. Their innate moderation had brought about *Völkerchaos*, "robbing areas of influence of pure blood and unbroken vigor and depriving them of the rule of those with the highest talents" (Chamberlain 1968: 1.494).

Aryans versus Jews

As elsewhere among the Western authors we have read, Chamberlain's discourse on the Aryan exists primarily as a foil to vilify the Jewish people (Chamberlain 1968: 1.243–44, 264, 402–5, 434–40). Chamberlain read the Veda to construct an idealized portrait of the Aryan world that stood in sharp contrast to that of the Jew. Where exactly in the Sanskrit text Chamberlain culled his information is left vague. We only learn that the Veda shows the Aryan Gods to be bright, true, and friendly. They were without malice, cruelty, or perfidy (Chamberlain 1968: 1.436). They treated others as their children and not their slaves. Unlike the Jew, the Aryan did not fear his gods, since they showed no capricious autocracy. Theirs was not a religion of superstition, but an introspective state of mind. Because the Aryan was in direct contact with the world beyond reason, he was primarily a thinker and a poet—in short, a creator. Aryan religion did not consist of a hard and fast chronological cosmogony and theogony. The Aryans' lively feeling for the infinite rendered their religious conceptions flexible, replacing, as need arose, old gods with new gods (Chamberlain 1968: 1.243). Creativity in secular and religious matters stemmed from the great Rig Vedic truth that Aryans sought the core of nature in their hearts (Chamberlain 1968:

1.215–16). Recognizing the relationship between the inner self, nature, and God within the Self, the Aryans were moved by the desire to unravel the mysteries of the world. Religion, for the Aryan, was an expression of self-esteem and self-respect (Chamberlain 1968: 1.259–60), a belief that one lived and died not for oneself, but rather for the whole world. The Aryan had a feeling of all-embracing duty and responsibility. Action thus took on an everlasting importance; it became a religion (Chamberlain 1968: 1.438). The Vedas afforded the Aryans the freedom to think as they pleased (Chamberlain 1968: 1.429). It provided an inclusive yet flexible scripture in which all gods could be viewed as orthodox (Chamberlain 1968: 1.431). Its flexibility highlighted the freedom of thought in Aryan religion. In this respect, it differed from the rigid chronology of the Old Testament. As the *Rig Veda* instructed (6.9), the Aryan mind was infinite, freedom was its element, and creative powers its joy (Chamberlain 1968: 1.243). In contrast, the Hebrew God meted out punishment (Chamberlain 1968: 1.438). The Jewish faith consisted of commandments, customs, and ordinances; it lacked any creative element (Chamberlain 1968: 1.216). It differed radically from Aryan religion, whose goal consisted of bringing to perfection the highest act of creation in the reformation of man's soul and its merging in the All (Chamberlain 1968: 1.438).

Compared to the Indo-Teuton's dedication to God, the Jews manifested violence and fanaticism. The Aryans were freely metaphysical (Chamberlain 1968: 1.243), while the Jews were historical and mechanical. Aryan freedom of thought resulted in the Indo-Teutons being a more tolerant people than the Jews (Chamberlain 1968: 1.404). What the Aryan created as art, appeared in the hands of the Jew as mere expression; science for the Aryan became mere industry for the Jew (Chamberlain 1968: 405).[21] Aryan religious literature, by far the greatest that the world has created (Chamberlain 1968: 1.402), differed from Hebrew scripture in the intensity of its religious feeling (Chamberlain 1968: 1.402) and individualism. Hebrew religious poetry was subjective (lyrical) and egotistical. The Jew's need to pour out his soul prevented him from creating epic or drama that would have demanded less subjectivity. The Jews stole their philosophy from the Indo-Teutons (Chamberlain 1968: 1.403), just as they pilfered their other great achievements from foreigners (Chamberlain 1968: 1.401). While the Aryan incorporated religion into all aspects of life, the Jew banished it from art, science, and literature. Whereas Indian literature was rooted in faith, Jewish thought, as exemplified by that "anti-Aryan" Spinoza, was based on obediance (Chamberlain 1968: 1.431).

Compared to the tender, sympathetic, and pious Aryan (Chamberlain 1968: 1.434), the Jew was hard-hearted and stunted in his spiritual development (Chamberlain 1968: 1.213). Chamberlain claimed that the *Rig Veda* portrays the Aryans as joyous, spirited, and ambitious people. They drank, hunted, and robbed. Yet they also questioned the great riddle of existence, seeking to discover the Self in all phenomena, and all phenomena in the Self (Chamberlain 1968: 1.214). He contrasted Aryan religion, viewed as cosmic in scope, to a rigidly national faith of the Jews (Chamberlain 1968: 1.434). Chamberlain read in the *Rig Veda* (x.129.7) how the Aryans questioned the origin of the world and continually aspired toward uplifting their soul to God (Chamberlain 1968: 1.229–30). From this hymn, Chamberlain concluded that Aryan moral speculation did not narrow itself to questions of good and evil, as did that of the Jews (Chamberlain 1968: 2.109). Rather, the Aryan was motivated in all matters by the will.

According to Chamberlain, the Aryan striving of the will was akin to the Faustian ideal expressed by Goethe (Chamberlain 1968: 1.230). It was this will that created supermen (Chamberlain 1968: 1.215). Because of their direct contact with the world beyond reason, Aryans could be thinkers, poets, and creators. They had discovered the great truth expressed in the *Rig Veda*—that one must seek the core of nature within the heart. This truth never dawned on the Jews (Chamberlain 1968: 1.216) because their will had a retarding effect. Although the Jew was capable, the Jewish will stood in the way of loftier activity; it hindered a profound knowledge of the universe, artistic work, and a noble thirst for knowledge. The Jew's faith was superstitious. The Aryan faith impelled its believers onward and upward. The Aryan's will obeyed; it did not command as did the abnormally developed will of the Jew (Chamberlain 1968: 1.242).

Moreover, the Aryans invented monotheism in the *Rig Veda* (i.164.46) and provided its most sublime form. The Jews stole monotheism from the Aryans. In fact, all Christian dogma found its source in Aryan religion. The *Rig Veda* supplied Christianity with the concept of God becoming man. The Aryan doctrine of the *Ātman* became a tenet of the religion of Jesus and later found expression in that essentially Aryan author Meister Eckhart (Chamberlain 1968: 2.412–13).[22] The notion of the Virgin birth also derived from Vedic nature symbols, as did the altar and sacraments originate in Vedic nature cults rather than in Jewish peace offerings to an angry god (Chamberlain 1968: 2.26).

As a figure overflowing with life (that is, attending banquets, forgiving sins of the flesh, proud, and combative), Jesus was specifically Aryan (Chamberlain 1968: 1.259). In no way could he be considered a Jew (Chamberlain 1968: 1.256). In the first place, Jews had no aptitude for religious thought. Moreover, the history of Galilee discredited any delusion of Christ's Jewishness. In looks and speech, Galileens were racially distinct from the Jews; their area was populated by Greeks and Indo-Europeans. More significantly, however, Christ had the character of an Aryan. The most important teaching of Christ was linked to the idealist religion of the Aryans and not the legalistic and materialistic faith of the Jews. In his attitude and religious thinking, Jesus was the "God of the young Indo-European peoples" (Chamberlain 1968: 1.245). As such, Jesus was God's representative of the Teuton soul (Chamberlain 1968: 1.893). The religion that he created and its mysticism find their models among the Aryans. Unfortunately, the Jews, "men of chaos," disfigured these Aryan elements and bequethed them to Christianity in their present distorted form (Chamberlain 1968: 2.23–27; 109–10),[23] making Christianity a mere annex of Judaism (Chamberlain 1968: 1.417).

From a creative and unsubstantiated reading of the Veda, Chamberlain constructed the history of the Aryan people that allowed him to argue that the Jew was the purveyor of materialism, intolerance, and social dissolution as well as the destroyer of civilization. Furthermore, his "reading" of the Veda enabled him to show that the Teutons in their antimaterialistism, idealism, mysticism, loyalty, and freedom must be Aryans and, as such, the antithesis to the Jew. Through miscegenation with Jews, Teutonic Aryans had broken all the laws of racial breeding and brought on their own destruction. Chamberlain, therefore, implored Germans to undertake a valiant fight and recapture their heritage from the alien grasp of the Jew, *Völkerchaos*, and the Semitized Church.

ALFRED ROSENBERG AND THE NORDIC ARYAN

The Fall of the Indian Aryan

At Nuremberg, twenty men were tried and eleven were executed for their active involvement in the brutal mechanism of the Third Reich. The defendants were indicted for conspiracy to commit crimes alleged in other counts, crimes against peace, war crimes, and crimes against humanity.[24] Alfred Rosenberg, an early Nazi and editor of the party organ, the *Völkischer Beobachter*, was tried in his capacity as Reich Minister for the Eastern Occupied Territories. Responsible for the Germanization of Eastern populations, he supervised slave labor and facilitated the extermination of Jews. His office was specifically responsible for rounding up quotas of workers assigned to labor under inhuman conditions. Although his defense tried to make the case that he did not play as active a role as Sauckel, who oversaw slave labor, or Speer, who directed armaments, Rosenberg was found guilty on all four counts and was executed on October 16, 1946. Rosenberg was condemned in large part for his role as party "philosopher" and chief ideologue of National Socialism. His depiction of the Aryan aptly concludes part I of this study.

Rosenberg's racial theories were influenced by the tradition of German political Romanticism as well as by the cultural criticism of Gobineau and Chamberlain.[25] The title of his "masterpiece," *Der Mythus des Zwangzigsten Jahrhunderts* (1930),[26] clearly pays homage to Chamberlain's *Grundlagen des Neunzehnten Jahrhunderts*. Rosenberg's writings also exhibit the manner in which National Socialism distorted and developed upon key themes found in Nietzsche's work. Finally, as in the case of all those we have studied in these pages, Rosenberg appropriated "Aryan" scripture to analyze European cultural decay and develop a plan for the future.

Rosenberg's chief work and Hitler's *Mein Kampf* provided the "philosophical" bases of the National Socialist movement. In the *Mythus*, Rosenberg explicated how world history consisted of nothing but an unending struggle between the Nordic spirit and the corrupting influence of inferior races. This superior and creative Aryan race originated in a lost semi-Arctic continent. Rosenberg traced the historical development of the Aryan race in its numerous branches among the Amorites of the Middle East, the Aryans of India, the early Greeks, and the Romans. Although the Aryans once peopled the entire earth, they survive in modern times only as Germans. The *Mythus* sets out to explain this historic phenomenon and to chart a course for the German Aryans' future prosperity. Rosenberg begins his work by describing the fate of the Indian Aryan.

Upon entering India, the Aryans segregated themselves from the dark indigenous populations.[27] As a natural consequence of this separation, they formed the caste system. Caste gave meaning to blood, as it pertained to color (*farbigblutvollen Sinn*). Although the caste system soon lost its initial meaning, becoming technically tied to the organization of professions (Rosenberg 1937: 30), it nevertheless promoted racial segregation and a worldview that has never been surpassed by any other philosophy (Rosenberg 1937: 28). In places like Goa, where Indian Aryans took on the Portuguese, we can see how they must once have been a people of stern mettle. But, just as Goa was overrun by the jungle and snakes, so too was the Aryan race overrun by half a million mixed breeds (*Mischlingsbevölkerung*). Humanity degenerated in the swamps and fever of India. White blood intertwined with the dark, thick, and unfruitful native racial strength (Rosenberg 1937: 664). Except for a small group of survivors, the racial soul that had created Aryan thought and civilization disappeared. Where there had once been an embodied nation of *Feldherrn*, there remained Gandhi and his pacificism (Rosenberg 1937: 663). India's near total racial degeneration explained her need of a *Herrenhand* to rule over her.

Rosenberg traced the golden age of the Aryan to the Vedic period, when the *kṣatriyas* waged a spiritually brave and resistant battle against degeneration (Rosenberg 1937: 488). Theirs was a life of action. Rosenberg contrasted the heroics described in the Veda to the later decadent Hindu reliance on magic, ecstatic cults, and blood sacrifices. Whereas the Aryans had held lofty belief in *Brahman*, their degenerated descendants worshipped magic and demons. Although the Aryan spirit tried at times to reassert itself, it could not rise above the non-Aryan superstitious mire under which it was submerged. The aristocratic, kingly, and warrior ethos of the Aryan, vainly maintained by brahmins, ultimately succumbed to racial decay (Rosenberg 1937: 29).

In Rosenberg, as in other authors we have examined, racial decay was tied to textual decay. The Indian Aryans disappeared just like the heroic songs recorded in the Vedas. The once profound Vedic philosophy became wild (*dschungelartig*), establishing a system of racial chaos (Rosenberg 1937: 662). Brahmin custodians of Aryan spiritual achievement falsified Vedic texts. The distortion of Vedic teachings destroyed the racial preconditions for Aryanhood. The post-Vedic philosophy of *Brahman/Ātman* that denied race and fostered breeding with indigenous groups introduced dark mixed breeds (*Mischlinge*) into the highest positions (Rosenberg 1937: 488). Indians thus irretrievably lost the meaning of blood and the Aryan life of action (Rosenberg 1937: 30).

Rosenberg claimed that the philosophical recognition of equality between *Ātman* and *Brahman* was a falsehood nowhere present in Vedic Aryan thought and only a later Upanishadic invention (Rosenberg 1937: 448). This falsehood, however, had struck the deathblow to the Aryan personality, leading to its eventual racial destruction. Rosenberg characterized modern India, absorbed in the All, wallowing in brotherly love and cherishing pity, as irremediably weak. The real Aryans had never sought personal happiness or an escape from suffering as an aim of existence.[28] Rosenberg saw them as dedicated to the fulfilment of duty and the maintenance of honor (Rosenberg 1937: 147–48). Those Aryans, who were born masters, felt their individual soul expand into the universe and their hatred for the world internalized. They waged a grandiose battle against those obsessed with the spiritual. However, once their aristocratic quest lost touch with any living racial reality, they could not prevail. The monists' abhorrence for nature had destroyed the racial instinct. The belief in the identity of *Brahman* with *Ātman* obliterated any notion of personality (Rosenberg 1937: 30) and sense of blood (Rosenberg 1937: 661).

With the destruction of personality, the Indian Aryan ceased being creative. The foreign dark blood of the *shūdras*, now seen as the equal bearers of the *Ātman*, annihilated the Vedic vision of race. It destroyed the original concept of caste, and bastardization began. Indigenous snake and phallic cults proliferated, as did the grotesque symbolic representations of the gods. Bastard art grew like the growth in a primeval forest. Glimpses of the Aryan worldview could still be found in places: the heroic sagas sung in the princely states and the lyrics of Kālidāsa and lesser-known poets. Shaṅkara too had attempted to reinvent Aryan philosophy. However, such flowerings failed completely. The arteries of the racial body had been severed and Aryan blood was allowed to flow forth and fertilize the dark thirsty earth of India. All that remained were dead technical rules of breeding cut off from their original philosophical meaning, whose insane distortion dominated contemporary Hinduism (Rosenberg 1937: 31). Aryan culture thus died in India. Racial disgrace alone remained in the form of those pathetic bastards who seek a cure for their crippled existence on the banks of the Ganges (Rosenberg 1937: 30).

The Scripture of Aryan Christianity

Just as in India, so too had Western Aryanhood in its Greek, Latin, and Germanic forms been destroyed. The cause of its demise was decadent Christianity, which consisted of nothing but lies perpetrated by bastardized Jews. Had Christianity retained its Aryan basis (that is, the true teaching of the Aryan Jesus), then all would have been well. However, Christ's message, dominated very early on by Paul's teachings, repudiated any Aryan heritage. Christianity became nothing but a Semitized version of Aryan ideals and a dumping ground for abusive Jewish concepts. It was Rosenberg's task not only to condemn the distortion of Christianity (primarily in its Roman Catholic configuration), but also to set the record straight. The most important error that needed to be rectified pertained to Jesus' true identity.

The figure of Christ had been falsified by Jewish fanatics like Matthew, materialistic rabbis like Paul, Africans like Tertullian, and mongrel half-breeds like Augustine. The real Christ was an aggressive and courageous revolutionary who defied Jewish and Roman systems and paid for his bravery with his life. Christ, in fact, was an authentic Aryan rather than a Jew. He was not of Jewish stock because the inhabitants of Galilee were descendants of Amorites, Aryans who had come to the region around 700 B.C. By 100 B.C., the Jews had established hegemony over the Aryan city of Jerusalem, forcing the non-Jews into the Gentile district of Galilee. When Joseph returned to Bethelem, he was returning not as a son of the tribe of David, but as the son of Aryan exiles who had been driven out by Jews.

Another important point that needed clarification concerned Jesus' teaching. What we moderns understand as the word of God is actually a gross distortion of His actual message. The Jew Paul totally subverted Christ's teachings by Judaizing them. Paul replaced the true, Aryan, and heroic Christ with a weakling seeking to mediate human salvation through love, humility, and brotherhood. Proud Nordic man should not prostrate himself before the Creator, as the Jew does before Yahweh. Not only did the Jews distort Christ's message, the popes and, finally, the Jesuits utterly destroyed the original Aryan Christianity. Even the heroic efforts of Luther and Calvin could not reverse the damage. Rosenberg's primary complaint with Roman Catholicism was its fundamental error that anyone, regardless of racial origin, could enter its fold. This tenet destroyed any ideal of racial purity. Doctrines of love and pity subverted Aryan virtues of heroism, honor, and blood.

Despite the present decay of the Church, Rosenberg felt it was possible to purify Christianity and return to its Aryan *Urform*. In fact, the time was ripe for the creation of a new, positive, and Germanic Christianity by restoring lost Aryan virtues, vitality, and racial consciousness. First, it was necessary to reject ideas of human universality and substitute race consciousness for the notion of the common nature of humanity. True Christianity had been Aryan in its contours: natural, brutally self-assertive, egotistical, powerful, and decisive. Rosenberg viewed Christianity in its present form as a moral code of weaklings (Rosenberg 1937: 147), in much the same manner as Nietzsche did. It had assumed its degenerate form when the Jew, who represented the polar opposite of the ancient Indian Aryan, took over Christianity (Rosenberg 1937: 265–66). The new Nordic Christian Church that the Nazis sought to establish aimed at leading men back to a heroic superhumanity. To return to the original Aryan faith, it was also necessary to restore the feeling of individuality that had previously existed.[29] Aryan individuality had first been destroyed by the hazy monism of the post-Aryan Indians (Rosenberg 1937: 389). It reasserted itself in Christ, only to be destroyed again by the Roman Church (Rosenberg 1937: 390).[30] The new Aryan religion of National Socialism sought to reinstate the individual will and commitment to action that Germans had lost during the post-Vedic era.[31]

Rosenberg identified several models of Aryan religious vision. He read into the *Chāndogya Upanishad* a vision of man as formed by the will and discovered in the *Bṛhadāraṇyaka Upanishad* lessons on the use of power (Rosenberg 1937: 240–41). Rosenberg also recognized an Aryan Christ of will and freedom in the mysticism of Meister Eckhart. By equating the "message" of the Upanishads with that of Meister Eckhart, Rosenberg textually tied the themes of will and power to the world of both the ancient Aryan and the medieval German. Rosenberg also admired Justin Martyr as a figure who had sought to free Christianity from its Ebionitic taint by returning to the teaching of Christ as it existed before the corrupting influence of Paul. Finally, Rosenberg sought inspiration from Zoroaster and his reformer Mani. Like Christianity, Zoroastrianism had been corrupted by the Jews and transformed into a ritualistic cult. It also had not been able to remain in

Aryan hands. The Babylonian captivity and Persian rule over Israel had led
to its Jewish corruption. Mani had tried to reinstate Zoroastrianism's
absolute dichotomy between good and evil that had been destroyed by the
Jews. But his attempt to revive the true teaching of Zoroaster was totally
suppressed. We only learn of Mani's existence through Augustine's bitter
attacks on him and his religious ideal.

Rosenberg identified the Manichaean worldview as the common
thread to all Aryan religious thought. It was precisely the dichotomy
between good and evil that had been intact in Vedic times but had disappeared in the Vedāntic union of *Brahman* with *Ātman*. It was at this point
that the Aryan virtues of duty, honor, faithfulness, and bravery had been
destroyed. In their place, the weak India of the post-Aryan period substi-
tuted love, pity, and the desire to escape from suffering (Rosenberg 1937:
147–50). Rosenberg extended the Manichaean dichotomy to the texts
themselves: The Veda recorded the saga of the children of light and the
Talmud was a document registering the history of the children of darkness.
It was only through a wide-ranging Jewish conspiracy extending throughout
history that Jews contrived to switch roles with the Aryans. First, they took
over Jesus through Paul. Next, they suppressed Mani and Persian Aryan
values. Finally, Augustine, the Jesuits, and various popes brought to fulfilment the Jewish conspiracy.

Rosenberg viewed human history as a repetitive reenactment of the
destruction of Aryan values. India had destroyed its Vedic Aryanness with
the adoption of Advaita Vedānta and Buddhism. Subsequent Aryan nations
too had been corrupted and destroyed. First Greece, then Rome, and finally
Germany was the third Aryan empire to be immersed by hither-Asiatics and
Jews. Rosenberg felt that it was still possible to save Germany's Aryan identity. The first task was to stem the tide of migration and eject the human
flotsam. Judaism should then be studied so that it might be more efficiently
combated. If one could scientifically uncover Judaism's core values, ferret out
where they had been imposed on Christianity, and expunge them from the
New Testament, one could then renew the true teaching of Jesus as it
appears in the mysticism of Eckhart and Justin Martyr. Of course, the Old
Testament had to be rejected as cattle herders' renditions of Jewish history.
Remaining Aryan texts were to be added to the new Christian canon. They
were to be supplied by inferring what a true Aryan/Nordic soul would place
in an Aryan religion.

In other words, Rosenberg called for the establishment of a purely syn-
thetic Aryan Christian canon: Dreams of honor and freedom would be culled
from Nordic and German fairy tales and sagas. Only expressions of the
Aryan worldview and eternal soul of the Germanic people would comprise
this canon. For the more sophisticated, religious representations from Aryan

Persia and India would be collected (Rosenberg 1937: 614–15). These texts need not necessarily be authentic. The modern Aryan was not interested in literal formalities, but in the philosophical and conceptual message of Nordic Aryan times. Rosenberg contrived an incredible circular logic. Since Jesus was God, he had to tell the truth; therefore, he must have spoken of Aryan nobility and race consciousness. The texts deemed authentic for inclusion in the National Socialist canon were those that dealt with these themes.

CONCLUSION

We have seen how the Enlightenment viewed man as subject to forces that shaped natural law. Humanity was depicted as endowed with the potential for living in conformity with nature. Although governments might vary according to geographical position, their success was believed to be tied to an ability to provide a framework for their population to fulfil its potential. States and constitutions were created according to the dictates of reason, with God as the impersonal clockmaker overlooking the process. Romanticism, and particularly the politicized Romanticism of Germany, appeared as a reaction to eighteenth-century rationalism. Herder had developed the concept of the unique nature of the *Volk* with its *Geist* reflected in its language, poetry, and myth. Herder himself had shied away from hierarchizing the various *Völker*. They all proceeded at their own pace toward humanity. Fichte, however, tied the notion of a people's fulfillment to the idea of nation. Fichte also brought anti-Semitism into the equation. The "philosophical" synthesis or, rather, the symbolic cluster of nationalism and anti-Semitism was subsequently popularized in the poetry and spectacle of Arndt and Vater Jahn.[32]

Until the mid-nineteenth century, Western discourse on the Aryans was largely limited to the scholarly domain of philosophy, linguistics, and the "scientific" fields of ethnography, botany, craniology, and so forth. Until the efforts of Max Müller, Western discourse on the Aryan based itself on the authority of absent texts and falsely present texts. We have seen how, even with the appearance of the Veda in the West, assumptions regarding the Aryans did not change significantly from a time-honored script. Once the Veda became a tangible source of reference, however, it virtually dropped out of the Western discourse on the Aryan. Once it became real, the Veda's use as an Aryan sourcebook greatly diminished. Max Müller's enthusiastic public relations work on behalf of the Vedic Aryans effected their entree into the public domain. A new generation of "philosophers" working outside of the institutional framework developed popular theories regarding the Aryans. Here, as in earlier discussions, the discourse regarding the Aryan based itself on loose attribution of Vedic sources, Indological scholarship, and translations of other canonical Sanskrit materials, regardless of their status or antiquity.

Gobineau popularized *Manu* because it was a significant point of reference for his source, Christian Lassen. From *Manu's* discussion of caste and its role in maintaining blood purity, Gobineau focused on the concept of racial decline. Since even *Manu* could not alter the Indian's fate, Gobineau concluded that blood poisoning was the eventual fate of all peoples. Nothing could prevent the inevitable destruction of race. The Germans, whom he identified as modern Aryans, would themselves eventually fall. Rosenberg rejected this dire prognosis. Through the force of a racial will (a concept found also in Renan, Gobineau, and, most significantly, Nietzsche), the German Aryans could maintain their purity. Rosenberg also revived the Romantic cult of the organic and sacred community. From Fichte and Pan-Germanists such as Paul de Lagarde and Constantin Frantz, he developed a German national religion in the form of Aryanism. Although many aspects of Nietzsche's thought would not sit well with the Nazis,[33] Rosenberg laid claim to and developed one significant *echt* Nietzschean element—the glorification of breeding. Rosenberg was also influenced by the "scientific" racism of Gobineau and Chamberlain. From Gobineau, he borrowed the concept of history as racial history, his identification of the Aryan with the German, and his emphasis on Aryan bastardization.[34] Similarly, it was Gobineau who had proposed that a nation's survival was tied to the purity of its racial composition.[35]

Chamberlain can be credited with supplying Rosenberg with the concept that German Aryan blood was superior to all others and that any mixing of blood led to racial extinction. Chamberlain viewed the German as embodying inner purity. Terms that would reappear in Rosenberg's writings, such as "German soul," "German religion," and "race-chaos," were first popularized by Chamberlain. Moreover, it was Chamberlain who proposed the idea that psychic conditions were reflected in physical forms with the corollary that blood (here, synonymous with *Geist*) could be judged by physical criteria.[36] Rosenberg developed this thesis, concluding that blood comprised that portion of the unconscious that determined race. The conscious rational life separated us from this obscure source of existence and alienated us from our national community. As in the case of Gobineau and Nietzsche, Rosenberg also focused on caste and its role (or failure) in maintaining Aryan blood purity.

Although the *Mythus* owed much to the racial doctrines of Gobineau and Chamberlain, it differed from them in its angry condemnation of Christianity. Gobineau had attributed Aryan decline to Buddhism's debilitating influence. Chamberlain had placed the destruction of the Aryans in the hands of the Jews. Neither Gobineau nor Chamberlain ceased believing in Christianity. Rosenberg, however, waged a relentless battle against Christianity and, in particular, Catholicism. In this respect, he was indebted to Nietzsche's and Chamberlain's vision of Christianity as a form of Semitized Aryanism. Nietzsche blamed Christian doctrines of compassion and love for destroying Aryan virtues. In his attack on Catholicism, Rosenberg owed much to Nietzsche's anticlerical fulminations. Finally, Rosenberg shared with Nietzsche and Chamberlain three important themes. They all emphasized the belief that Jesus was not a Jew. They all saw the possibility of reversing racial degeneration through breeding, and they all sought a return to their respective myths of an Aryan ideal.

In all instances, this return to the Aryan ideal was to be effected through an interpretation of "Aryan" texts. This documentation was "Aryan" in the loosest sense of the term, consisting of Indological scholarship and translations of Vedic and post-Vedic texts of different genres. Gobineau's Vedic sources were secondhand via Lassen. Nietzsche's point of Aryan reference was a distorted translation of the Hindu (read: post-Aryan) lawgiver *Manu*. Chamberlain cites the *Rig Veda* as a source for his speculation, but acknowledges the expedient need for myth-making. Rosenberg takes this interpretive creativity further still. Although he claims to base his vision of the Aryan on the authenticity of the Veda, rather than on the monistic distortions of Vedānta, he cites from the *Bṛhadāraṇyaka* and the *Chāndogya Upanishads* at length to complete his vision of Aryan masculinity. Other sources, such as Meister Eckhart and Justin Martyr, are included in the Aryan canon. In fact, with Rosenberg, the canon expands to include anything that articulated Aryan values as understood by the interpreter. We have come full circle from the Enlightenment and Romantic authority of an absent text to the authority vested in a virtual text. The myth of the Aryan gained authority in the West as a text-centered construct even before "Vedic" texts were discovered and deciphered. Later, when these texts became present, their authority remained on the level of the imaginary, unmediated by any bonds of textuality. The Aryan was initially and remained an object of pure fantasy. We are all aware of the dire consequences that resulted. All that was needed was an historical grudge and a demagogue to activate this phantasm.

PART II

Who Speaks for the Subaltern?

CHAPTER 5

Rammohan Roy

READING REFORM

In 1828, Raja Rammohan Roy (1774–1833) founded the Brāhmo Sabhā. Later renamed the Brāhma Samāj, this organization sought to effect a purification of traditional Hinduism by promoting the values deemed operative in Vedic times: belief in the unity of God, absence of idol worship and unnecessary rituals (Collet 1962: 220–24). The Raja based his reform on a reading of "Vedic" scripture, believing that its wisdom, once available to all, would effect the rejuvenation of Hinduism. The role of the Brāhma Samāj in the social and religious conditions of early nineteenth-century Bengal has been the subject of several fine studies and continues to inform critical assessments of Indian social history.

In *The Intimate Enemy: Loss and Recovery of Self under Colonialism* (1983), Ashis Nandy examines the Raja's relationship to colonialism as the flip side of a theory of progress. His identification with the colonial aggressor is presented as an ego defense mechanism. Nandy likens Roy's reform efforts to the response of a child in confronting the inescapable dominance of physically more powerful adults enjoying total legitimacy. First, Nandy reconstructs a psychological sketch of the Raja's relationship with his mother as the subtext for reform. He then posits the "unbreakable dyadic relationship" that ensues from such an identification as the *sine qua non* of colonial culture. Nandy views Roy's introduction of ideas such as organized religion, a sacred text, monotheism, and a patriarchal godhead as a response to the colonial subject's alienation from an older lifestyle and its values. Nandy also sees Roy's reform as a reaction to the colonial incursion into eastern India and an attempt to confront domination by redefining masculinity, traditionally based on the demystification of womanhood, and shifting the locus of magicality from everyday femininity to a transcendent male principle. Nandy's analysis, while brilliantly performative, lacks sufficient grounding in textual specificity, a defect shared by the feminist conflation of Rammohan Roy by Lata Mani.

In Mani's article, Rammohan Roy's appeal to scripture is attributed solely to a purported colonial institution of scriptural normativity. The privileging of brahmanic scripture and the equation of tradition with scripture are presented as an effect of the "colonial discourse" on India, where colonial power underwrites official discussion and ensures scripture's increasing normativity (Mani 1988: 91). Colonial authorities alone institutionalize assumptions by making texts the basis of law. Only under colonialism is scripture seen as the locus of authenticity. For this critic, there exists no positioning of scripture within the brahmanical tradition, as if scripture had not always been normative and privileged in the history of Sanskrit literature. Not only is the colonial subject's relation to a text completely disengaged from any Indian exegetical tradition, but Rammohan Roy, as colonial subject par excellance, can only stand in relation to a text in light of the colonial experience. Any call to textual authority becomes a strategy of colonalism. Colonial subjects, we are told, would not even believe their own pandits, were it not for the British making them do so (Mani 1988: 102). While these arguments are absurd within the historical and religious framework, from a critical vantage point we must pause. They suggest a logic wherein texts can only function as "forms of cultural coercion" in which an ideology (in this case, colonialism) can be "naturalized and skillfully upheld" (Fluck 1996: 219).

Let us descend from the artful argument of Mani's critique to touch down in the realm of exegetical reality. The privileging of brahmanic scripture and the equation of tradition with scripture is not an effect of colonial discourse on India. The colonial subject is not solely constituted by colonialism, nor is it the only form of discourse that really matters. Other inventories and traces occur beyond the archive of the postcolonial critic. Other competing traditions of protest existed.[1] The colonial subject did, indeed, have a voice that was not wholly contingent upon the colonial experience[2] and was textually audible without need of the critic's intervention.[3] However, to hear this voice, one must engage texts and cultural specificity. Both Nandy and Mani represent a trend in theory that views textuality as little more than a rhetorical tool in the interest of ideology and form as a deceptive promise of the possibility of individual agency (Fluck 1996: 225). A theoretical posture that minimizes the formal elements of literary representation, since texts only reveal manifestations of power relations, obviates the task of detailed reading and simplifies the demands placed upon the reader. It does not necessarily bring us any closer to engaging cultural complexities as mediated through language and other cultural translations. In the following analysis of Rammohan Roy's translations and exegetical writings, we will challenge the critical approach that seeks to reveal textual complicity without recourse to text or context. We will examine how Rammohan Roy used various literary strategies to set the groundwork for reform structured on a myth of an Aryan Golden Age. We begin the discussion by contextualizing Rammohan's work as an outgrowth of his cultural encounter with Europeans and critique of Indian traditionalism.

THE COMPLEXITY OF THE COLONIAL SUBJECT

Rammohan Roy's *oeuvre* defies simple categorization. It is misleading to view him as enacting a debate between liberalism and conservatism, East and West, modernism and tradition (Kopf 1969: 204–5). The tradition/modernity polarity, so optimistically accepted by mythographer-critics of the Raj, positions an image of primal precolonial innocence as the alternative to the victimized or collaborationist colonial Other. The tradition/modernity polarity diffuses specifics; it blurs the fact that variants of the concepts with which many anticolonial movements worked have often been products of the imperial culture itself and that these movements also pay homage to Indian cultural origins.

Rammohan Roy was the first Indian to establish his own press and publish newspapers, books, and pamphlets (Pankratz 1998: 335). In so doing, he was the first Indian distributor of Hindu and Christian texts. Roy was motivated by the belief that these two religions held similar traditions despite their formal diversity. In keeping with this universalist credo, Brahmo worship included public readings from the Bible in addition to selections from the Vedas, Upanishads, and the *Brahmasūtra* (Collet 1962: 224–26).[4] Furthermore, it embraced other "Christian" elements such as prayer, sermon, and hymn as integral parts of its service.[5] Underlying this attempt at synthesis was Roy's belief that all major religions were equal in value and only needed to substitute rational faith for the meaningless rituals, myths, and superstitions prevalent in popular practice. Christianity, he felt, had much to offer India. Utilitarianism, in particular, offered a vision of theistic progress, wherein human perfectibility could be best achieved by joining social reform to rational religion. In Utilitarianism, he recognized a Christianity purified of miracles and devoid of theological "rust and dust." Yet, this search for a purer form of Christianity was of secondary importance to Roy's primary goal of rehabilitating Hinduism by proving that Sanskrit scripture espoused monotheism and rejected idol worship.

Toward this immediate pragmatic end, he fashioned translations and commentaries of the Vedānta and five principal Upanishads (the *Īśā, Kena,*

Katha, Muṇḍaka, and Māṇḍūkya). These translations served as a defense of Hinduism against the pernicious assault waged by Trinitarian missionaries, in particular Alexander Duff and his followers. Roy answered Trinitarian attacks on Hindu superstition by establishing that Christianity also had its share of foolishness. Such a claim simply enraged Roy's missionary opponents, most notably Joshua Marshman of the Serampore Mission, who could not conceive of an Indian challenge to the hallowed inconsistencies of Christianity or faith in the Trinity (Kopf 1969: 202). Rammohan established his first journal, the *Brahmunical Magazine* (1821) with the expressed purpose of defending his belief in a monotheistic Hinduism against the critique of polytheism launched by the Serampore Missionaries.[6] Rammohan Roy's relationship to Christianity was, therefore, not uncritical. Although he had great respect for ethical Christianity, this esteem did not blind him to its doctrinal inconsistencies or deter him from challenging its abuses.

His relationship to Sanskrit learning was equally complex. Because he had studied in Benares and was not formed by Orientalist scholarship, his knowledge of Hinduism was greatly valued in his time (Kopf 1969: 59). Even though he did not garner his knowledge of the Sanskrit tradition from Western scholars, his quest for a purified Hinduism was considerably influenced by their utopian vision of the Aryan past. However, it also reflected the work of eighteenth-century pandits. Just as the pandits essentially "rewrote" the shāstras for the benefit of the East India Company judges, Roy "rewrote" them for the Indian intelligentsia. He differed, however, from the eighteenth-century pandits by relying on English translations as much as on the Sanskrit texts themselves (Joshi 1975: 145). For this reason, Roy's version of the Aryan past also owed much to the prejudices of Sir William Jones and H.T. Colebrooke.

Colebrooke's essay on the Vedas proved particularly significant in its attention to discrepancies between ancient textual requirements and contemporary practices (Kopf 1969: 198). Colebrooke first suggested that objectionable religious practices resulted from a misunderstanding of texts (Colebrooke 1802: 196). Roy adopted this strategy in his own readings. He also followed the Orientalists' preferance for the Vedāntic period as the authentic model for Aryan theology, law, and literature (Roy 1906: 573). He shared their devaluation of post-Vedāntic Hinduism as well as their identification of idolatry, *satī*, and polytheism as medieval excrescences. Although ideas regarding monotheism and the symbolic nature of idol worship had previously been discussed by learned Hindus, particularly the eighteenth-century poets Ramprasad and Bharat Chandra, Roy followed Western critics in their direct attribution of the degeneration of Hindu society to these customs (Roy 1906: 574–75). As did Jones and Colebrooke, the Raja likewise blamed the brahmins for social and religious decay, since they plotted to conceal the truth of the Vedant

"within the dark curtain of the Sanskrit" (Roy 1906: 3) rather than dissemi-
nate it to the people in the vernacular languages. It was to undo religious
degeneration and counter the brahmin hegemony over Hinduism that Roy
chose to translate scripture into the vernacular (Roy 1906: 199). Here too,
Roy continued an age-old struggle between Sanskrit and vernaculars that had
previously found expression in the works of Eknath (Ranade 1902: 219).

Quite simply, the strategy arguing for social reform in terms of scriptural authority existed in India outside the colonial era and did not depend
on "the emerging dominance of an official Western discourse on India"
(Mani 1988: 114). Before we accuse Roy of collaborating with colonial
administrators by prioritizing *smṛti* (with *Manu* as foremost among *smṛti*
texts), we must first question whether there existed a colonial discourse with
respect to scripture that differed from brahmin orthodox policy.

SCRIPTURAL AUTHORITY AND THE
HERMENEUTICS OF *SATĪ*

In orthodox tradition, *Manu* was a standing source of authority and not
just a text that was malleable to colonial administrative designs (Manu 1992:
xviii) and, by extension, Roy's need to imitate his colonial masters. It was the
subject of nine complete commentaries and more frequently cited than any
other *dharmashāstra*. In theory, Indians have always taken *Manu* very seriously. Whether its privileged status extended to actual use in legal courts is
another matter. Some historians have claimed that, before colonial rule,
Manu had been used by jurists (Manu 1992: ix). Orientalism did not give
Manu its authority.[7] *Manu* was the absolute authority of both Vedic knowledge and Vedic practice (Manu 1992: xli–xlii). In other words, there existed
a noncolonial precedent for Roy's reliance on *Manu*. Roy (and the colonial
officials) diverged from this exegetical tradition, however, in an important
respect. After identifying original authoritative sources, they felt it their duty
to correct these texts of the accretions suffered with the passage of time.
Whatever truth claims scripture originally held had been contaminated by
centuries of ignorant and sometimes wild accretions.

The Raja thus posed a serious challenge to scriptural inerrancy and
canonicity. A scriptural canon was established as original and authentic.
However, in order to prove valuable for Roy's larger project of reform, it had
to be corrected. For his needs, Roy gave centrality only to those texts that
could be read to support universalist and modern interpretations (Nandy
1983: 194). Toward this end, the Raja drew primarily from those texts that
easily lent themselves to reinterpretation suiting his immediate concerns for
social reform (Heimsath 1964: 154). His reliance on the Upanishads, the

Vedānta Sūtra, and *Manu* as sufficiently vague and complex authorities stemmed from this same need for adaptability.

Roy based his vision of the Aryan Golden Age on a "Veda," constructed to provide ample opportunity for self-realization. As a guide, even this extensive canon could not sufficiently reinforce the ethical basis that Roy felt lacking in Hinduism. Moral precepts that he found present in his "Veda" appeared only in scattered form. Since he felt Christian ethics presented the same system of morality in a manner better suited for the discharge of social duties, Roy incorporated the precepts of Jesus into his canon as a basis for teaching morality. He continued to champion the validity of "Vedic" texts, but acknowledged the unacceptable errors that they had accrued over time, clouding their moral focus.

It is important to remember that in his definition of the canon, Roy was guided both by the Orientalist reception of the "oldest" texts and method of reading as well as by the Indian normative view of a "Vedic" canon and tradition of interpreting it. Although eternal and immutable, this Veda could be employed to explain a process of change and provide a fluid sacred authority upon which an interpreter could impose a personal thematic. Canonical gerrymandering and free translation techniques restructured the authoritative texts. They could now be read "objectively," that is, to support the pillars of Rammohan's reform: the condemnation of *satī* and polytheistic idolatry (Roy 1906: 5).[8] The Raja read and sometimes rewrote the "Vedic" canon to depict an ideal Aryan past where these practices did not exist.

Of all the contemporary practices that diverged from ancient sources, *satī* was considered by Rammohan Roy to be the most destructive force threatening society: engendering prejudice, superstition, and the total destruction of moral principles. In the *Conference between an Advocate for and an Opponent of the Practice of Burning Widows Alive* (1818), Roy presented his textually grounded condemnation of *satī* in the form of a debate. The opponent of *satī* claims that it is suicide and, as such, forbidden by the various shāstras. The advocate for *satī*, however, cites the *Rig Veda* in support of the ritual.

> O Fire! let these women, with bodies anointed with clarified butter, eyes coloured with collyrium and void of tears, enter thee, the parent of water, that they may not be separated from their husbands, but may be in union with excellent husbands, themselves sinless and jewels amongst women. (Roy 1906: 327)

The opponent's response to Rig Vedic authority relies on a fundamental thesis of Roy's commentaries and translations: pure religion degenerated into cultic practices that aimed at accommodating less gifted adherents. Citing the *Bhagavad Gītā,* the opponent claims that even a Vedic passage may be superceded, if it is directed toward readers who are occupied with or trapped within sense desires. Thus, the *Rig Veda* passage, the ultimate authority condoning *satī*, can be discounted as a lesser authority intended for lesser minds.

The opponent/Roy also points to the obscurity of the Rig Vedic passage and questions its authenticity (Roy 1906: 367–72). He notes that it does not specifically enjoin women to sacrifice themselves and contains no reference to women performing voluntary death with their husbands' corpse. The phrase "these women" can only be taken to refer to particular women and not women in general. Roy adds, moreover, that no commentary has ever given this passage the interpretation of commending widows to burn themselves on their husband's pyre. In a gesture of overkill, Roy has now both rejected as an invalid authority the Vedic passage cited in favor of *satī* and called into question its reliability.

He next questions whether support for this problematic ritual has ever been found in *smṛti*, texts which rank second to the Veda in authority. Among *smṛti*, *Manu* is the most authoritative. Roy claims that *Manu*, by enjoining the widow to live a virtuous life, is decidedly against concremation. Although contradictions to *Manu* can be found, Roy rejects them for the same reason that he discounted the Rig Vedic passage—their promise of future carnal fruition (Roy 1906: 368). In addition to the *Gītā's* injunction to discount texts that promise reward, he cites *Manu* and modern law experts who also discredit behavior done in the hope of future gains. Roy's condemnation of *satī* rests, therefore, upon three claims of validity. Passages are first assessed according to intent. A text, whatever its status, that promotes superstition, idolatry, or the promotion of selfish ritual must be discarded. Secondly, passages are judged by authenticity and reliability. These factors are judged by corroborative textual evidence. Thirdly, corroboration is sought in the most authoritative text. Barring Vedic corroboration, it is to be found in the next most authoritative source. Roy reads *Manu* as inviolate and claims a text valid only insofar as it agrees with *Manu* (Roy 1906: 343). *Manu*, therefore, can overrule all other lawbooks and, in this case, the Veda itself. At the expense of the *Rig Veda*, *Manu* is deemed truly "Vedic." As such, *Manu's* assessment is deemed valid and original. Roy reads *Manu's* enjoinder for widows to live virtuous lives as the legitimate condemnation of the rite. The condemnation of *satī* thus pivoted upon the rhetorical use of scripture, its shifting authority, and conflicting truth claims. Rammohan Roy's critique of idolatry further developed this line of argument.

MISREADING MONOTHEISM: IDOLATRY
AND BRAHMIN PERFIDY

By shifting scriptural authority and translating select Upanishads and the Vedānta Sūtra into vernaculars ("Hindoostani" and Bengali) and English,

Roy did not merely construct a specific normative reading. By making the texts available, he prioritized scripture as it had never been before, substituting the texts themselves for the priest as the ultimate source of authority and, thus, subverting the traditional hermeneutic process. In this manner, Roy created a vision of the Vedic past wherein objectionable aspects of modern Hinduism were absent, since they existed only through misreading and abuse of textual authority.

In the introduction to his translation of the *Kena Upanishad*, Roy asserted that in India, no less than in the West, there had developed a notion of monotheism (Roy 1906: 35). In subsequent epochs, this belief had degenerated into idolatry for two reasons: believers are often ignorant and priests are often liars. There exist many who are incapable of grasping higher truths, yet are entitled to religious principles lest they remain in a primitive state. For the sake of those who possess limited understanding, worship of figured beings is allowed. This rationale explains how an infallible text such as the Veda can appear paradoxical; it is so by design, with the interest of the common man in mind. Where the Veda suggests a tolerance for idolatry, it actually reveals a strategy for accommodating the unsophisticated (Roy 1906: 23).[9] Subtleties in Vedic rhetorical style aimed at providing divine access to all persons, including those incapable of subtlety who may choose lesser paths.[10] Roy thus delimited a subtext within the Veda, a meta-Veda, that demanded an allegorical reading aimed at an alternative audience. As a literary device, however, allegory proved baneful, since Indians showed themselves to be particularly skilled in this art. When literature and philosophy subsequently decayed, clever allegorical representations were misinterpreted to condone idolatry as the foremost and preferred form of worship.

The prevalence of Hindu idolatry, therefore, should be seen as an error in interpretation. Different genres coexisting within a single scriptural text presented different claims to authority and validity. To decipher Vedic truth, one must determine which passages should be read as scriptural injunction and which as poetry. The Raja could then, having established rules for textual validity, dismiss the poetic (and symbolic) passages that had been "misread" and correct those "excrescences" that had led to "exceptionable practices," depriving Hindus of common comforts and bringing about societal ruin. Rather than anything intrinsic to Hinduism, it was the Indian genius for allegory and democratizing scriptural strategies of revealing God to all, the gifted as well as the unsophisticated, that led to confusion. The reader's inability to judge the respective truth claims of poetry and scriptural injunction enabled the practice of idolatry to flourish. Roy's translations and commentaries aimed at enabling Indians to cast aside prejudice and release themselves from the fetters of accumulated misreadings.

In addition to misreadings stemming from interpretive misperceptions, Vedic wisdom was also undermined by a well-organized brahmin conspiracy.

Roy directly accused the brahmins of keeping the true scriptural knowledge concealed from their brethern (Roy 1906: 66) by permitting "themselves alone to interpret or even touch any book of this kind" (Roy 1906: 3). Roy claimed that textual inaccessibility had allowed religious practice to stray from orthodoxy to the point that it stood at a considerable distance from precept. Brahmins read the Vedas in support of ceremonial observance as necessary for the acquisition of divine knowledge in order to monopolize profits from the rites and festivals of idol worship (Roy 1906: 93). Zealous brahmins thus sacrificed scriptural authority for "the preservation of their fertile estate of idolatry" (Roy 1906: 108, 118). They were fully aware of the absurdity of idol worship (preface, Iśopanishad, 1816), yet they nevertheless encouraged its practice since it provided their fortune and comfort. Their motives as promoters of image worship were, therefore, base, shameless, and mercenary (Roy 1906: 114, 116). These self-interested guides, motivated by vulgar caprice (Roy 1906: 71), conducted believers to the temple of idolatry (Roy 1906: 73). They succeeded in promoting idol worship only because the average Hindu was unversed in scripture and believed that religion really consisted in the observance of rituals and rules of caste. Whereas the worship of idols had existed in other civilizations (notably Greece and Rome) in equally "impure, absurd and puerile" forms, the Hindu variety was far more pernicious, since it was perpetrated by trusted authority figures "hardly deserving the name of social beings" (Roy 1906: 120), who destroyed the comforts of life and the very texture of society.

Rammohan believed that idolatry ultimately effected the total destruction of morality. As an external form of ritual palpable only to gross instincts, it countenanced criminal intercourse, suicide, female murder, and human sacrifice. All prejudices and superstitions derived from it, since the worship of objects resembling one's own nature deadened the senses and led to grosser abuses (Muṇḍaka Upanishad, 1819). He laid the destruction of society's moral fabric directly at the feet of the brahmins, who acted as false guides and consciously defied scripture. Roy chided traditional brahmins for distorting scripture and withholding religious truths. But he primarily blamed "modern Brahmins" for sanctioning the practices of satī, child marriage, dowry abuses, and Kulinism.[11] They promoted "the most heinous crimes that would make even the most savage nations blush to commit unless compelled by most urgent necessity" (introduction, Kaṭha translation).

In his translation of the Kaṭha Upanishad, Roy elaborated upon his condemnation of self-interested brahmin leaders who foster superstitions. He accused them of actually fashioning scripture to suit their greed and selfish aims. Roy exhorted his readers to use common sense, follow reason, and put faith only in those who translate scripture for them out of disinterested motives rather than those who conceal truth, demand goods, and require obeisance. In contrast to the traditional (and flawed) interpreter, the Raja positioned himself as the ideal reader committed to reason and not motivated by greed. His desire to reform Hinduism, however, conflicted with his ideal of objectivity. Although he claimed to translate the Upanishads faithfully (Roy 1906: 63), his renditions differ considerably from the Sanskrit texts, particularly in those passages (noted in italics) that he added to the original to "facilitate comprehension." Upon closer inspection of Roy's translations, one realizes the extent to which he editorialized scripture to promote his reform agenda. In the interest of space, a representative example of Roy's creative emendations should suffice.

The attributeless God of the Upanishads becomes in Roy's translations a patriarchal deity viewed as "spiritual father" and parent (Roy 1906: 39, 42). This was a difficult divine image for the Raja to have extracted from the attributeless *Brahman* of Vedānta or the monism of Advaita. Nevertheless, he read into Shaṅkara's commentary a revival of monotheism and evoked a patriarchal God who was "the author and governor of the universe" (Roy 1906: 174). He is a God who rewards the faithful and bestows grace upon them in the form of knowledge (Roy 1906: 58) and faith (Roy 1906: 26). Unique and paternal, God responds to those who rationally approach Him. Although human forgetfulness allows for the identification of this God with a multitude of celestial representations (Roy 1906: 12), no competing divinities really exist. In the *Īśā*'s invocation of the Sun (verse 16), Roy supplements the text with the comment that such prayers are "meaningless since the sun is the same as He who possesses Divine Nature." Throughout his translations, Roy consistently explains away multiple gods and promotes a vision of Vedic monotheism. The Raja reads the text to say that idolatry is as much an error as is ritual excess.

Roy introduces the subject of ritual into texts (Roy 1906: 26, 76) where it does not appear. A passage from the *Īśopanishad* is literally translated as:

Those who are covered in darkness and who despise the Self die and become demons.[12]

Rammohan Roy rendered this passage in the following manner:

Those that neglect the contemplation of the Supreme Spirit either by devoting themselves solely to the performance of the ceremonies of religion, or by living destitute of religious ideas, shall after death, assume the state of demons such as that of the celestial gods, and other created beings, which are surrounded with the darkness of ignorance. (Roy 1906: 76)

Here as elsewhere (Roy 1906: 47, 51–52), the Raja introduced the subject of ritual into the text only to condemn it as a false goal of worship, motivated by vain desire of future gain, a form of superstition (Roy 1906: 15), or something purely optional. Ritual is equated with religious ignorance. Demons are likened to the multiple gods worshipped by lesser minds. In this manner, he rewrites the Upanishadic text to condemn both ritual and idolatry.

These polemical works and translations show that the Raja fully recognized the authority wielded by the "Vedas" as absent texts and the abuse of authority exercised by their brahmin "readers."[13] Rammohan Roy's entire project was directed at making present these texts and wresting power away from their custodians. In his polemical works, Roy developed strategies to alter the canon so that it supported his arguments. With his translation of principle portions of the "Vedas" and the Vedānta, authority came to rest solidly on a tangible archive. Here the canon, now fixed, underwent rewriting. Through the manipulation of his canon, Roy set about redressing errors concerning the nature of the "invisible Supreme Being" and suggesting models for "pure worship" untainted by idolatry. The condemnation of idolatry ultimately rested on the conflicting truth claims of poetry and divine injunction.

RAMMOHAN ROY'S SYNCRETISM AND ITS CHALLENGE TO POSTCOLONIAL THEORY

Christophe Jaffrelot has identified two theoretical positions that historians generally use to describe the origin and development of ethnic movements in India: the primordialist and the instrumental. The primordialist position maintains that cultural specificities lead to ethnic consciousness. The instrumentalist position holds that cultural identities are malleable and can, as symbols, be manipulated by elite groups to mobilize a given community. Jaffrelot suggests a third perspective, what he terms "strategic syncretism." He terms this position syncretic because the content of ideology is taken from the behavior of groups deemed antagonistic to a given population. The syncretism is strategic in that it aims, through psychological and mimetic processes, to dominate those same antagonistic groups (Jaffrelot 1993: 519).

We have tried to show how Rammohan Roy constructed a canon and used it in a manner consistent with what Jaffrelot has termed strategic syncretism. He borrowed from the Orientalists a preference for Vedāntic texts. He shared their devaluation of modern Hinduism. Here, he was less motivated by the missionaries' contempt for a debased faith and more from belief that it did not suit the social needs of the population. However, he shared their distrust of brahmin power. Rammohan Roy took what he liked about Christianity, borrowed the methods wielded by missionaries and Orientalist scholarship, and devised strategies, based on traditional Indian normative approaches to textuality (that is, that texts *need* interpretation), to challenge scriptural inerrancy and canonicity.

He waged a battle on two fronts, one against the heavy-handed techniques of Christian missionaries (a problem that does not seem to go away, as witnessed by recent events in India with American Baptist groups) and another against brahmin power. His reform was strategic in the sense that it sought to dominate both missionary and brahmin discourse. Through the evocation of a Vedic Golden Age constructed out of alternative readings of canonical sources, he condemned those very practices that had elicited the scorn of Christian missionaries. By evoking a monotheistic Vedic *Urreligion*, he placed Hinduism on equal footing with Christianity. By exposing the idolatrous nature of the Christian Trinity, Roy silenced any critique of Hindu polytheism.

However antagonistic the Trinitarians might have been as a group and however necessary it was to neutralize them, the enemies who existed closer to home were far more daunting opponents. To combat them, Rammohan Roy waged a battle of literary proportions. By prioritizing textuality over and above priestly exegesis, the Raja dealt a severe blow to brahmin authority. If there was a brahmin conspiracy, wider accessibility to authoritative texts would do much to countermand it.[14] By grounding his reform in the reinterpretation of sacred texts and appending onto these texts core values borrowed from the rhetoric of Christianity, Roy legitimized his arguments according to existing Indian concepts of scriptural sacredness. He sought to establish a means whereby Hinduism, whose conventional sacred duties had been confined to ceremonial rites and offerings, might be transformed and brought into the service of the community. He expressly sought to promote the comfort of his people and unite them by reviving the "Vedant" and disseminating religion in book form.

In this study of the Aryan myth as it expresses itself in the literary consciousness, it is our intention to stress at all times the hermeneutic event, the individual's relationship to inherited tradition and the specific experience of encounter. Rammohan Roy's translations of the Upanishads brought into focus a fundamental disagreement over man's natural capacity to understand religious truth. This hermeneutic problem stemmed from the hierarchization of Hindu social and religious life founded on the premise that significant differences in capacity and competence exist between individuals. Rammohan Roy seriously challenged this *adhikārabheda* tradition when he translated the texts. He asserted that all but a very small minority could understand the basic teachings of the Upanishads. He did not expect all to benefit fully from these teachings, but the success rate would be proportionate to one's state of mental preparation (Roy 1906: 133).[15]

There was even another level of syncretism in his work—his promoting Christian precepts grounded in Western rationalism. He did not see contemporary Hinduism as permanently inferior to Semitic-based creeds, but as a once great but now fallen religion which still had possibilities. His efforts at reform were motivated by a desire to improve the lot of his countrymen and modernize their faith. In his harkening back, via a "Veda" that could wield authority in India's present-day malaise, Roy sought to reconstruct a purified Hindu community and a sense of history for that community (Nandy 1983: 103). To borrow Jaffrelot's terminology, we may say that his syncretism was strategic in the sense that the resulting neo-Hinduism originated out of a purely indigenous golden age that depicted a unified religion and a single cultural strain (Nandy 1983: 193). By revealing the essential truth embedded in scripture, Rammohan Roy sought to separate scriptural authority from the false accretions of time and the literal teachings of idolatrous, self-promoting brahmins who continued to practice a socially destructive system. His methodology provided a powerful tool of social engineering to the next generation (Nandy 1983: 193). His efforts represent far less the colonial's intellectual dependency on the Western Other and need to mimic his values, and far more an individual interrogating his own tradition and wielding the tools of Western religion as they are useful to him. In Rammohan Roy, we find the "voiced" subaltern.

No one doubts the acknowledged limitations of nationalism within the colonial context, nor the influence of nineteenth-century intellectual models upon nationalism. Colonialism does define, limit, and distort contact between cultures. However, it does not follow that a weak and dependent intelligentsia's admiration for its master's civilization is exclusively a result of dependency (Sen 1978: 4). The hermeneutic possibilities of cross-cultural encounters are simply not exhausted by identifying a "drive" in the European psyche suffering from ego-anxiety or its aggressive objectification of the other in order to constitute its own coherence (Said 1978: 72). Quite simply, we must question the dynamics involved in Eastern appropriations of Western constructs. Indian responses to specific elements in British culture, for example, were not necessarily linked to colonialism, even though responses may ultimately have reinforced imperial dominance (Raychaudhuri 1988: 5). The oppressor/victim binary of colonial discourse analysis does not account for patterns of admiration and positions adopted within the receiving culture. Dominance can provoke revulsion and rejection as well. While negative responses are frequently interpreted as ambivalence, they might also be explained by the fact that particular components of the cultures involved determine what is admired or rejected. Ideally, theory should explain how appropriations are rooted in the specific cultural traits of the receptor society and its literary tradition. Equality and inequality are not the sole determinants of cultural encounters.

Encounters are determined from the evolving values of a people and their specific historical situation. Rammohan Roy lived at a time when one could envision incorporating the ideas of science, history, and progress as forces of criticism within Indian traditions. He was a product of an age which was culturally self-confident (Nandy 1983: 101), when individuals thought themselves capable of self-definition. Rammohan's political consciousness was based on a good deal of self-esteem and autonomy. As recent assessments of Rammohan Roy have shown, directing our theoretical task to unmasking his complicity in colonial rule limits any need or desire to engage in more nuanced literary or philosophical investigations of his work. It is important to stress the power of ideas themselves acting as autonomous forces and as catalysts (Sen 1978: 5). It is important to avoid complacently dismissing Indian responses to the West as motivated either by slavish admiration or xenophobic rejection. Epistemological binarism is problematic in itself. In this particular instance, structure and history collide.

Since structuralism, critical theory is largely based on some idea of structural power that determines all behavior, both political and personal. To this fundamental systemic feature, the critic questions whether there can, in fact, be a true representation of any thing (Ahmad 1994: 192). The desire to know the world and the claim that it is open to rational comprehension can then be dismissed as contemptible attempts to construct "grand narratives" and totalizing (totalitarian?) knowledges.[16] In Orientalist and postcolonial criticism's narratives of oppression, complex subjects such as Rammohan Roy tend not to exist. Representation is always already misrepresentation; human communication is "a ruse of illusory subjectivity [that] precludes the possibility of truthful statements on the ground that evidence that . . . writing, is always already prejudiced by the very nature of language itself " (Ahmad 1993: 194).

On a historical level, such theory gives colonial discourse a status that it did not possess in the world as power. If colonial discourse as knowledge had the power ascribed to it, colonialism would probably not have been overthrown. There would have been no room for local power elites to collaborate with colonialism or synthesize their own form (Clark 1996: 29). By replacing reading with theoretical strategems intent on shaping the contest over decolonization, colonial discourse analysis can overlook areas of response that are not wholly determined by relationships of colonial power and undervalue causal links in areas such as eighteenth- and nineteenth-century nativist concerns. It can neglect those positive responses to specific elements in an alien culture that are not necessarily linked to dominance, even though the latter may reinforce them (Raychaudhuri 1988: 5). It can dismiss most claims of individual agency. It can refuse to acknowledge textuality as anything but a representation of inner contradictions of systemic violence. Theory prioritizes itself as the necessary device with which one can decode how textual inconsistencies and contradictions reenact or deconstruct the power relations of a system.

It allows us as readers to embrace the rather shallow critical assumption that all human communication is deceptive. The notion that systemic limits determine all struggles for self-realization stems from the belief that the individual is always subject to forces beyond his or her comprehension. If texts are considered mere effects of systemic violence, if representation is conceived as already an attempt to impose boundaries, then promises of reform ultimately reveal themselves as shrewd strategies of containment. This critical position points to reactionary and self-serving impulses dominating literary theory today. As we have seen in the case of Rammohan Roy, it has little basis in fact when actually applied to the production of any number of colonial subjects. In the following chapters, we might want to ask ourselves what politics of projects foreground the theoretical dependence on epistemic power and the rejection of intersubjectivity.

CHAPTER 6

Text-based Identity: Dayānand Saraswatī's Reconstruction of the Aryan Self

INTRODUCTION

In chapter 5, we saw that the founding of the Brāhmo Samāj in 1828 by Raja Rammohan Roy initiated a religious and political movement for the cultural purification of Hinduism. It was his belief that India had strayed from the true model for Indian culture and religion, the ancient Aryans. As a cure for India's political subjugation, he proposed a recuperation of the former Aryan vision and glory. Rammohan's method of reading the past as a means of reaffirming or undoing the present set a precedent. Indeed, throughout the nineteenth-century, Indian readings of the Aryan past revalorized ancient Indian history and contributed to social reform. Perhaps the most radical reformer was Dayānand Saraswatī (1824–83), who founded the Ārya Samāj in 1875. In much the same manner that Rammohan Roy based his reform on the translation and dissemination of the Upanishads, Dayānand developed his notion of the Aryan through a continued rearticulation of the authority vested in Vedic texts.

Like the Brāhmo Samāj, the Ārya Samāj was a movement that rejected much of what passed as current Hinduism. It based its reform on eradicating differences in language, religion, education, customs, and manners that prevented Indians from fully effecting the mutual good of society as a whole. The ten principles (*niyams*) of the Ārya Samāj (written in 1877) provide a summary statement of Dayānand's position with respect to social reform and ethics. Many of the issues raised in the *niyams* address ethical concerns for the physical, spiritual, and social welfare of others that the Brāhmo Samāj and Western critics had found lacking in Hinduism.[1]

As did Rammohan Roy, Dayānand rejected polytheism and posited the existence of a single and abstract God. He also condemned idol worship. Since God is formless, He cannot be captured by plastic representation. For both thinkers, the issue of idolatry was emblematic of a degenerate Hinduism as opposed to an earlier pure faith. Both focused on idolatry as a medieval excrescence totally foreign to Aryan religion. By debunking idol worship, both sought to reform Hinduism and return to its source. However, Dayānand took arguments against idol worship one step further. He asserted that idolatry led to India's political slavery and degradation. By depending on idols and not exerting themselves, Indians had lost their government, independence, wealth, and pleasures. Dayānand maintained that the Indians themselves were responsible for having become a subject race.

In addition to approximating the Brāhmo Samāj's stand on monotheism and idolatry, Dayānand also advocated other issues that were fundamental to Rammohan's reform: female equality in education, postponing the age of marriage, marriage by choice (Dayānand 1981: 315), and widow remarriage (Dayānand 1981: 282). In matters of caste reform, Dayānand far exceeded the efforts of the Raja.[2] While the Brāhmo Samāj challenged caste with arguments based on Western Enlightenment concerns for social utility, Dayānand condemned caste as a Hindu distortion of Aryan social values.[3] The means for rehabilitation existed and could be rediscovered in the Vedas. It was, therefore, a question of relying on Aryan solutions to social and religious problems. No foreign inspiration or models for reform were necessary. The Ārya Samāj rejected the universalism of the Brāhmo Samāj, particularly in its later configurations.[4] Rather than accommodating different religious writings, the Ārya Samāj challenged scriptural eclecticism. Hinduism was not equal in the brotherhood of religions, but superior to all others (Jordens 1978: 278–79).

Underlying the Ārya Samāj's mandate was its founder's profound belief that modern Indians needed only to return to Aryan values articulated in the Vedas in order to effect reform and regain independence.[5] Since the techniques for a return to the Aryan social system were to be found in the teachings of the Veda, Dayānand based his entire program on these texts. They possessed the necessary learning (Dayānand 1981: 117), including all scientific knowledge (Dayānand 1981: 404, 130). Unfortunately, the fundamentals of all types of knowledge do not appear in the Veda in their fully developed form. To access this knowledge, one needed the interpretive skills that Dayānand's reading of the Veda purported to offer.

With the *Satyārth Prakāsh* and the *Rgvedādibhāshyabhūmikā*,[6] Dayānand sought to liberate the Veda from brahmin control, make it accessible to all Hindus,[7] and reveal the Aryan Golden Age. In the following discussion, we will examine how the *Satyārth Prakāsh* (1875, revised 1883) and Dayānand's commentaries on the Vedas present a series of interpretive strategies enabling him to extricate Vedic revelation from its hermeticism and narrow ritualism and promote a vision of Hindu nationalism that resonates up to the present day.[8]

DAYĀNAND'S CANON AND HERMENEUTICAL STRATEGIES FOR READING THE ARYAN WORLD

Vedic textual reference was traditionally known only as memorized utterance. In order to reconstruct a universal system based on the Veda, it was first necessary to fix the revealed text as a written text in the form of a book edition or a translation before invoking it as a canonical authority. Rammohan Roy had begun this process by physically disseminating his "Veda" in the form of vernacular and English translations of the Upanishads. Max Müller continued this process of fixing the Veda with the monumental task of "collecting the ancient MSS" and "publishing for the first time the text and commentary of the *Rig Veda*, the oldest book of the whole Aryan race" (Müller 1970: 25). Before Dayānand, however, no modern Indian scholar had exhaustively studied the Vedic mantras. Although Hindus paid homage to the Vedas, the Purāṇas were the scriptures used by the masses and the elites alike. Even for rituals, priests did not rely on the Śrauta Sūtras, but on medieval glosses of their commentaries that had been written in Sanskrit (Sen 1979: 328). The perception of scriptural value was often more important than content or authorship.

Like Rammohan Roy and Max Müller, Dayānand realized that the Veda's authority was contingent upon the text's accessibility, its availability to the public, and its release from brahmin control. In fact, the entire issue of Vedic authority and canonicity really entailed the liberation of Vedic revelation from its brahmin appraisers. Witness the format that Dayānand initially chose for his polemic, the *śāstrārtha* or book disputation (Llewellyn 1993: 104).[9] The most notable book disputation took place in Benares in 1869. Here, Dayānand challenged the pandits to prove that idol worship had Vedic sanction by demanding that they physically produce references. They, of course, could not prove Vedic authority for idolatry. Only the Purāṇas sanctioned it, and Dayānand 's opponents based their claim on this authority.

The site and the theme of this book disputation are noteworthy: Dayānand chose Benares, a center for brahmin learning, as the site to debate idol worship, one of the major sources of priestly pecuniary gain. Although the topic was idolatry, the ensuing debate ended abruptly in the midst of a discussion concerning whether the Purāṇas were an expression of the same religion as was found in the Vedas. Legend has it that one of the pandits produced some pages containing the term *purāṇa* ("old"), and while Dayānand was reading them, the pandit declared victory. Dayānand was pelted with stones and police whisked him away (Jordens 1978: 68).[10] It is important to note that the debate rested more on the issue of canonicity than on idolatry. Even at this early stage in his career, the book-bound nature of his canon and the physical existence of a Veda were significant factors.[11]

With time, Dayānand focused even more on textually grounded Vedic
authority (Jordens 1978:54-58).[12] Throughout his career, he consistently
emphasized the legitimacy of physically present texts. After he abandoned
the medium of the book disputation and public debate, he focused his attention on translation and commentary. Through these efforts, Dayānand established a canon from which he could create a portrait of an idealized,
monotheistic Aryan world devoid of idolatry.

Dayānand's initial task consisted of identifying a canon of authority. In
an innovative move, Dayānand limited the Vedic canon to include only the
saṃhitā portions of the Vedas.[13] It was a curious move on his part to posit the
Vedic saṃhitās as the sole authority, since they were historically viewed as
ritualistic texts. Dayānand, however, insisted that the saṃhitās be read exclusively in order to gain knowledge relevant to life. Since the Vedas alone were
considered divine in origin and other texts were composed by seers,
Dayānand deemed that whatever was found in any text contradicting the
Veda must be rejected. As the only texts composed by God, they alone were
infallible; other texts depended on them for their respective authority. By
delimiting his canon in this manner,[14] Dayānand sought to discover the earliest strata of religion in its purest form. The movement back to the earliest
text, predating any and all practices, provided an impregnable position from
which to launch an attack on contemporary abuses.

Regarding the rest of Hindu scripture, Dayānand only considered those
texts written before the Mahābhārata War in the Vedic Golden Age,[15] the
ārsha literature, as authoritative. While this corpus contains some error (since
it was composed by humans), Dayānand judged it valid to the extent that it
reflected God's knowledge as manifest in the Veda. He judged the anārsha
texts, those written after the Mahābhārata War, devoid of authority and
unworthy of study. They may contain some truth, but it is hidden under
much falsehood, amidst "a lot of rubbish, myths and fabrications" (Dayānand
1915: 74). Given the fact that Dayānand clearly delineated those texts that
he viewed as authoritative, it is interesting to note the extent to which he
held to his valuation of textual legitimacy and adhered to his preestablished
canon of authority. Dayānand scholar J.T.F. Jordens compared the first and
second editions of the Satyārth Prakāsh and discovered that, in the first edition, Dayānand provided few Vedic references to support his portrait of the
Aryan world. It was only after the long and arduous work on the
Vedabhāshya that he compiled the second edition and cited the Vedas more
frequently (Jordens 1978: 102). In both editions, Dayānand also relied heavily on Manu, the principal Upanishads, and the six schools of philosophy
(Jordens 1978: 250).[16]

In an exhaustive statistical analysis of Dayānand's use of source material,
J.E. Llewellyn has further shown to what degree Dayānand relied on ārsha

literature when the *saṃhitā* portions of the four Vedas did not offer sufficient material to substantiate an idealized vision of Aryan reality. Llewellyn has quantified the extent to which Dayānand based his portrait of the Aryans on a limited Vedic canon supplemented by alternative authorities from *ārsha* literature that were not Vedic as Dayānand defined it, but could be used canonically in conjunction with the Veda to support argumentation (Llewellyn 1993: 207).[17] In order to develop a full theory of polity, for example, Dayānand relied primarily on *Manu*. Expediency overrode his self-imposed canonical strictures. The important point in this regard is that, textually, Dayānand's Vedic world was no more "Vedic" than Rammohan Roy's translations of the Upanishads. Moreover, in order to read this "Veda" in support of an idealized vision of the Aryan world, Dayānand devised a series of hermeneutical ploys that further facilitated his thesis that the Vedas embody a totality of truth.

Llewellyn has shown how, in general, Dayānand was not truly consistent in his use of citations (Llewellyn 1993: 231).[18] References to sources frequently did not even follow the authority quoted (Llewellyn 1993: 240). In the great majority of cases, Dayānand presented his own interpretation of the Vedic passage without any reference to supporting material (Llewellyn 1993: 231, 238). When he chose to support his readings, he prominently featured non-Vedic *ārsha* texts noteworthy for their interpretive flexibility (Llewellyn 1993: 235–37).[19] Dayānand also allowed himself considerable freedom through an impressionistic treatment of verbs. If the Veda was indeed timeless, Dayānand felt justified in changing verb tense or person to fit his interpretation (Llewellyn 1993: 237-38). Because God's knowledge is eternal and infallible, the relation of words, letters, and meaning remains the same in the past and in the future (Dayānand 1981: 40, 301). Thus, Dayānand could easily transform the past into the present. Semantic contortions allowed him to render historical events or geographical features into statements of principle (Jordens 1978: 271–72). The latitude that such tinkering afforded his translation cannot be overstressed. It virtually liberated his "authoritative" reading of the ultimately canonical text from any bonds of textuality.

However, Dayānand's most effective strategy for reading the Veda to support his argument was to be found in his fanciful etymologies and translations. Creative etymology allowed Dayānand to draw his rather baroque conclusions—that the Aryans possessed sophisticated scientific data regarding air filtration and water purification techniques (Dayānand 1981: 327), the science of aeronautics (Dayānand 1981: 264), and techniques of medicine (Dayānand 1981: 267). Grammar and semantics were enlisted to support Dayānand's unique notion that the Vedas were the repository of all scientific truth (Jordens 1978: 272). Creative translations also allowed Dayānand to reveal the Aryans' historical commitment to social progress. The *Yajur Veda* text 20.10 is literally translated thus : "I take my stand on princely power and kingship." Dayānand renders this passage:

> I live in a kingdom which is administered righteously and in the country which is awakened, due to the widespread literacy and morality.

Two sentences later in the same passage, the Sanskrit can be rendered thus: "I stay on welfare, on upper regions and earth and I recline on sacrifice," to which Dayānand offers the following reading :

> Those who carry on duties of government regarding me as their supreme Lord, achieve always triumph and progressive prosperity. All government officials therefore should strive to enlighten the people with knowledge and justice and should protect them so that injustice and ignorance may be uprooted. (Dayānand 1981: 293)

Creative translations also allowed Dayānand to reveal the Aryans' commitment to scientific progress by proving Aryan knowledge of telegraphy and modern chemistry.[20] Reading the results of scientific investigations into the Vedas may well have functioned as a strategic ploy aimed at defusing the modern encroachments of scientism or attacking the scientific pretenses of modernism. However, Dayānand's linguistic flights of fancy also served a serious practical purpose: They were directed in service of religious reform.

Broad translation enabled Dayānand to draw his most significant conclusions regarding Aryan religious belief. A free rendering of the term *pratimā*, as "measure" rather than "idol" or "image" (Llewellyn 1993: 250) allowed Dayānand to confirm that the Veda actually prohibits image worship (Dayānand 1981: 383–87).[21] Morphosyntactic switching allowed Dayānand to affirm the existence of Vedic monotheism (Dayānand 1981: 91–92).[22] Although Dayānand ascribed ten separate meanings to the term *deva*, he concluded that it in no way referred to a multiplicity of divinities (Dayānand 1981: 76).[23] In this manner, Dayānand's reading of the Veda supported his critique of Hindu polytheism and idolatry, constant themes in his attack on traditional beliefs and practices. In other words, Dayānand's interpretive strategies established a hermeneutical structure that foreclosed all competing value systems: scientific, religious, and, finally historical.

The Veda eternally existed prior to all history.[24] It cannot, therefore, relate to any particular event or individual (Dayānand 1915: 240). Those instances where the Veda seems to refer to proper names or events actually express statements of principle or injunction clothed in dramatic or poetic form. Moreover, the Veda cannot contain anything that offends reason and morality (such as miracles or myths). Seemingly supernatural or historical events must be interpreted allegorically (Dayānand 1981: 369). Names, particularly the names of various gods, can indicate general sense only (Dayānand 1981: 120).[25] In short, Dayānand used a "shadow" Veda or alternative canon, miscitations, creative etymologies, and mistranslations to support his central thesis of the Veda's universal applicability and usefulness as a protomodernist tool for reform. This methodology had far-reaching implications: It ultimately allowed him to mythologize history and demythologize myth.

Dayānand's vision of text-centered authority, his delimitation of the canon, and the hermeneutical strategies he devised enabled him to attack the very type of religion that brahmins identified as "Vedic" and Dayānand deemed false and superstitious. His creative method of reading also challenged the modernism represented by the Brāhmo Samāj and Indian scholars whom he felt were under the spell of Western ideological presuppostions.[26] The layers of deception were manifold: Indian modernists depended upon Western scholars who, in turn, had fallen prey to brahmin falsehood in the form of traditional Sanskrit commentaries (Dayānand 1981: 405). Dayānand thus rejected the authority of traditional exegesis (in the form of scoliasts and commentators) as well as modern (yet traditionally trained) scholars both at home and abroad. After rejecting all competing exegetical authorities, his canon and interpretation alone remained valid.

Beyond imposing a personal idiosyncratic reading on the canon as he defined it, Dayānand's strategies for reading presented a serious attempt to liberate the Veda from the limited readership of brahmin priests and pundits who controlled access to the texts. Rammohan Roy had first sought to liberate the text by redefining access to it through translation. By rejecting traditional and contemporary readings, Dayānand directed his efforts to the same end—freeing the text from brahmin readings and bequeathing it to a more general public. Rammohan's efforts had been limited. Dayānand understood that, with the consolidation of colonial power and its print culture, Indians had the opportunity to reclaim their scripture from "unworthy" brahmin custodians. Dayānand's response was forcefully directed at undermining the system of age-old authority, overthrowing the traditional reader, and installing an ideal reader.

Dayānand 's discourse on the Aryan world thus challenged tradition in the form of brahmin textual power as well as incursions of modernity into tradition. Given the traditional Hindu attitude toward scriptural authority, Dayānand 's interpretive play with citations, etymology, syntax, and tense were truly innovative. They provided the textual apparatus for the reinterpretation and valorization of what it was to be Aryan. However, this text-based Aryan identity necessitated the rehabilitation not only of the text, but the reader as well.

ARYAN MASCULINITY AND THE TELEOLOGY OF DECAY

The task of rehabilitating the textually bound Aryan and his reader necessitated the revaluation of human actions and the spirit that animates them. Dayānand represented the human soul as an active and creative energy, not a passive spectator (Dayānand 1915: 226). In fact, the *Satyārth Prakāsh* at numerous reprises drives home the message of man's involvement in the moral world.[27] Underlying Dayānand's recuperative efforts was the acknowledged conviction that the primeval truth of the Veda had been distorted by the Advaitan belief in the oneness of God and the human soul. According to Vedāntists, neither good nor evil exist because God is the only reality. It is the Advaitan goal to realize this identity, and the *sannyāsī* dedicates himself to this ideal. The world, where good and evil seem to exist, is an illusion. The *Satyārth Prakāsh* sets out to disprove the notion that the world is unreal and evil nonexistent. Common sense, Dayānand claimed, established the existence of objects independent of our perception of them. Objects have a reality of their own, and the world must exist or souls could not reap the rewards of previous deeds (Dayānand 1915: 221).

Dayānand presented the soul alone as the seer, doer, and reaper of the fruits of actions (Dayānand 1915: 290). It is the soul that thinks, knows, remembers, performs actions, feels individuality, enjoys, and suffers. Only the soul can perform good and evil deeds (Dayānand 1915: 221–30). Dayānand discouraged belief in concepts such as transmigration and *karma* because he felt that their determinism made people lazy and indolent. There were no shortcuts through ritual or devotion. Action alone led to *moksha*. In his estimation, passivity sanctioned by religion had deprived the Indians of their independence, happiness, wealth, political power, and learning. They sit idle, praying for relief and charity that is never forthcoming. Such behavior, he maintained, had completely ruined Āryavarta (Dayānand 1915: 318).

Dayānand enjoined his readers to revert to their Aryan selves, to become again men of energetic and active habits (Dayānand 1915: 250). He urged them to reject ignorance and promote public good, justice, and righteousness (Dayānand 1915: 279). Rather than focusing on the casting off of bodily concerns with a view toward emancipation, Dayānand promoted an image of active masculinity, laying special stress on the efficacy of good works ordered by the Veda, the mastery over sense gratification, and behavior beyond the standard personal virtues. These traits had previously made the Aryans great and should be revived in modern India. Clearly, for Dayānand, the Aryans serve as models for human achievement. Their historical downfall, however, provides an equally important lesson, whose message has less to do with racial somatology than with textual politics and potency.

Dayānand's "history" of the past begins with a panegyric to Aryan glory. Humanity consisted of two classes: the good (*ārya*) and the wicked (*dasyu*) (Dayānand 1915: 266). The Aryans were God's chosen people to whom the Veda had been revealed and whose language was the source of all languages. The *Dasyus*, also called *asuras*, were dacoits (Dayānand 1915: 264). Warfare broke out between the Aryans and *Dasyus*. Dayānand did not, however, use the terms *ārya* or *dasyu* in a racial or a religious sense.[28] *Ārya* simply meant an "excellent man" as opposed to a "wicked man." He did not suggest that the Aryans were a particular race or tribe who had conquered aborigines and named them slaves (*dasyus*) (Dayānand 1981: 266).

Regarding India as the best place on earth, the Aryans emigrated there from Tibet "sometime after creation" (Dayānand 1915: 265) and colonized it. They named this land Āryavarta, the abode of the Aryans.[29] Before the Aryans had colonized it, Āryavarta had no name and had been uninhabited. From their new home, the Aryans governed the whole world (Dayānand 1915: 320) and preached the Vedas throughout their dominion (Dayānand 1915: 266). All peoples embraced the Aryan morality, since it taught universal brotherhood. Only under the rule of the Aryans did peace and happiness reign upon this earth (Dayānand 1915: 326–27). Āryavarta was the center and source of Aryan power; all knowledge, righteousness, and all religions originated there (Dayānand 1915: 265). The Aryans were the true Indians. Unlike the Bible or the Koran, the Veda was meant for all nations. Sanskrit was the universal language, since it was no people's mother tongue and all had to learn it. The Aryans taught Egypt, Greece, and Europe whatever initial learning they possessed (Dayānand 1915: 238). They were sophisticated, generous (Dayānand 1915: 39), and cosmopolitan (Dayānand 1915: 326). Their system of rule was so perfect that it formed the basis for all subsequent world governments (Dayānand 1915: 201). Devoted to the acquisition of knowledge and bodily perfection, endowed with ideal social structures and religious customs, the Aryans kept India free from disease and misery. Despite their efforts to maintain a perfect society, however, the Aryans brought destruction upon their culture.

The Mahābhārata War marked the end of the Aryan Golden Age. During this conflict, Āryavarta was dealt a blow from which it never recovered: When the princes, kings, sages, and saints of the golden age perished, their teaching of Vedic literature and religion died with them (Dayānand 1915: 316-18). Superstition and degenerate cultic practices took root and began to flourish in the form of Hinduism's distortions of Vedic religion.[30] Dayānand's philosophy of "history" installs this aetiology of loss and corruption as the root cause of Indian's contemporary malaise. However, what sets Dayānand's teleology of decay apart from Western theorists of degeneration, such as Spengler or Nordau, was that the degeneration Dayānand found in history was intimately related to textual degeneration.

Dayānand held that God communicates the Vedas to man at the beginning of each *kalpa*. Just as He has done in the previous *kalpa*, so will He reveal the Veda again in future *kalpas* ad infinitum (Dayānand 1981: chapter 1). Of the three eternally existing entities, God, souls, and the material universe, the universe and souls cease to exist in their present form at cosmic dissolution (*pralaya*). In the beginning of the next *kalpa*, however, they come into existence again (Dayānand 1915: 281, 284). Like the universe and souls, the Veda too, while not manifest in the period after *pralaya*, is communicated anew to humanity as each world is created (Jordens 1972: 372). Thus, God's knowledge in the form of the Veda is revealed to humanity at the beginning of each *kalpa* and, we are to assume, suffers a similar process of degradations through successive readings. Racial degeneration is thus tied to textual decline.

Textual degradation was partially defined by brahmin agency. Since the Mahābhārata War, brahmins had denied textual access to non-brahmins, thus bringing to a close the tradition of studying Vedic scriptures rationally. Without necessarily understanding the texts, they made their living by controlling and distorting them (Dayānand 1915: 158). Dayānand tied the degeneration of Vedic Hinduism to the proliferation of spurious works of a sectarian nature. Brahmins furthered India's degeneration by sponsoring superfluous rituals for financial gain. Hence they bequeathed to Hinduism belief in idols, miracles, pilgrimages, astrology, and the like, all absent in the Aryan world of the Vedas. Dayānand held that brahmin preoccupation with absurd rituals stemmed from greed and ignorance. He noted that when uneducated persons became preceptors, hypocrisy, fraud, and vice got an upper hand (Dayānand 1915: 317). Their behavior directly brought about the ruin of Āryavarta (Dayānand 1915: 318).

Given the brahmins' abuse of their privileges, Dayānand maintained that they were no longer worthy of the respect paid to them by their birthright (Dayānand 1981: 321). Out of selfishness, they destroyed Vedic knowledge. Lest their fraud be revealed, they contrived to undermine and repress all dissenting voices (Dayānand 1915: 157). They prevented people from educating themselves and ensnared the population in a net of hypocrisy (Dayānand 1915: 317). The authors of "current Sanskrit books or vernacular books" that "wrangle over trifflings" completed the degradation of Vedic truth (Dayānand 1915: 260). Brahmins abused and misdirected the power placed in their hands.

Dayānand directly associated this power with textual power. He claimed that the Vedic source of brahmin power, the *Purusha Sūkta* of the *Rig Veda*

(10.90), had intentionally been misinterpreted. While there were indeed four hierarchical classes, as evinced in this *sūkta*, Dayānand described them as born out of the collectivity's needs for socioeconomic complementarity. Rather than the dismemberment of a primordial man into elements representing social hierarchy,[31] the true meaning of the *sūkta* related how the universe was created and sustained by an omnipresent God who oversees human merit, allowing individuals to enter their hierarchical station only by faithfully discharging the duties of that station (Dayānand 1915: 98–99).[32] According to Dayānand's interpretation of the *sūkta*, even the lowborn should be recognized as brahmins as long as they possess the requisite qualifications. Similarly, the highborn should be demoted if they fail to fulfil duties. Thus, righteous conduct alone determines the achievement of a "higher order of caste" (Dayānand 1981: 397). Dayānand claimed that the status distinctions, the actual "evil" of caste, were a later distortion read into the *sūkta* by brahmins; they did not exist in Vedic times.

Dayānand proposed to replace the current caste system with a meritocracy, where all classes were determined according to the individual's qualifications, accomplishments, and character. Individuals would be assessed some time between their sixteenth and twenty-fifth year of age (Dayānand 1915: 100). Dayānand allowed that the *shūdra* could attain brahmin status and enjoy the privileges of a brahmin, if he evinced the qualities of a brahmin — if he possessed wisdom, piety, charity, and chaste conduct. The same criterion held true for the brahmin, who would become a *shūdra* if he were impure, stupid, dependent, or subservient (Dayānand 1981: 396). For Dayānand, therefore, a brahmin is not born, but self-actualized. One whose mind is a repository of Vedic learning and devotion to God becomes a brahmin.[33] Self-realization is, however, tied to textuality or textual literacy. One can read and understand the Vedas only if one's mind and speech are pure and controlled (Dayānand 1915: 45). Such an individual represents for Dayānand the ideal reader of the Veda, someone capable of returning to true Aryanhood.

Dayānand's attack on the traditional brahmin and redefinition of the true brahmin intersects with his discourse on masculinity, which, in turn, is intimately related to his ideology of the Aryan. False brahmins (that is, traditional brahmins) are false readers of the Veda. They do not exhibit the traits of the Aryans. True brahmins have recuperated Aryan values by returning to the Veda. These "restored Aryans" differ radically from present-day "emasculated Aryans," who are the object of Dayānand's invective. In fact, Dayānand took pains to dissociate his followers from the fallen Aryans of Hinduism. For the 1881 census, Dayānand gave the direction that Ārya Samājists should enter themselves as "Ārya" in the column on community or race and should note

"Vedic Dharma" in the column on religion.[34] When he once inadvertently used
the term "Hindu" in one of his sermons in Poona, he immediately corrected
himself.[35] He urged his audience to give up the name "Hindu" and take pride
in "Ārya" and "Āryavart." He noted: "You have degenerated in your qualities,
which is bad enough but you should at least not corrupt your name."[36]

Dayānand chose a series of persuasive metaphors to describe the
manner in which modern "Aryans" had rejected Aryan values and adopted
evil customs (Dayānand 1915: 320). One metaphor that Dayānand chose
to illustrate past Aryan glory and present "Aryan" dissolution was that of
the *sannyāsī*. Rather than focus upon renunciation as the path by which one
seeks personal liberation, Dayānand devalued the renunciant's role in
Hindu society.[37] Dayānand "Aryanized" the *sannyāsī*. Like others, the true
sannyāsī should be an active member of sociey, dedicated to the good of the
people, rather than a worthless parasite (Jordens 1972: 377).[38] Dayānand
juxtaposed Aryan worldliness with what he considered to be modern
Indian provincialism. He cited dietary regulations as symptomatic of the
general malaise. How, Dayānand asked, could Indians fight and persevere
over their enemies (as the Aryans had done) if they worry about who pre-
pares their food, where they eat it, and with whom? Real Aryans had trav-
elled abroad learning good qualities from other peoples and rejecting bad
influences. They traded, wielded political power, and were fearlessly bold.
Rather than obsessing on foolish injunctions, modern Indians should emu-
late Aryan cosmopolitan sophistication.

The loss of Aryan values was thus tied to the loss of true *kṣatriya*hood
(Nandy 1983: 24–26), as the loss of knowledge was directly tied to the loss
of worldly power. Perhaps this is why Dayānand never took a stand against
the British. In his view, foreign rule had occurred through the Indians' own
failings. A country cannot progress when it indulges in mutual feud, child
marriage, carnality, untruthfulness, neglect in the study of the Veda, and
other evils. When brothers fight against each other, then only an outsider
can pose as an arbiter (Dayānand 1915: 320). Unless a country trades effectively with foreigners and extends its rule over others, it can only expect
misery and poverty.[39]

Dayānand's Aryan thus stands in stark opposition to the tendency in
Hinduism to draw men away from the world and active involvement in it
(Jordens 1972: 378). Indeed, this thematic expresses itself throughout his
commentaries. The message of activism, a vision of an active Hindu and a
new Hinduism, finds expression most significantly in the purified, vital, and
progressive India that Dayānand hoped to see reborn on the model of the
Aryan Golden Age (Jordens 1972: 379). Dayānand tied the loss of
Aryanhood to the very behavior and customs that his reform sought to
attack: communal and sectarian violence, idolatry, lack of education, child
marriage, and the neglect of Vedic study. These malpractices brought about
the loss of Aryanhood and, as a consequence, caused India's foreign subjuga-

tion. To reverse Āryavarta's degradation, one merely had to reestablish the Aryan utopia with its undistorted institutions. The necessary palliatives for modern Indian malaise could be found in Vedic times. One need not resort to other proposed cures, such as Christianity or modern science. The cure was in "reading" the wisdom that the Aryans left behind, as in Dayānand's interpreting the ancestral *varṇa* system to incorporate individualistic values. Such "correct" readings of the Veda would usher a new Aryan age into being.

CONCLUSION

Contemporaneously with European flights of scholarly imagination within the domains of linguistics and philosophy, India was creating its own autochthonous myth of origin in the Aryan past. A myth of a Vedic Golden Age was first promulgated by the Brāhmo Samāj. Rammohan's reinterpretation of the Indian socioreligious tradition led to conflict on two fronts: against Christian missionaries on the one hand and Hinduism on the other. It was Rammohan's belief that Hinduism had strayed from its true model, the ancient Vedic period. He condemned the later period, identified as that of Hindu idolatry, for destroying the texture of society.

The belief that India had degenerated from Aryan ideals also found support in the commentaries and debates of Dayānand Saraswatī. Dayānand's cure for India's political subjugation was to recover past vision and glory. Like Rammohan, who based his version of the Aryan myth on the interpretation and authority of canonical sources, Dayānand also sought a textual basis to reconnect with the Aryan past. The Ārya Samāj, founded in 1875 by Dayānand, provided a social context for interpreting the Vedic canon (Llewellyn 1993: 7). In fact, throughout the nineteenth century, a myth of the Aryan, grounded in arbitrary readings and authoritative definitions of what was considered "Vedic," was used by social reformers to mobilize public opinion. Reformers devised interpretations of the Aryan tradition in order to diffuse Western missionary propaganda, battle against modernity, and combat social inequity. Out of a need to reassert self-esteem under colonialism, caste Hindus regarded themselves as descendents of ancient Aryans and stressed the continued historic superiority of their culture. Since philology had deciphered the relationship between Sanskrit and Greek, the Indo-Aryans could now be recognized as the true originators of civilization. The historian Romila Thapar has correctly noted that the theory of the Aryan race was the most influential theory to come out of nineteenth-century Indology (Thapar 1992: 3).

In Dayānand's discourse regarding the Veda, the loss of Aryanhood and the degradation of values from the Vedic Golden Age was intimately bound up with textuality and the hermeneutic process. Cultural regression was due to the loss of interpretive skills that had previously ensured the survival of Aryan values. If the glorious past of great achievement rested on Vedic knowledge, Dayānand explained India's modern decline as a distortion of that knowledge through inaccessibility and/or misreading of its textual basis. He proposed a plan for the revival of that glorious past through the restoration of Vedic textual knowledge and readership. In short, he assigned to the Veda an authority that far exceeded its traditional status within orthodoxy. While still the locus of truth and authority, it now became the measure of all knowledge and the only tool whereby the reversal of India's sociocultural decline could be effected. Prior to his interpretation, Dayānand felt that the Veda had either been foreclosed or incorrectly read. "Unworthy" modern Hindus had limited access to the text or intentionally misinterpreted it. All Indians were entitled to the text. Through a correct reading for which Dayānand provided the hermeneutic tools, they would be guided back to its true meaning and its ideal *Weltanschauung*.

Dayānand's ideology of the Aryan framed, therefore, a larger discussion wherein Indian masculinity was placed in the balance and found to be sorely lacking. The biographies (hagiographies) of Dayānand tend to ennoble his cultivation of physical powers. The soteriology of moral activity that he devised codified engagement as opposed to contemplation. Dayānand's myth of the Aryan brings into focus the larger reformulation of Indian masculine identity in nineteenth-century social reform. Ashis Nandy has shown just how, in coming to terms with India's subjugation, certain Indian thinkers both attributed England's use of power to masculine superiority and India's defeat to the loss of the ideals of Aryan manhood. The task now was to seek in Indian tradition those "cultural differentiae" (Nandy 1983: 25) that enabled the West to stay on top. Dayānand found these values, or rather read these values, into a flexible Vedic canon.

Through an idiosyncratic reading of essentially non-Vedic sources, Dayānand revealed the Vedic truth of active masculinity that had been destroyed by distortion and brahmin greed. This truth revealed the character of the Aryan as a cosmic force to be reckoned with—a figure engaged in good works and fearlessly bold. This ideology of the Aryan was not intended as an alternative frame of reference by which Indians might confront their colonizers. For Dayānand, colonialism did not represent an absolute evil. Britain did not appear as a juggernaut, but merely as one conquerer among others who had profited from Āryavarta's decline. Dayānand's aetiology posited the crises of Indian identity not as a result of colonialism, but as an ongoing degeneration dating from ancient (mythological) history.

It is not surprising that postcolonial critics have neglected a seminal colonial figure like Dayānand. He does not serve their theoretical criteria. In Dayānand, there is no systemic effect; struggles for self-realization are not subject to forces beyond one's comprehension. He knew who the enemies of Aryanhood were; they were close to home and identifiable. Their power could be questioned and challenged. The texts themselves tell us how to deconstruct brahmin power. The reader possesses individual agency and wields it through formal textual strategies. Under colonial rule, liberal visions of individual agency functioned in widespread and sophisticated forms. Dayānand represents a subaltern voice railing against home-grown oppression, reordering society through the rearticulation of myth, and building a hermeneutic structure to assert a new national identity. By distinguishing the modern brahmin from the ancient Aryan, Dayānand justified the need for a new social order and provided a model for redefining authority. His ideology of the Aryan became a means of redefining the role and position of the brahmin elite.[40] By liberating the text from its traditional custodians, documenting their misreadings, and offering an alternative reading, Dayānand rewrote the caste system as a meritocracy and "Aryanized" Hindu masculinity.

British colonial rule was the symptom, not the cause, of India's real tragedy. The cause was to be found in the loss of Aryan manhood. Emasculation had brought about India's legitimate defeat at the hands of the British. Dayānand's strategies for reading created a myth of the Aryan that allowed Indians rather to "redeem their masculinity and become the counterplayers of their rulers according to the established rules" (Nandy 1983: 11). Dayānand's textual construction of the Aryan exhibited a political strategy enabling Indians to access a discourse of power and, as reified Aryan overlords, share in it.

CHAPTER 7

Aryan Identity and National Self-Esteem

INTRODUCTION

The translations of Rammohan Roy and the Vedic commentaries of Dayānand Saraswatī were predicated upon the belief that India had degenerated from Aryan ideals partially because the Aryan texts themselves had decayed. The cure for India's political subjugation was thought to be found in the recuperation of past glory through a canonized image of the past and in the reinterpretation of canonical texts. Their readings of the Veda created portraits of the Aryan that carried considerable ideological significance. These reformers created a foundation myth worthy of a new nation.

An idealized vision of the Aryan necessitated reenvisioning Indian masculinity, since the nineteenth-century Indian male, under the yoke of foreign oppression, did not measure up to his valorous forebears. Indian masculinity, like Aryan values and Aryan texts, had decayed from its ideal in the Vedic Golden Age. Thus, the recuperation of Vedic texts and their reinterpretation represented a response to a general detour from the true Aryan path and a loss of its imagined virility. The process of "remasculinizing" the modern Indian, however, necessitated reformulating femininity through social reform.

Since identity was text-centered, the Aryanization of the modern Indian male centered on reading the Vedic canon as texts written against the female body. As such, the retrieval of the Vedic canon and its reinterpretation expressed a will to power over one's own degenerate male self and over the female whose social position threatened that effeminate self. The retrieval of the Veda also expressed a will to identify with those superior qualities that had previously been attributable to the West but could now be situated in the fictive Aryan past. It also enabled reformers to allocate lost Aryan strength to the Indian present. Rammohan Roy and Dayānand Saraswatī had set this process in motion when they tied the themes of Aryan degeneration and textual decay to the reformulation of gender. In this chapter we will examine how late nineteenth-century social reformers further developed this theme. We base our discussion on the work of Justice Ranade, Lokamānya Tilak, and Swami Vivekananda.

JUSTICE RANADE AND LOKAMĀNYA TILAK

The Mythic and Historical Context

The Marathas comprised the last great Hindu empire in India. Maratha power, consolidated under the rule of Shivājī Mahārāj (1627–80), had seriously challenged Muslim rule during Aurangzeb's reign. Under the Peshwas (1713–60), the Maratha confederacy expanded power beyond Mahārāshtra into the subcontinent. Shivājī had been a *kṣatriya*; the Peshwas were brahmins and, as such, were unique in their position as both the spiritual elite and temporal rulers. The Peshwas came from the Chitpavan brahmin community. With the fall of the Peshwas (1818), the British unified India under colonial rule. However, the Chitpavans continued to wield considerable power and were formidable adversaries to the British. Claiming to have directed Maratha power at its height and overseen its demise when the last of the Peshwas fell, they naturally resented their new vulnerability. The British took this potentially volatile situation seriously and sought to placate Chitpavan wounded pride by continuing to support their pandits monetarily (as the Peshwas had done). They also instructed missionaries to give them a wide berth.[1]

By and large, these efforts to placate the Chitpavan community failed. As a group, they consistently presented problems for the British as evinced by their representation among opponents of colonial rule. The Chitpavan community supplied India with some of its greatest nationalists (such as Vishnu Krishna Chiplunkar and Bal Gangadhar Tilak), its greatest revolutionaries (such as Vasudeo Balwant Phadke and Vinayak Savarkar), and its most effective terrorist assassins (the Chapekars and Godses).[2] However, the Chitpavans have also provided India with some of its greatest reformers, such as Mahadev Govind Ranade and Gopal Krishna Gokhale. To this day, Chitpavan brahmins remain a proud community. When modern Mahārāshtrians think of the Aryans, they associate them with the Chitpavans, who pride themselves on their fair complexions and greenish gray eyes. Their superiority and "otherness" is reflected in the community's myths of origin. The term "Chitpavan" either means "pure of mind" or "pure from the pyre." The former etymology is popular in contemporary community representation; the latter finds support in the creation myth preserved in the Sahyádri Khand of the *Skanda Purāṇa*.

In this mythological account, the community's patron deity Parashurāma ("Rāma with an axe") slaughters so many warrriors and has become so defiled that brahmins refuse to perform purification rituals on him. In retaliation, Parashurāma takes the bodies of fourteen shipwrecked foreigners he finds on the Western shore of India, purifies them in a pyre ("chita"), and restores their corpses to life. He works this miracle so that he might teach these resuscitated outsiders to perform purification rituals on him (Wolpert 1962: 4). Several aspects of this myth of origin are of interest. First, the Chitpavans define their position of superiority within caste hierarchy by means of a myth highlighting their very marginality to society. By coming to India from the West by sea, they are eminently impure as *mleccha* (barbarian foreigners). Moreover, they are Westerners, Europeans, or even Jews, who undergo purification to become purifiers.[3] Finally, they are exemplary purifiers in the sense that they purify god, usurp the position of the mythic brahmins, and become the best and the brightest of the historic brahmin families. This myth of identity is fraught with ambiguity and contradiction. It reflects the intricacies of brahmin notions of identity and otherness that informed brahmin-based nationalism. Bal Gangadhar Tilak and Justice Ranade were both born in Chitpavan families. It was their respective responses to their religious and secular privilege and jurisdiction that inspired their nationalism. Ranade represented the progressive forces of reform, while Tilak allied himself with the traditional orthodox camp.

Aryan Degeneration, Textual Decay, and the Rights of Women

In 1897 in a lecture at the National Social Conference, Mahadev Govind Ranade defined revival as a return to the old ways, an appeal to old authorities and sanctions. A society, unlike a living organism, can undergo revival (Ranade 1902: 169–70). For a culture, the doom of death was not irrevocable. It merely needed to stimulate the stifled seeds and lop off dead excrescences (Ranade 1902: 107). Decay could be stemmed and death averted.

> Without a survey of the past, it is not possible to understand intelligently the present or correctly to forecast or guide the future. The theory of evolution has, in this country, to be studied in its other aspect of what may conveniently be called devolution, when decay and corruption set in, it is not the fittest and the strongest that survive in the conflict of dead with living matter, but the healthy parts give way, and their place is taken up by all that is indicative of the

fact that corruption has set in, and the vital force extinguished. (Ranade 1902: 27)

By calling upon the authority of revered texts, Ranade sought to retrace the pristine glory of India's Aryan past and revive Hindu society.

Ranade felt that such a return to the golden age could be achieved under a *Pax Britannica* (Ranade 1902: 246). Providence had sent England to India to provide a living example of pure Aryan customs, untainted by non-Aryan traditions, to aid in the restoration of healthy old practices (Leopold 1970: 283).

> Fortunately, the causes which brought on this degradation have been counteracted by providential guidance, and we have now a living example before us of how pure Aryan customs, unaffected by barbarous laws and patriarchal notions, resemble our own ancient usages, to take up the thread when we dropped it under foreign and barbarous pressure, and restore the old healthy practices, rendered so dear by their association with our best days, and justified by that higher reason which is the sanction of God in man's bosom. (Ranade 1902: 169)

A theist like Rammohan Roy, Ranade praised the Christian virtues that he perceived were at work under colonial rule: fraternity, philanthropy, and the battle against indifference. A similar commitment to human dignity likewise animated his reform (Ranade 1902: 23). His regard for "Christian" values was as pragmatic as that of the Raja. He too felt that neither Hindu nor Moslem civilization had trained virtue in a way to bring the races of India on a level with those of Western Europe. The British connection was, therefore, just and humane. It could bring about a positive social change and stem India's further decline (Ranade 1902: 183).

Ranade did not advocate an indiscriminate return to ancient practices without considering whether they suited society. He distrusted the efforts of certain revivalists and condemned any irresponsible nostalgia for the past:

> We are asked to revive our old institutions and customs, people seem to be very much at sea as to what it is they seek to revive. What particular period of our history is to be taken as the old— whether the period of the Vedas, of the Smritis, of the Purāṇas, or of the Mahomedans, or the modern Hindu times? Our usages have been changed from time to time by a slow process of growth, and in some cases of decay and corruption, and you cannot stop at any particular period without breaking the continuity of the whole . . . What shall we revive? Shall we revive the old habits of our people when the most sacred of our castes indulged in all the abominations, as we now understand them, of animal food and intoxicating drink, which exhausted every section of our country's Zoology and

Botany? The men and the gods of these old days ate and drank
forbidden things to excess, in a way that no revivalist will now venture to recommend . . . Shall we revive the old liberties taken by
the Rishis and by the wives of Rishis with the marital tie? Shall we
revive the hecatombs of animals sacrificed from year's end to year's
end, in which even human beings were not spared as propitiatory
offerings to God? . . . Shall we revive the *satī* and infanticide customs, or the flinging of living men into rivers or over rocks, or
hook-swinging, or the crushing beneath the Jagannatha car? Shall
we revive the internecine wars of the brahmans and the kṣatriyas or
the cruel persecution and degradation of the aboriginal population?
(Ranade 1902: 170–71)

In response to the question of what one should revive, Ranade followed the
inspiration of a long tradition of indiginous reformers. In particular, he emulated the work of the universally respected Maratha saints. He recognized in
their efforts an attempt to modify caste exclusion, endow the *shūdra* with
spiritual power, and raise the status of women. Since Ranade viewed the
Aryan past as a time of enjoyment in which woman played a necessary part,
women's rights became for him emblematic of the good old times. As a consequence, Ranade's reform became intimately bound up with the status of
women in Hindu society. Activities of reform included female education,
widow remarriage, caste intermarriage, and infant marriage.[4]

Ranade saw the rise of female rights in Aryan India and their subsequent fall as a history much like the rise and fall of institutions among the
Roman Aryans. In early Vedic times, women were devoid of rights. Their lot
gradually improved as Vedic texts show: there grew a chivalrous regard for
women and concern for their freedom and comforts. Aryan women ultimately were allowed to choose their marriage partners. The Vedas speak of
women poets, philosophers, and rishis (Ranade 1902: 97). Vedic texts such
as the Gṛhya Sūtras recognized female liberty. According to Ranade, the
Aryan society articulated in the Vedas celebrated monogamy, intercaste marriage, and non-infant marriages.

This idyllic Aryan past, however, gave way to a philosophy that devalued earthly existence, with women appearing as just one of the many snares
of *māyā*. As a consequence, the status of women diminished. Aryan society
in general lost its vigor. Non-Aryan barbarians who had earlier been driven
to the hills reemerged. They easily overran the weakened and demoralized
Aryans. The victors' morality, decidedly of a lower type, asserted itself. The
non-Aryan conquerers circumscribed female liberty and lowered the dignity
of women in social and family arrangements (Ranade 1902: 29). The subsequent rise of other non-Aryan tribes to power and Buddhism's "horror of

female society" further eroded Aryan cultural values (Ranade 1902: 32). Non-Aryan races from central Asia such as the barbarian Scythians and Mongolians then invaded. They too conquered India and drastically altered what remained of its Aryan institutions and usages. All these "lower civilizations" further curtailed women's rights. Islam, however, dealt the final blow: The Moslems had an especially low ideal of family life and respect for the female sex. Women now became a symbol of corruption and vice.

Aryan civilization did not recover. It had tried to reassert the values of the Vedas, but Moslem outrages interrupted restoration (Ranade 1902: 100) by degrading Aryan spiritual values (Ranade 1902: 192–93). It is important to note that Ranade did not attribute loss of Aryanhood to brahmin corruption. Aryan institutions had been pure and healthy until they were assailed by the Scythians from the north and attacked by the aboriginal Dravidians in the south (Ranade 1902: 230–31). Hindu institutions had even tried to revive and return to their old pristine glory, only to be assailed by the Jains and Buddhists, who sapped Aryan spirituality with the introduction of idol worship (Ranade 1902: 221). To fight off all these forces, brahmins allied themselves with barbarians whom they had previously treated as *shūdras*. They deteriorated even more through this intercourse (Ranade 1902: 188–91). Brahmanism, having failed to conquer non-Aryan forces, was thus overrun by the very multitudes that it had failed to civilize (Ranade 1902: 191–92). Although the Aryans had once been a chosen race, they were now submerged by Dravidians and tribals. Finally, they were conquered by the Moslems.

Non-Aryan influences caused all those practices (infanticide, Kulinism, communal land tenure, *satī*, polygamy, polyandry) that reformers sought to change. Ranade advocated, therefore, a return to the true Vedic past where these practices did not exist. His aim was to undo the process of degeneration that had beset Hindu society.

> We have not to unlearn our entire past,—certainly not—the past which is the glory and wonder of the human race. We have to retrace our steps from the period of depression, when, in panic and weakness, a compromise was made with the brute force of ignorance and superstition. If this unholy alliance is set aside, we have the brahmanism of the first three Yugas unfolding itself in all its power and purity, as it flourished in the best period of our history. (Ranade 1902: 193)

Reform was nothing but the liberation of superior religion, law, polity, and institutions from restraints imposed upon them by brute force (Ranade 1902: 194). The procedure that Ranade advocated was textually bound. By retracing the status of women in Vedic texts, Ranade hoped to show the process by which Indians had generally departed from the healthy customs of their Aryan ancestors.

In "The Age of Hindu Marriage," Ranade surveyed the growth and decay of Aryan social usage regarding the institution of marriage. He pinpointed two distinct stages in the development of the present practice. First, there existed the old, venerable, and noblest stage in the Vedic age. This epoch was followed by the period of arrested growth, when the internal decay caused by foreign invasions had paralyzed activity. It was in this second (and degenerate) stage that Indian society in Ranade's time was living (Ranade 102: 28). When *shāstrīs* evoked the past, they did not venerate the "ideal" Vedic past, but rather the "developments" of the Purāṇic period. This was unfortunate, Ranade claimed, since exegetical practices of the Purāṇic age had distorted old texts to make them fit what was hopelessly irreconcilable with them (Ranade 1902: 29). If one returned, however, to Vedic sources, one would discover through textual analysis that the dependant status of women, child marriage, and seclusion of women were not authentic Aryan practices. Moreover, prohibitions against widows remarrying, intercaste marriage, and foreign travel were also distortions of the old Aryan standards (Ranade 1902: 285). Interpolations had been made on authoritative texts in order to support changes that had been introduced as Aryan society decayed (Ranade 1902: 286). Reform, therefore, entailed taking a stand to defend the letter of the ancient ordinances. In order to return to the customs of the Aryan forefathers, it was necessary to confront the textual obstacles that obscured meaning (Ranade 1902: 287).

Widow Remarriage and the Age of Consent Controversy

Ishvara Chandra Vidyasagar, the renowned Bengali Sanskrit scholar, was the first to agitate against the prohibition of widow remarriage. In 1855, he submitted a petition to the Legislative Council of India pointing out that this prohibition was a cruel and unnatural custom. He claimed that forbidding widows to remarry prejudiced the interests of morality and was not in accordance with the shāstras and the true interpretation of Hindu law. Acting upon Vidyasagar's petition, the Legislative Council passed Act XV of 1856, legalizing widow remarriage. However, this legislation had little impact, since there existed throughout India popular feeling against this reform.

In Mahārāshtra, reformers sought to arouse the public conscience against the prohibition and enlist the sympathy of the orthodox community. In Poona, a center of orthodoxy, the Shaṅkarāchārya of Sankeshwar[5] convened a meeting in 1870 to debate the issue of widow remarriage. The orthodox community argued in favor of the prohibition and claimed textual support for their position.

To counter their claim, Ranade specifically enumerated Vedic authorities (Ranade 1902: 57–61) that allowed widow remarriage (Ranade 1902: 62ff).[6] He maintained that the orthodox party had cited prohibatory texts that were general and culled from inferior *smṛti* writers, such as Babhravya, and not the likes to be pitted against Manu, Nārada, Vashiṣṭha and Parāshara, whom he judged more authoritative. The gist of Ranade's reform argument was that Parāshara was the guiding authority, and he expressly allowed remarriage in five instances.[7] Parāshara was particularly important because he enumerated the particular cases where remarriage was allowed, referred specifically to the three castes, and permitted remarriage even though a first marriage had in every sense been completed. Ranade presented Parāshara's text as an earlier attempt to revive Aryan law regarding widows.[8]

The orthodox objection to Parāshara hinged upon his use of the Sanskrit term *pati*, meaning 'husband' or "protector." The orthodox camp claimed that in the text, *pati* did not mean "husband," but rather signified "protector." What the sages meant, they averred, was that the widow should have another protector. Ranade countered this argument by claiming that such a reading, given its context, was false. In the text, the injunction was immediately followed by other cases in which "another husband" (*pati*) is allowed. In the latter cases, there is no question regarding the meaning of the disputed term *pati*. One who has lost one *pati* is to take "another *pati*." If "protector" was meant, he cannot be "*anya* (another) *pati*." He can be "*anya*" only with reference to the first. Besides, another "protector" would be no help in remedying the affliction that the loss or incapacity of a first husband brings. Ranade concluded that there exist numerous specific authorities in the shāstras and the Vedas (Ranade 1902: 79) as well as in *smṛti* law allowing widow remarriage. He judged the prohibitory texts to be vague and general (Ranade 1902: 80). He relied on Parāshara's authority and, by means of a close reading, rejected the orthodox interpretation of the passage. Despite Ranade's strong argument and the weak case presented by the orthodox contingent, the Panch (council) nevertheless voted in favor of maintaining the prohibition. Although there would be no immediate improvement in the cruel conditions assigned to widows, the movement to reform widow remarriage prohibitions continued. Ranade now turned his attention to the matter of infant marriage.

In 1884, the Gujarati reformer Behramji Merwanji Malabari published his "Notes on Infant Marriage and Enforced Widowhood."[9] The time was right for agitation against this abuse. The Criminal Procedure Bill amendment, known as the Ilbert Bill, had recently sought to place accused Europeans on equal footing with native Indians in criminal proceedings.

Although this amendment was later modified, it had roused much enthusiasm for colonial reform among the Indian public. Malabari took the offensive: If Indians wanted equality in politics, why did they not exercise it in their own homes?

Ranade wrote a commentary on Malabari's "Notes" that supported legislation against infant marriage (Ranade 1902: 105–6).[10] As in the case for widow remarriage, Ranade's argument was text-centered. Reminiscent of Rammohan Roy's earlier strategy, Ranade claimed that infant marriage was never included among the pure customs of the Aryans but rather, like *satī* and infanticide, reflected degenerate excrescences on the once healthy Aryan society (Ranade 1902: 108, cited in Wolpert 1962: 49). The tendency to lower the age of consent marked degenerate Purāṇic India. Ranade concluded that, in clinging to the existing order of things, the orthodox school was really setting at naught the traditions of their own best days and the injunctions of their own shāstras. As in the case of widow remarriage, Ranade advised his readers to follow the rule laid down in Vedic times (Ranade 1902: 51) and return to the true and legitimate order.

Ranade began his commentary by vouching for the authenticity of his sources (Ranade 1902: 45, 49). The various law treatises he cited were unanimously in favor of late rather than infant marriage. The majority of the authorities cited the age of twelve or puberty as ideal for females.[11] Ranade maintained that it was later added texts that promoted the notion that girls should be married before the age of eight. Moreover, those sources that the *shāstrīs* cited to condone infant marriage were actually obscure *smṛti* of which complete texts were not preserved. Ranade also rejected the passage from *Manu* cited in favor of infant marriage, claiming it to be a misinterpretation (Ranade 1902: 48). He felt that the problem with the orthodox argument in favor of infant marriage was its penchant for lumping all *smṛti* together, major and minor, original or later accretions. Applying a faulty method of exegesis, they sought to reconcile divergent texts by inventing fictions. Ranade also accused the *shāstrīs* of twisting and torturing texts absurdly. He claimed that, rather than attempting to show the true and natural meaning (Ranade 1902: 90), the *shāstrīs* bent the texts for desired meanings. Ranade called for Hindus to take the texts as they exist, arrange them in intelligent order, and determine where the balance of authority rests (Ranade 1902: 38). He personally concluded that the texts support post-pubescent female marriage (Ranade 1902: 38 ff). The Vedic age of the Gṛhya Sūtras did not set an age limit for females (Ranade 1902:33), but the majority of the texts favor the age of twelve or the age of puberty (Ranade 1902: 41). Just as in the argument favoring remarriage for widows, Ranade's justification of post-pubescent marriage depended on a close reading of texts and canonical legitimacy. This strategy of explicating and hierarchizing canonical authority was also adopted by Bal Gangadhar Tilak in the next stage of the orthodox resistance to infant marriage reform.

As in the case of Ranade, Tilak's great battle for Aryan authenticity revolved around women's rights. After initial skirmishes over female education and the Rakhamabai case,[12] Tilak joined the infant marriage debate. Ranade had condemned the practice of infant marriage and advocated its voluntary prescription. Tilak, as editor of *Kesari* and *Mahratta*, approved this measure, but vigorously protested over its official state regulation (Wolpert 1962: 46–47). The government remained passive until 1890, when the eleven-year-old Phulmani Bai died from injuries sustained during sexual intercourse with her considerably older husband.

The Legislative Council decided to act, since Phulmani Bai's husband was not liable to any criminal charge. Malabari saw in this tragedy the test case with which to take his cause to London and enlist government support for reform. Tilak's contention was that the English as foreigners had no jurisdiction over matters of religion, a strategy he applied also to the Parsi Malabari (Wolpert 1962: 49). Moreover, Tilak defended his position by resuscitating the claim that legal treatises from the pure Aryan past did not support reform (Wolpert 1962: 51). Tilak positioned law books as the ultimate religious authority, invoking them as male texts written against the female body. Tilak claimed that Phulmani Bai died from having "an unusually dangerous organ." Her husband had justifiably omitted "to speculate upon the comparative dimensions and vigour of the sexual organs of both either before or at the time of his marriage or intercourse." Tilak blamed the girl's death on her being one of those "dangerous freaks of Nature." How, he asked, could a husband reasonably be punished because of "defective female organs" and persecuted "diabolically for doing a harmless act?" (cited in Wolpert 1962: 53–54).

The final battle in the Age of Consent controversy had begun. In the *Proceedings of the Council of the Governor-General*, orthodox anti-reformers renewed their strategy of alluding to textual support for the custom. Tilak implored the Viceroy not to interfere in religious and social customs with the passage of the Age of Consent Bill (Tilak 1992: 7). Justice Telang of Bombay's High Court rearticulated the reformist position that the dharmashāstras viewed infant marriage as a distortion of ancient practice. Finally, the renowned Sanskrit scholar Ramkrishna Gopal Bhandarkar presented the most eloquent defense of reform and most authoritative challenge to orthodoxy's vague and rhetorical reliance on textuality. Bhandarkar quoted references to claim that Hindu religious law allowed consummation three years after puberty because medical science felt a female could not give birth to a healthy child before sixteen years of age (Bhandarkar 1891: 23, cited in Wolpert 1962: 55). Tilak countered that reformist readings of shāstra were attempts to "oppress dharma." To which Bhandarkar replied that present practice did not always reflect ancient usage. Moreover, Bhandarkar accused Tilak and the orthodox anti-reformers of abusing scripture by enlisting authoritative texts to support ideological projects.

> He twists a passage in an old work so as to harmonise it with that practise, in spite of grammar and propriety. He thus belongs to the school of those who find the steam engine and the electric tele-graph in the Vedas. (Bhandarkar 1891: 37, cited in Wolpert 1962:56)

Tilak's bluff had been called. The tradition begun by Rammohan Roy, exploited so artfully by Dayānand and manipulated by Tilak, was unmasked by an unimpeachable Sanskrit authority. Either one respected the letter of the text or left one's references vague. One could no longer miscite the canon.

The Scoble Bill (1891) settled the infant marriage debate by raising the marriageable age of consent from ten to twelve years. Its passage represented a significant defeat for Tilak. As a consequence of this debacle, Tilak may have felt the need to reassert his position of authority and competence within the orthodox community (Wolpert 1962: 63). His subsequent Aryan scholar-ship might well be viewed in this context: as a means of enhancing his tar-nished reputation as the most vocal and effective supporter of orthodox Hinduism. By rewriting the history of the Aryans, Tilak continued his nationalist efforts in a more subtle vein. He had learned a valuable lesson from the Age of Consent battle. The Orthodox community did not suffer defeat gladly. It was now the moment to pamper its wounded collective male ego. To do so, Tilak needed to reaffirm his community's respect for Sanskrit scholarship and their identification with their Aryan forebears. What better way to achieve both ends than by reading the Veda and deciphering the true story of Aryan glory? By valorizing those ancestors with whom his people identified, he effectively valorized his own community. Moreover, glorifica-tion of the Aryan past validated nationalist faith in present-day Indian (read: brahmin) capabilities and future potential.

Arctic Aryan Hegemony

As Bhandarkar correctly noted, Dayānand and Tilak read the Vedas lit-erally. Both believed that they could be read as plain and simple points of fact. Both denied the poetic nature of these texts and sought to find in the Vedas factual information regarding the fate and mission of the Aryans. As a *Realpolitiker*, Tilak realized that textual legerdemain was no longer an option. What had been acceptable for a holy man such as Dayānand was not acceptable for a politician. If the texts themselves could not be manipulated, the history they told was still open to revision.

In *The Orion or Researches into the Antiquity of the Vedas* (1893), Tilak rewrote the history of the Aryans. He began by calculating the age of the *Rig Veda* from astrological data. By examining the zodiacal positions culled from the Vedic hymns, he placed the Aryans on the plains of Central Asia between 5,000 and 6,000 B.C. In a subsequent work, *The Arctic Home of the Vedas* (1903), Tilak turned to the specific mythological descriptions found in the *Rig Veda* to determine the Aryan's original home and describe their lifestyle. Rejecting the theories of Western racial theorists of the time whose conclusions, he believed, were formed by their personal ethnic identities rather than "objective" truth,[13] Tilak proposed that the original home of the Aryans was situated near the North Pole. He based this conclusion on meteorological data supplied by the hymns of the *Rig Veda* themselves: The poetry of the Veda described physical phenomena only visible in Arctic regions.[14] Commentators such as Yāska and Sāyaṇa could not have known anything about the Aryans' Arctic region, since the key to this discovery had only been recently unearthed. The ignorance of earlier interpreters had seriously compromised their readings and subsequently India's entire understanding of its Aryan ancestors. Previous commentators had been forced to rely on explicating the verbal texture of passages (Tilak 1971: 342). Because opaque passages could not be explained, the general impression made by these commentaries was that the Aryans and their product, the Veda, were illogical. This judgment was clearly erroneous. Earlier interpreters just did not possess the necessary scientific data, and they misread plain and simple points of fact as metaphor. Armed with the proper interpretive tools, Tilak could read the Veda, analyze the fate of the Aryans, and predict the proper course of action for their descendants.

When the Aryans lived in the Arctic zone, they flourished. They were able to thrive because, at the time in question (that is, interglacial period), the polar regions were mild and temperate like a perennial spring. The Aryans led a happy life, only inconvenienced by the long polar night (Tilak 1971: 358). Around 8,000 B.C., however, catastrophe struck: The mild climate was destroyed by the onslaught of the glacial period. The land became covered by ice and the Aryans were forced to abandon the Arctic region. For the next three thousand years, they wandered through Northern Europe and Asia searching for a suitable new home, cherishing throughout this period memories of their civilization.[15]

Through religious zeal and industry during their exile, the Aryans incorporated their traditions in religious hymns, making them the exclusive preserve of a few to hand down scrupulously to future generations (Tilak 1971: 262). By oral tradition, the Aryans were thus able to maintain their culture intact for thousands of years. Tilak dated the oldest Vedic hymns at 4,500 B.C. Whatever shortcomings the texts may exhibit must be understood within the larger context of the Aryans' catastrophic loss of home, forced migration, and fragmentation during the Neolithic age (Tilak 1971: 345).

It is only when Tilak elaborated upon this chronology that the ideological parameters of his thesis become clear. Tilak presented the Aryans as the first globally victimized people. He discounted any "shortcomings" attributable to the Aryans of the hymns as a natural relapse into barbarism following great catastrophe (Tilak 1971: 361). They were simply unable to preserve in a pure form their civilization among non-Aryan savages. Only the Asiatic Aryans, the ancestors of the Hindus, significantly maintained their civilization. Considering what they had undergone since the Neolithic age, the intrinsic superiority of the Aryans is a foregone conclusion. It is not customary for a race to suffer such a catastrophic loss of home and forced migration. What we have in the Veda are the necessarily degenerated expressions of a truly superior antediluvian civilization. The very fact that, even after compulsory dispersion from their motherland, the Aryan survivors could carry with them fragmented culture and establish supremacy over all the races that they encountered in their migrations is significant. That they were able, under such adverse circumstances, to "Aryanize" these peoples in language, thought, and religion proves just how superior these Aryans were to the non-Aryan races (Tilak 1971: 360–64) that they encountered in their colonization of northern Europe. Their superiority manifested itself in an ability to preserve Aryan civilization by conquering and ruling over others.

Although the culture of the Neolithic Aryans was but a relic or imperfect fragment of pre-diaspora Arctic Aryans, it was exponentially greater than that of modern savage races. The very fact that so much of this sophisticated culture can be discerned in the Vedas, and that the Vedas, representing merely a fragment of Aryan genius, are so well preserved, further indicates the mettle of these people. The Vedas exist, therefore, as testimony to the temporary regression of the Neolithic Aryans when exiled from their antediluvian home (Tilak 1971: 375-76). More importantly, even in their fragmented form, they testify to the interglacial glory of the Aryan race.

The message of *The Arctic Home of the Vedas* was tailor-made to appeal to the chauvinism of the orthodox community. While its pseudoscientific thesis in no way revolutionized the way historians view the Vedic period, Tilak's theory did have significant implications: The Vedic texts need not be deciphered. They described what actually existed in the pre-diasporic Aryan world. The Aryans were neither primitive nor illogical. In fact, they were almost superhuman to have survived in the form that they did. If the Aryans were, indeed, the first to attain a level of civilization higher than that reached by any other group in the age of metals, how could they now justifiably remain dependent on the West? It was this vision of the Aryan's intrinsic ascendancy over others (both foreign and domestic) that came to fuel nationalist rhetoric. This racialist script was exported to the West by Swami Vivekananda.

SWAMI VIVEKANANDA

Text-Centered Identity amidst Scriptural Loss

Like others we have examined in this study, Swami Vivekananda's vision of Hinduism also depicted a glorious past and a degenerate present. His prescription for the future consisted in reactivating past Aryan glory by empowering Hindus through the rediscovery of their superior spirituality. By retrieving an Aryan ideal, Vivekananda hoped to implement it in the Indian present. In one important aspect, however, Vivekananda differed from other nineteenth-century social reformers. His reform, while primarily directed toward the domestic front, was also intended for export abroad. The West, possessing mere techniques in the form of technology, work ethic, and organizational skills, was in dire need of Hindu spirituality. Vivekananda proposed to remedy this deficiency by spreading Indian wisdom throughout the world. His mission was all the more necessary because the Aryan God was the true Father to all peoples, while the Semitic God was "only a thunderer, only a terrible one" (Vivekananda 1991: 8.151).[16]

In order for the modern inhabitants of Bharata to gain the strength and courage of their convictions and rise up from the dust of the earth where they were presently mired, they must study their past and set out working the great plan laid out by their ancestors (Vivekananda 1991: 3.368). To rediscover its Aryan core, India must first return to the Vedas, the oldest Aryan texts (Vivekananda 1991: 1.344) and the oldest literary works in the world. They are the foremost, most complete, and most undistorted texts. Accessible to all, regardless of caste distinctions (Vivekananda 1991: 6.208–9), they furnish the basis for all other scriptures (Vivekananda 1991: 6.182) and the model for all society (Vivekananda 1991: 7.174). Indeed, the religion of the Vedas is the foundation and authority of all religions (Vivekananda 1991: 6.48).

Vivekananda claimed that there was no truth or law absent from the Vedas (Vivekananda 1991: 5.206). They provided the "eyeglass of evolution" containing the whole history of the progress of religious consciousness (Vivekananda 1991: 6.103). Their authority extended to all ages, climes, and people as it alone expounded universal religion (Vivekananda 1991: 6.181). Reminiscent of Dayānand, Vivekananda held that the germ of every Aryan science (Vivekananda 4:427) and all religious ideas (Vivekananda 6:105) were found in the Vedas.[17] Creation comes out of the Vedas; they represent "authority with a vengeance" (Vivekananda 2:336–37). All things exist in the Vedas. If one thinks that there exists something not found in the Vedas, then one is prey to delusion (Vivekananda 1:148). The Vedas were not written: they are eternally coexistent with the infinite God (Vivekananda 3:512). God spoke once and he spoke Sanskrit (Vivekananda 3:512).

Vivekananda recognized, as did others, the textual limitations of his blueprint for the future: The Vedas provided a damaged source of reference. One must, therefore, use caution in reading them, adopting as revelation only what agrees with reason (Vivekananda 5:315), since its knowledge arises at the beginning of each cosmic cycle and degenerates with time (Vivekananda 5:411). Moreover, since most of the Vedas have disappeared (Vivekananda 3:232), what remains is a mere fragment. For this reason, Vivekananda claimed that the Vedas' canonicity was malleable. They could be altered to suit the needs of the reader. Anything sanctioned by the Vedas that proved to be problematic could be dismissed as a degenerate distortion. The Vedas were thus absolute, sacrosanct, and eminently interpretable.

Vivekananda further circumscribed his canon: The Vedas only consist of those portions of the remaining fragmentary Vedic corpus which did not refer to purely secular matters and which did not record tradition and history (Vivekananda 6:182). Vivekananda thus rejected the Saṃhitās and the Brāhmaṇas. He judged the highest form of spirituality to be found in the later Upanishad sections. In short, he structured his interpretation of the Veda to provide a scriptural basis for a socially concerned Vedānta.[18] Calling upon the authority of the Veda, Vivekananda created an idealized myth of the Aryan in a negative manner. His conception of the absolute malleability of the Vedas is as striking as the way he restricted the canon to fit his needs. The Aryan could be anything that was not specifically proved to the contrary in the Veda. The issue of Vivekananda's use of the Veda as a negative authority is, however, a moot point. At no time does he refer to any text to support his ideology of the Aryan. An absent authority, the Veda is invoked rather than cited.

The Racialist Script

The Aryans originally lived to the North and possessed a warm, poetic nature (Vivekananda 1:492). Vivekananda inferred this knowledge from the existence in the Himalayas of a unmiscegenated brahmin type, pure in thought, deed, and action. This pure brahmin-Aryan is honest and beautiful. In fact, he represents the most handsome human specimen in the world, a being so perfect that degenerate Westerners can only dream of his existence

(Vivekananda 5:466). Aryans, Vivekananda noted, possess regular features and dark eyes. They dress well.[19] Their hair and skin are "like drops of milk." Aryans are kind and generous. They dedicate themselves to elevating persons of brutish habits (Vivekananda 2:482). They possess superhuman genius. Beastly practices have never found a place in their world (Vivekananda 5:537). The Aryan is, by nature, totally untainted and unsexist (Vivekananda 8:28). His wife's dowry belongs to her alone. These Aryan-brahmins possess trusting natures; they allow their women to circulate within the community. Since they live in isolation, few people know of the survival of this hidden Aryan tribe of supermen in modern times. Missionaries have not found them nor have they suffered Muslim influences (Vivekananda 3:506).

While Vivekananda's understanding of the historic Aryan was as ficti-tious as any other, he did take the argument one step further by specifically identifying his mythic Aryan with racially "pure" modern brahmins. While this depiction of the Aryan feigned inclusivity, embracing the "ethnological museum" that was India (Vivekananda 4.296),[20] it was clearly restrictive. Although he proposed that all Hindus, whether pure or of mixed blood, were Aryans, Vivekananda presented very definite criteria for the true Aryan: They have straight noses, mouths, and eyes; they are white-complected, their hair is black or brown, and their eyes are dark or blue (Vivekananda 7:366).

As opposed to the "so-called Aryans of the philologists" (Vivekananda 5.466), Vivekananda clearly delineated the moral fiber of his Aryan. During the Vedic period, the climatic conditions had not yet begun to have a negative effect upon race (Vivekananda 6:158) and it was the custom of the ancient Aryans to work incessantly.[21] One Aryan branch went to Greece. Surrounded by a "beautiful, sweet, tempting and invigorating" cli-mate, they studied the "outer infinite," or the macrocosm. Due to their continual activity, these Aryans also turned politically outward. They and their descendants, the Europeans, developed arts and sought political lib-erty. The other branch migrated to India. There they found the subconti-nent's climate inconducive to physical exercise. These Aryans developed the "inner infinite," studied the microcosm, and sought spirituality. They developed their religion (Vivekananda 6:86) and provided the world with its spiritual giants (Vivekananda 4:316). Aryan man has always sought divinity within himself (Vivekananda 6:3).

Vivekananda felt that each branch of the Aryan family had distinct parts to play in civilizing the world (Vivekananda 3:434). In fact, Vivekananda held that there exists only one really civilized race in the world, the Aryan. Until endowed with Aryan blood, no race can be deemed civilized. Civilization cannot be taught: It necessitates the Aryan giving his blood to a race for it to become truly civilized (Vivekananda 3:535). The Aryans were lovers of peace and cultivators of the soil. Vivekananda contrasted these

Aryans with India's first inhabitants, races of wild people and cannibals who were neither Aryan nor Hindu. Exposure to the sun had turned their skin black. The Aryans did not swoop down and steal land from these aborigines. Nor did they settle India by exterminating the native population (Vivekananda 5.534), as Christians were wont to do (Vivekananda 2.282). Rather they absorbed them, making modern India a totally Aryan nation (Vivekananda 3:292). The only vestige of this successful miscegenation was the alteration of the "transparent glow of the white complexion of the Himalaya dwellers" into the bronzed hue of the present-day Hindu (Vivekananda 3:506). Once again, apparent inclusivity masked social, racial, and political exclusionism.

When not constrained by nationalist rhetoric, as in a 1900 lecture in Oakland, California, Vivekananda elaborated upon the racial subtext that there is no kinship between the northern and the southern Indian. The North, Vivekananda maintained, belongs to the great Aryan race to which all Europeans (except the Basques and the Finns!) belong. The South stemmed from the same race as did the ancient Egyptians and Semites (Vivekananda 8:241–42), racially and culturally distinct from the Aryan center. While the great Aryan race comprises the top three castes, the non-Aryan race consists of *shūdras*, aborigines (who aspired to become civilized), and the Dravidians.

This racialist argument foregrounds the larger political concern of validating caste distinctions. Rather than evolving toward a civilized mode of existence, non-Aryans are presented as "schemers" trying to live as did the Aryans, coopting their lifestyle by entering schools and colleges, wearing the sacred thread, performing ceremonies, and enjoying equal rights in religion and politics (Vivekananda 3:520). Too many different uncivilized and uncultured races tried to flock to the Aryan fold with their superstitions and hideous forms of worship. While appearing civilized, they clearly were not. These barbarians wreaked havoc by introducing "mysterious rites and ceremonies" to the old faith. They destroyed Aryan vigor and chaste habits. They defiled India with their superstitions (Vivekananda 3:263). Their rank imitation of the Aryan lifestyle initiated a process of decay. The central Aryan core, forced to succumb to the allurements of sensual forms of worship prevalent among these various low races, lost its integrity. In the past, when contact with "outcastes" had threatened to "destroy Aryan civilization," the Aryans had struck out in a natural reaction of self-preservation, as when they destroyed Buddhism (Vivekananda 6:164). But, the successful seduction of the Aryans by sensualists resulted in blind allegiance to usages "repugnant to the spirit of the Śāstras" and ultimately destroyed the Aryan race (Vivekananda 6:182). Āryavarta became a deep and vast whirlpool of the most vicious, most horrible, and most abominable customs. It lost all internal strength and became the weakest of the weak (Vivekananda 4:445).

The racialist tone of these passages starkly contrasts with the nationalist script where Vivekananda presents Aryans warmly embracing others within their fold, despite their cultural superiority, or where, by mixing with the blood, speech, manners, and religions of Dravidians, *shūdras*, and aborigines, the northern Indian Aryan emerged as a stronger and more organized race. Vivekananda might claim that by "clinging on with great pride to its name of Aryan," the "central assimilative core gave type and character to the whole mass." However, he is quick to note that Aryans were by no means willing to admit other races within the Aryan pale (Vivekananda 6:159), even if willing to share with them the benefits of their civilization. The political argument ultimately bows to the force of genetic constraints. An Aryan cannot be born out of lust, suggesting that Vivekananda only viewed as Aryan those born from civilized rather than barbarian types. Civilization meant adherence to the Veda. In fact, only a child whose conception and birth proceed according to the Vedas can be called an Aryan. The very fact that fewer such "Aryan" children are being produced these days in every country accounts for the mass of evil in the modern world (Vivekananda 3:409). Vivekananda's vision of progress is thus tied to the production and maintenance of Aryan racial types.

Caste and Racial Chaos

In Vivekananda's schema, caste becomes necessary insofar as it prevents the destruction of blood heredity. One does not want to mix, for example, with Negroes and American Indians; "nature will not allow you" (Vivekananda 3:534). Caste provides the "unconscious" means whereby the Aryan race will be saved. Amidst disingenuous disclaimers of inclusion—that the non-Aryan is equal to the Aryan and should be afforded equal rights— Vivekananda upholds a strict adherence to caste exclusionary practices. Caste Hindus must not mix with non-castes, lest the Aryan be degraded. Already in India, the barbarian has overrun the civilized as "hordes of these out-landish races came in with all their queer superstitions and manners and customs." These barbarians were "not decent enough to wear clothes. They ate carrion. They introduced fetishism, human sacrifice, and superstition in their wake. With time, they degraded the whole race" (Vivekananda 3:534). Thus, while ostensibly supporting the equal rights, Vivekananda focuses on the racial distinctions between Aryans and non-Aryans, civilized and barbarian, northern Indian and Dravidian, caste Hindus and Tribals, and the threat of diluting Aryan blood in a process of racial degradation.

This racialist script should not be confused with the political script directed against the West. The former aimed at maintaining the caste status quo; the latter evoked the fiction of Indian social and religious superiority to the West. Vivekananda thus directed a public relations coup against foreign critics of caste and Indian social reform. In this scenario, Aryan civilization is a fabric; its cotton consists of its highly civilized, semicivilized, and barbarian tribes; the warp is the *varṇāshramadharma*, and the woof is represented by the conquest over strife. Europe has been able to produce nothing of this magnitude. All the West can do is exterminate the weak like wild beasts (Vivekananda 5:537), acts of which India is incapable. Unlike Europe's extermination policies, Aryans have established a system of inclusion. Through the implementation of *varṇa*, Aryans raise everyone up to their own level or even higher than themselves. While Europe metes out death to the weak, Aryan civilization devised social rules for their protection.

Vivekananda conceived of caste as a liberating force. While individuals have every chance of rising from a low caste, "only in this birth-land of Altruism" are they compelled to "take" their whole caste with them (Vivekananda 4:297). Vivekananda viewed caste as one of the greatest social institutions that the Lord gave men (Vivekananda 4:299). Although it evinces some unavoidable defects (which Vivekananda blames on foreign persecutions and undeserving brahmins),[22] it has worked wonders in India and "is destined to lead Indian humanity to its goal." Exactly what Vivekananda envisioned to be India's goal was clear.

Prevention of race chaos appears as the central message Vivekananda believed India could impart to the world. Just as Sanskrit provided the linguistic solution for humanity, the Aryans provide the racial solution with the caste system. *Varṇa* ensured the social stability necessary to form a race of superior strength (Vivekananda 3:534). Vivekananda championed its continuation as a social system, since it had established the conditions wherein a superior race could develop over time. The only problem with caste, as Vivekananda saw it, was that it occasionally needed to be readjusted (Vivekananda 5:215).

Although Vivekananda saw all social and political problems solved (Vivekananda 4:309) by the formation of "brahminhood," at crucial junctures in his argument the language of race competes with his theology of decay. While Vivekananda upholds upper-class descent from Aryan ancestors, he also condemns them as ten-thousand-year-old mummies or walking corpses with antiquated possessions, manners, and customs. In the world of *māyā*, they represent the real illusions; they are void, unsubstantial nonentities of the future (Vivekananda 7:326). The fact that an ideal past had degenerated justified Vivekananda's subversion of traditional social hierarchy.

The vitality in India is not found in the hereditary elite, but rather in those whom the ancestors called "walking carrion" (Vivekananda 7:326). Vivekananda could call for the new India to arise out of the peasant's cottage and the huts of the fisherman and sweeper. He could maintain that the common people who suffer oppression and misery have become vital through suffering. He could claim that their strength derived from their pure and moral lives. He could even portray the common people as possessing unparalleled love, power of incessant work, and manifestation of strength (Vivekananda 7:327). But such claims were most often made at a safe distance, among Californian and Chicagoan society matrons. Effective reform or actual amelioration of the disenfrancised was never an issue at home. Vivekananda held to the status quo, camouflaging his orthodox politics in a mystification of caste. Without caste reform, any romanticization of the downtrodden is foreclosed. What remains is a glorification of an India in which the brahmin descendants of Aryans are the only real beneficiaries.

Vivekananda's plan for India's future consisted of a recreation of the past glory. In order to achieve his end of moral regeneration, he first established an Indian utopia in the Aryan past. He read into the Veda, or rather, invoked the Veda to portray an India that seeks the common good through caste and liberation through austere religious vows, fasting, and retreat. The language of the Veda becomes the means by which renunciation is attained. Vivekananda juxtaposed this ideal fiction of the Aryan past with an equally fictive West fraught with rank materialism, power, sense-pursuits, and strange luxuries in the form of fashion, food, drink, magnificent palaces, manners, and transportation. The West is guided by self-interest. The goal of Western society is individual independence attained by a language of money-making, education, and politics (Vivekananda 4:476). Vivekananda presented the Aryan ideal as an alternative to the decadent West. India will lead the world in the regeneration of man the brute into man the god (Vivekananda 4:315). For the colonized, this message was, indeed, uplifting. However, behind the rhetoric of the holy man lies a disingenuous will to power: the determination to maintain traditional structures of power and domination.

CONCLUSION

In this chapter, we examined in detail three nationalist configurations of the Aryan myth. What is particularly striking about these stagings of the past is their literary aspect, specifically their modernism. In reading Ranade, Tilak, and Vivekananda, one is reminded of certain short stories by Borges, where history is presented as inevitably limited and parochial in focus. Facts are only interpreted according to the ideology of the time, just as memory is activated by conventional scholarly wisdom. History and memory are potentially radically different phenomena than they appear to be. What is remembered or recorded is paltry in comparison to what actually took place. Great races have existed, but have been lost or forgotten. Outside recorded history, there was once a golden age with mythic forebears who accomplished astounding feats. The central insight here is that myth holds greater truth value than history. As opposed to history, myth absorbs contradictions into its own system. Myth is permitted to ignore details, since it contains the true spirit of the past—its essential legacy. This arbitrary and fragmented construction of history commonly fetishized in literary modernism also appears in popular culture's attempts to recuperate an idealized past.

In a 1980 article coauthored with Dominique Julia and Jacques Revel, Michel de Certeau defined popular culture as the vision of a culture's infancy, whose purity of social origin lies buried in history and needs to be preserved or recaptured (Certeau 1986: 127). Popular culture creates an explicitly political fiction of a national heritage and a cohesive geographical community. The establishment of popular culture correlates to specific acts of political repression. All recuperations of an idealized past present a strategic process of homogenization in the interpretative treatment of a community (Aherne 1996: 131), wherein diverse populations are brought into conformity with prescribed political programs. A fictional model of authenticity is created by interpreters and presented in terms of a seductive origin, whose traces are presumed discernible in interpreted texts. Authors thus mask the nature of their own interpretative intervention and presence. They provide a reassuringly idealized image of a people, despite the inevitably corrupted nature of their product. It has been our intention to show that the Aryan presented in Indian social reform and nationalism functions as an icon of popular culture. This figure inhabited an idealized past, and its textual rediscovery enabled interpreters to bring into supposed conformity diverse segments of the population without publicizing the politics behind their production of authenticity.

The fictional model of the Aryan addressed a variety of psychological and political needs. We have seen how some nationalists sought to bolster Indian self-esteem by portraying the Aryans as the most superior race that the earth had ever produced. The nationalist vision of Aryan superiority promoted belief that India's regeneration was attainable only through the restoration of Hindu culture. In this respect, they were indebted to the Ārya Samāj, whose vision of Aryan moral superiority and its recuperation provided a model. Following a trend set by Dayānand, reformers like Tilak and Vivekananda emphasized the uniqueness of Aryan physical and mental prowess, courage, bravery, and conquest. Vivekananda also stressed the spiritual ascendency of the Aryans over other nations and particularly over their Western cousins, who had lost their spiritual edge through contact with non-Aryan religions. Faith in the Aryan past thus became a tool in the fight against foreign oppression.

Some nationalists focused on Indo-European solidarity. They were inspired by the Brāhmo Samāj under Rammohan Roy and its emphasis on Anglo-Indian sympathies in the service of liberal and social reform. The belief that the white masters were distant cousins of their Aryan subjects provided a salve for the egos of the Indian intellectual elite and bolstered cultural self-confidence. It provided the Indian elite with a forceful psychological weapon against British power politics. Through identification with the aggressor, the Indian elite raised morale under colonialism. Justice Ranade viewed colonialism as a predestined event in order that a pristine Hinduism might be reborn from the model provided by English Aryan customs (Ranade: 1902: 101). Caste Hindus could thus identify with their British rulers, the representatives par excellence of European Aryandom. Keshab Chandra Sen could thus view English rule over India as a reunion of parted cousins, descendants of two different families of the ancient Aryan race. Colonialism was destined in order to rescue India and return it to a pristine form of Hinduism (de Bary et al. 1988:2. 48–9). Significantly, caste Hindus' racial rapprochement to their British rulers effectively distanced them from their benighted brethren and allowed them to sidestep the pressing issue of domestic inequality.

As the preceeding discussion has sought to show, the different strategies of nineteenth-century Indian nationalists, regardless of their politics or religious orthodoxy, held to the cultural, moral, and intellectual inferiority of non-Aryans. Justice Ranade believed that the Aryans were the chosen race whose civilization had been submerged by lower Dravidians, Huns, and Moslems. Hindus who had been contaminated, for example, by contact with the Moslem world and customs needed to restore former healthy Aryan practices. This belief expressed itself in the knowledge that the conquest, assimilation, and extermination of non-Aryans proved Aryan superiority. Caste Hindus, regarding themselves as descendants of ancient Aryans, could stress the historic superiority of their culture and its racial and religious unity. As Lokamānya Tilak formulated it, the superiority of the Indian Aryans manifested itself in their survival and conquest over the non-Aryan, who had migrated to northern Europe and immediately lapsed into barbarism. For Vivekananda, the Indian Aryan could even assert racial superiority over Western Aryans who had lost their moral fiber upon foreswearing Aryan spirituality. Groups that had previously been marginalized could be "Aryanized" by renewed access to Aryan scripture and religious ritual. Vivekananda even sought to take this mission worldwide and reintroduce Aryan ideals to the spiritually depraved West. When reformers and nationalists called for the racial unity of all Hindus, they inevitably defined Hindu culture as Vedic, Aryan, and upper caste.

Hindu identity was defined "by those who were part of national consciousness and drew on their own idealized image of themselves resulting from an upper-caste brahmin dominated identity" (Thapar 1992:85-86). Geographically, the seat of culture favored the north, and the center of national culture always gravitated to Sanscritic Hinduism, Vedic culture, the Vedānta, and the Sanskrit epics. It did not focus on Buddhism or *bhakti*. Given its marked bias for defining culture in favor of the upper castes, nationalist reform tended to support the caste system. In fact, the Aryan theory of race provided a triumphant pseudoscientific justification for caste exclusion. Discourse regarding the Aryan was used to differentiate upper castes from the lower castes believed to be of non-Aryan origin (Thapar 1992: 8). Caste became seen as a means whereby different racial and cultural groups had been brought together and subjected to the civilizing influence of the Aryans.

As we have seen throughout this volume, Aryan racial identity was often text-centered in the Vedas. Like Dayānand, Tilak read the Vedas literally, as plain and simple points of fact. Like Dayānand, Tilak denied the metaphorical nature of these texts and sought to find in the Vedas factual information regarding the fate and mission of the Aryans. Whereas Dayānand, Ranade, and Tilak sought support for their notion of the Aryan past in the letter of the text, Vivekananda eschewed basing his vision of Aryan superiority on any textual reference. On the one hand, Aryan superiority was a foregone conclusion. On the other hand, the Vedas were so distorted that they afforded no reliable reference. As in the case of Dayānand, Vivekananda's pronouncements on scripture had credibility due to his status as a holy man. Laymen were held to a different accountability when invoking scripture. Tilak and Ranade refered to specific texts when they described their Aryans. Whether supported by textual evidence or not, nationalist discourse presented the Aryans and their scripture as exempla of high culture.

The Aryans alone were responsible for their creation. One could not view these texts as monuments created by "the hostile Dravidians . . . freely cursed in the hymns themselves" (Aurobindo 1964: 1). The Dravidians could not have influenced the hymns for the very simple racial reason that they never evolved beyond savagery. The Aryans were seen as the bearers of culture while the Dravidians represented the barbarian. The binary civilized/*barbaros* would shift, with the barbarian variously represented by lower caste Dravidians, tribals, or Moslems. However, the Aryan always represented the civilized who had been contaminated by various barbarian Others. Even as enlightened a figure as Justice Ranade held to this scenario of cultural degeneration. It was non-Aryan influences that had inspired India's worse abuses (communal land tenure, *satī*, polygamy) and degrading social patterns (Ranade 1902: 31, 32, 98–100). Aryanhood in India had been sorely tested, if not destroyed. In short, the search for an Indian national identity was as bound up with the search for a superior race living in an unchanging utopian past as was the Western quest for origins. For European and Indian nationalism, Aryanism came to define the true and pure Hindu community (Possehl 1982: iv, 84). Some sought to reclaim it; others knew this to be an impossible task.

We have seen how reformers rhetorically sought to include those very persons who had been excluded (outcastes, tribals, Moslems, Jews) from Western- and brahmin-based Aryanism. They declared Aryanhood to be culturally attainable. Previously excluded groups were supposedly allowed to unite with the Aryan fold, once they espoused its spiritual values, as if Aryanhood could ever be dissociated from heredity. However, certain thinkers outside the brahmin fold would challenge the sincerity of the caste Hindu's call for unity in diversity. In chapter 8, we will see how Jotirao Phule and Dr. Ambedkar subverted this nationalist script in their portrait of the anti-Aryan. They recognized in Aryan historical revisionism a brahmin ploy to maintain the caste status quo and deny their people any equality with their so-called co-religionists. Phule and Ambedkar eloquently and effectively played the Aryan race card against brahmin reformers.

CHAPTER 8

The Anti-Myth

INTRODUCTION

In our previous discussions, we have seen how texts possess the power of composing and distributing narratives of space that underlie and organize a culture (Certeau 1986: 67–68). Indian evocations of the Aryan past, like all creations of popular culture, presuppose this unavowed operation of censorship (Certeau 1986: 119–21). Representations must be abstracted from historical conditions in which they are produced. The deceptive plenitude of a national identity is founded on an unavowed absence of those excluded (Certeau 1986: 133–34). Creating a myth of the people necessitates the excision of less comfortable or convenient forms of alterity (Aherne 1995: 134). Populations (in our case, the non-Aryan), must be converted into a reassuring Other, the utopia of a new political relation between the masses and the elite. The Other is then set up as an inert body which can be manipulated and controlled by a ruling elite. Such an elite becomes, according to Certeau, blind to what it excludes by means of such an operation—it occults a panoply of other kinds of operations that run through those regions of society which it supposes to be passive (Aherne 1995: 136).

According to Certeau, however, acts of excision produce certain symptoms that remain discernable in the language of interpretation. They leave behind questions of lost origin or a fantasmatic presence of a putative origin. The Other, excluded from interpretation, returns to "haunt" the production. The truth of the people is thus set back from their texts. Subsequent interpreters work with these predefined models of what constitutes the authentically popular or original. They offer a reassuringly idealized image of the people and remain deaf to anything that unsettles that ideal. In the following pages, we will show how two great untouchable reformers dealt with the historical exclusion of their respective communities from true national identity. Mahatma Phule and Babasaheb Ambedkar recognized how, through a displacement of traditional boundaries, they could delimit a new cultural field for their communities. We will examine how their reading of the Veda functioned as just such a redistribution of cultural space. Before we begin our analysis, however, the racial parameters of the Aryan myth require some clarification.

THE ARYAN AND ITS OTHER

It has been noted that the Western quest for origins received its initial formulation in the late Renaissance when philological similarities were noticed between Sanskrit, Greek, Latin, and other languages of Europe. We have seen how in the Enlightenment, theories concerning Aryan culture developed out of such linguistic theorizing and were never really discarded. They resurfaced in Orientalist scholarship, Romantic mythography, nineteenth-century linguistic science and race theory. Once philology had showed the relationship between Sanskrit and Greek, it was assumed that the Indo-Aryans were the originators of civilization. Nineteenth-century Indian racial theorists and reformers allowed themselves to be guided by this then-current and flawed philological thesis.

Orientalist scholarship had given the term *ārya* a racial meaning of physical and cultural alterity. The Aryans were other than the indigenous population of India; they came from the margins. This definition differed significantly from the textual use of the term *ārya*, where it signified an honored person of high status as distinct from a *mleccha* or barbarian *(an-ārya)*. Western scholars believed that the etymology of the term *varṇa* linguistically supported the Aryan racial theory by its association with color and its reference to caste.[1] They were wrong. In the Vedic context, *ārya* only signified one who spoke Sanskrit and observed caste regulations (Thapar 1992: 4). The textual criteria for difference between the *ārya* and *anārya* were determined not by race but by language, observance of the *varṇāshramadharma*, appearance, and religious worship.

The racial connotation did, however, enter the discussion because of the juxtaposition of the *ārya* with the *dāsa* in the *Rig Veda*, where the *dāsa* was described as dissimilar to the *ārya*.[2] Since Vedic references to the *ārya* contrast him with the *dāsa*, who was described as short and dark-complected,[3] both were taken to represent two distinct racial types. The Aryans were believed to have invaded India, subjugating the natives *(dāsa/dasyu)*, who were believed to be racially different from them. The *ārya* evolved later into the upper three castes with the *dāsa* remaining the lowest. The Aryans were believed to be the white race. They enslaved the Dāsas, a dark race, who eventually became the *shūdras*. This racial interpretation of the *ārya/dāsa* as white/black largely prevailed among scholars and is still a common scholarly perception (Hock 1999: 4). The linguist Hans Hock has recently shown, through an examination of Rig Vedic passages in which the terms white/black appear, that a racial interpretation is "not required by the textual evidence" (Hock 1999: 6). The Sanskrit terms in question are elastic. In the passages customarily cited to support a racial reading, Vedic terms of "white" can equally be translated as "light," with the sense that the Aryans were forces of light or goodness. Similarly, the Sanskrit term for "black" (most often, *kṛṣṇa*) can signify "darkness." In an "ideological" reading, those terms racially translated white/black can justifiably be rendered good/evil.

Those references to black skin also can elicit an alternate reading. The Sanskrit terms for skin in the pertinent Vedic citations (*tvac*) can just as easily signify the surface of the earth. These references could actually refer to the "dark world" of the Dāsas as opposed to the "broad light" of the Aryans (Hock 1999: 9). The compounds *kṛṣṇayoniḥ* and *kṛṣṇagarbha* have customarily been translated as "those with blacks in their wombs" or "pregnant with blacks." However, the Sanskrit also supports a reading of "having dark interiors" as in "those whose forts have dark interiors" or "the dark world where forts are located" as opposed to the light world of the Aryans.[4]

Racial interpretations based on skin color do not generally play a significant role in premodern societies. They are more "an invention of (early) modern European colonialism and imperialism" (Hock 1999: 15) and its construction of racial superiority. It is not surprising, therefore, that nineteenth-century European Indologists would have read Vedic texts racially, especially since the British takeover of India seemed to parallel the assumed takeover of prehistoric India by the invading Aryans (Hock 1999: 23). Nor is it surprising that the racial interpretation of *ārya/dāsa* persists among Indian Indologists, given modern India's color prejudice.[5]

The Aryans, deemed the founders of European and Asian civilization, entered from the borders and spread over the subcontinent. They settled Āryavarta by subjugating the indigenous Dāsas.[6] As victors, the Aryans were assumed to be superior to non-Aryans. They maintained their position of ascendancy through strict rules against racial miscegenation. With the implementation of the caste system, they protected their racial exclusivity, with the brahmins viewed as having preserved the purest Aryan strain. Already by the mid-nineteenth century, it was this racial rendition of the Aryan myth that had taken root in the collective consciousness. This was the script that Phule and Ambedkar sought to overthrow.

Lest we lose sight of the historical praxis of this racist ideology, it is worthwhile to describe to what degree such racial notions found expression. The treatment of untouchability was truly horrific. Let us cite Ambedkar's historically recognized examples. He wrote that in Poona, under the Peshwas, Untouchables were not allowed to use public streets if a Hindu was approaching, lest they pollute the Hindu with their shadow. Untouchables were required to wear a black thread on their necks or wrists to ward off Hindus, lest the Hindus be inadvertently polluted. They were to carry a broom strung from their waist to sweep away the dust that they tread. They were to hang an earthen pot from their neck to catch their spit, lest they defile the dirt upon which Hindus walk. Ambedkar noted that as recently as 1928 in central India, Untouchables could not wear clothing with colored or fancy borders. Women could not wear gold or silver ornaments. Untouchables must work without requesting any remuneration. They were not allowed to draw water from village wells or let their cattle graze on village lands. They were not allowed to walk through Hindu fields, and so forth. No fiction or mystification of caste by brahmin reformers could refute or obscure this brutal state of affairs.[7]

MAHATMA PHULE

Jotiba Govind Phule (1828–1890) was born a *shūdra* of the gardener (Mali) caste. Educated at the Scottish Mission High School in Poona, he was a militant advocate for the rights of the Untouchables and the peasants. He entered the field of reform by championing the cause of education for women and the lower castes. He opened the first girls' school in Poona and established an untouchable school. He is also credited as the first Hindu to found an orphanage with the aim of preventing infanticide (1863). In 1873, he founded the Satya Shodhak Samāj (Society of Seekers of Truth) to liberate the Untouchables from brahmin exploitation. He viewed British rule as a godsend, welcoming English conquest as a means whereby the disabled *shūdras* would be liberated from the slavery of the "crafty Aryans" (Wolpert 1962: 7).

Phule called for a reinterpretation of theories of the past by locating the struggle of the low castes within the historical perspective of the Aryan conquest of India. He launched an attack on the notion of Aryan racial superiority by identifying the Aryans as the perfidious barbarian aliens who had conquered the indigenous powerful social groups of the time, the *shūdras* (Mahars and Mangs). Mere subjugation did not satisfy Aryan lust for power; they instituted caste isolation so that they and their descendants, the brahmins, could continue to oppress the indigenous population. Aryan brahmins sought to punish the *shūdras* for eternity by depriving them of their rights and condemning them to ignorance.[8] Phule's revision of the Aryan invasion theory served him as the paradigm for subsequent Indian history. He framed the Moslem invasion as a repetition of Aryan conquest. Thus, Moslem social and religious power was no more alien than that of the Aryans. The Moslems distinguished themselves from the Aryans by bringing a sophisticated culture with them when they invaded India. Aryans only brought repression.

Phule's intention, like that of other social reformers, was to reaffirm or revitalize culture. In his case, however, culture was defined by the subculture. Like the nationalists, he aimed at identifying the national culture that would form the basis of a new state. The Indian bourgeois and upper-caste elite had offered a politically expedient response to the question of national identity: all India formed the basis for the state. However, it was clear that by "all India" they meant Hindu society and, in particular, Hindus who traced their origins to a Vedic Golden Age. In other words, the state consisted of the traditional *varṇāshramadharma*, wherein other Indian cultures (non-Aryan, Moslem, tribal, and low castes) were relegated to an inferior position. Phule's response was to identify national culture as consisting of those very persons that high-caste social and religious reformers had relegated to the margins. He did so by turning the argument of text-centered identity back upon the elite. Phule took those very strengths and virtues that had been attributed to the Aryan in Romantic mythography and Orientalist scholarship and subsequently coopted by brahmin reformers and transferred them to the lower castes.

If culture descended from the Aryan conquerers, then the traditional elite were essentially foreigners (*Irani Aryabhats*) who had overrun and enslaved the original and true Indians, the mass of peasants, tribals, and Untouchables. The original inhabitants should overturn the hierarchical system, now revealed as fraudulent, and usurp power from the high-caste Hindu, who was no less foreign than the English. In fact, as foreigners go, the British scored well in Phule's estimation: They, at least, aimed at an enlightened vision. The brahmins, however, were bound by villainous and treacherous traditions that had been devised as weapons by foreign forebears and wielded by their alien descendants. It was time, according to Phule, to put an end to oppression and to turn the brahmin foreigners' most effective weapon, the Veda, against them. For Phule, as for other social and religious reformers, the Veda provided the key to unravel the mysteries of Indian identity. He, too, undertook to reveal its true message. This process involved a demonstration of how the invading Aryans had treacherously conquered the natives and established socioreligious structures for their continued deception and exploitation.

Instead of an appeal to return to an Aryan Golden Age, Phule called for the reestablishment of an alternative mythical age, the reign of King Bali,[9] which predated the Aryans' treacherous coup d'état.[10] In retelling the legend of Bali, Phule posited the *ārya* as the invidious invader and the *dāsa* as the indigenous population made up of enlightened kings and warriors. By invoking the figure of Bali, Phule constructed an essentially non-Aryan myth or a

Dasyu myth wherein the Chitpavan brahmins of Mahārāshtra, who prided themselves on being close descendnts to the Vedic Aryans, were revealed as frauds and cheats. Phule identified those groups traditionally relegated to the lowest positions in caste hierarchy, the Mahārāshtran peasant majority, the tribal community, and the Untouchables, as the true Indians, distinct from and morally superior to the Aryans. His small treatise, *Gulamgiri* ("Slavery"), in fact, presents a paean to their intrinsic worth and calls for them to assert group solidarity and end oppression. In short, Phule sought a return to a former non-Aryan Golden Age.

It was through the authority vested in the Vedas that the alien Aryan usurpers fabricated their identity as brahmins and enslaved *true* Indians with draconian laws.[11] By passing off "idle fantasies" as divine revelation, brahmins forced those whom they had conquered into serving them faithfully as the consummation of devotion. By "stealthily producing heaps of new scriptures," brahmins "brain-washed" the Dāsas' descendants, the *shūdras*, into believing them to be the descendants of Aryans. They further duped the *shūdras* into thinking that by serving them and performing menial tasks, they fulfilled their religious obligations. Moreover, brahmins conspired to keep the *shūdras* in ignorance by denying them access to true knowledge and controlling them with "unholy" law treatises. Finally, as custodians of Vedic knowledge, brahmins vouchsafed their power to alter the so-called divine revelation as need arose (Phule 1991a: 1.34).[12]

As a weapon devised and wielded by the religious elite, the Veda's "palpably absurd legends" distorted God's revelation in order to consolidate brahmin ascendancy. Priestly control over the text's accessibility only highlights the brahmins' need to defraud: The hermeneutical conspiracy could only succeed if the Vedas remained a closed and hermetic canon of authority that could shield brahmins from the lies their ancestors had perpetrated in the name of religion and absolve them of associative guilt (Phule 1991a: 2.21).[13] Textual control enabled the brahmins to commit the even greater sin of rendering themselves godlike.[14]

Phule specifically designated the Vedas as a form of false consciousness. As fictions of religious authority enshrined in scripture and given additional force through custom, the Vedas express nothing but brahmin greed.[15] The brahmins transgress God's designs by denying the text to others (Phule 1991a: 2.104–5) and misusing it for selfish gain. Their continual textual subversion of scripture incurred God's wrath in the form of foreign conquest of India by the Mughals, Pathans, Portuguese, French, and finally, the English. The pen being mightier than the sword, God punished the Aryan brahmin in the nineteenth century through the texts themselves. Under the harsh light of foreign scholarship, God allowed Western scholars to reveal how the brahmins had persecuted the *shūdras* with spurious readings of the Veda.

God used Western Indological scholarship to punish the Aryan brahmins and publicize their treachery worldwide "so that the eyes of the *shūdras* will be opened and the sins against them will be brought home in a blinding flash" (Phule 1991a: 2.22–23).

Phule called for the victims of Aryan perfidy to use reason (Phule 1991a: 2.83), recognize what had been inflicted on them, and revolt against brahmin treachery by discarding the scriptural instrument of this fraud and enslavement (Phule 1991a: 2.32). Once the spurious Vedas are rejected, the true Vedas can be unearthed. Phule did not reject the concept of textual authority or legitimacy. He rejected rather the false readings of the Veda that held his people in thrall. Read correctly, the Vedas reveal a different message—that the Dasyus were the original inhabitants of the land; they were brave, pure at heart, and upright in their conduct. Phule exhorted their descendants to acknowledge this alternate rendering, recognize the degradation to which they have been reduced by the Aryans (Phule 1991a: 2.83), and reject it.

By introducing this new category of reason into the discussion, Phule effected a dissociation of "thing" from "name," or objects from what they were called (Certeau 1986: 70). Reference did not determine the *signifié*, but rather the application of a sign (Aryanhood) to an object (the Dāsa) categorized and interpreted that object. By challenging the myth of a utopian past, Phule launched a radical attack on Vedic revivalism. He realized full well that the brahmin and upper-caste intellectual (that is, the new middle class) would represent the Aryan in any return to origins. He also understood how any glorification of supposedly Aryan values further consolidated brahmin ascendancy. Finally, he suspected that opposition to the West, another key component of revivalism, often masqueraded as patriotism when, in reality, it masked hegemonic desire on the part of high-caste reformers.

DR. AMBEDKAR

B.R. Ambedkar (1892–1956) belonged to the Untouchable Mahar caste of Mahārāshtra. When only 1 percent of his caste was literate, Ambedkar received a B.A. in Bombay, M.A. and Ph.D. at Columbia University in New York, D.Sc. at London University, and passed the bar from Grey's Inn, London.[16] He was able to achieve what none of his caste had ever done because his father had joined the British Army and his family had found the means to secure him an education. Ambedkar dedicated his life to working for the advancement of his people. Initially, he worked as a social advocate in the field of journalism, later as a representative for his people testifying at government commissions, and finally as their guru and leader.

By the beginning of the twentieth century, the lower strata of Indian society had awakened to the inequities of their existence and begun to question the brahmanical face of reform. Ambedkar's witness before the Southborough Committee (1917) had sought treatment for the Untouchables as a distinct community (like that of the Muslims, Sikhs, and Hindus) and defended their legitimate political demands (Ambedkar 1979: 1.250). The Montague Chelmsford Reforms of 1919 and the Reform Act of 1919 acknowledged the changing social reality. The British government was beginning to address the low-caste needs that had gone unheard by caste Hindu society for centuries. Ambedkar contributed to the cause of low-caste reform by serving as a delegate to the London Round Table Conferences (1930–33), where he made the case for the recognition of Untouchables as a minority with a separate electorate.

Ambedkar would have been successful in London had not Gandhi manipulated the situation. Gandhi believed that the Untouchables should remain within the Hindu fold and seek redress for their treatment there. Ambedkar suspected this strategy to be a caste Hindu ploy to continue control of the lower castes and avoid strengthening the Moslem cause. He, therefore, opposed Gandhi's initiative. When it appeared that Ambedkar's opposition might succeed, Gandhi began a fast. The possibility that Gandhi might actually die put Ambedkar in an impossible position. The "Mahatma's" death would have certainly unleashed a bloodbath against the Untouchable community. Gandhi was as aware of this inevitability as was Ambedkar. Ambedkar had no choice but to acquiesce to Gandhi's strategem and capitulate, thereby forfeiting the opportunity of securing viable representation for his community under British rule.

Ambedkar understood fully the extent to which his people were persecuted. He suspected that behind the rhetoric of reform was the caste Hindus' concern with maintaining control. In the case of Gandhi, this control took the form of usurping the role of spokesman for the subaltern and directing their future in an eventually free India. Many of Ambedkar's efforts in the years leading up to Independence involved campaigning against what he felt to be the hypocrisy of the Congress Party and Gandhi toward the Untouchable community. While Gandhi proceeded with his method of pleading with caste Hindus to abolish untouchability, Ambedkar sought to secure basic rights that his community continued to be denied despite Congress's promises: He sought to obtain his people's rights of a temple entry, use of community wells, and other basic human rights. But here too, he failed.

Ambedkar founded the Independent Labor Party that won fourteen seats in the Bombay Legislature in 1937 and served as a Labor member in the viceroy's executive council. His greatest service to India, however, was his chairmanship of the drafting committee of the Indian Constitution. When need arose, it was to the Untouchable barrister upon whom high-caste clerks had spat, that the fathers of Indian democracy had to turn. Even in this venture, Ambedkar had to wage a pitched battle for his people's rights to reasonable representation. By 1956, Ambedkar had had enough. He was disgusted with the continued impossibility of his people's condition. He was tired and ill. With the claim that he was born a Hindu but had no intention of dying a Hindu, since the religion offered him no human dignity, he converted to Buddhism, as did his followers. His commitment to the plight of his people spearheaded the mobilization of low-caste Hindus that took shape with the Dalit revolt in the seventies and continues to this day in the social and political struggle of the scheduled castes.

Ambedkar had begun his mission where Phule left off,[17] by pointing out the fallacy of Indian social reform: Brahmin-based reform was a contradiction in terms. To expect a brahmin to revolt against social inequity was like expecting the British Parliament to pass an act requiring all blue-eyed babies to be murdered (Ambedkar 1979: 1.71) was Ambedkar's harsh analogy. Ambedkar particularly poked fun at the Ārya Samāj's pretense of determining caste by worth (Ambedkar 1979: 1.58–59). Ambedkar deemed all such efforts futile. He believed that if reformers really wanted to destroy caste, then they would have to destroy the authority of the Veda (Ambedkar 1979: 1.69), since the *Purusha Sūkta* of the *Rig Veda* gave the *caturvarṇa* its eternal and sacrosanct status as a system. By invoking the sanction of law, it presented caste as natural, ideal, sacred, and divine (Ambedkar 1990: 7.26). The *Rig Veda* thus codified caste and ensured its continued application. Given the damage produced by the *Purusha Sūkta*, Ambedkar felt that to preach the Veda as the basis of everything, as did the Ārya Samāj, was pure mischief. Throughout his writings, Ambedkar sought to destroy the Veda as the basis of society and debunk its eternality, status as revelation (Ambedkar 1987: 4.29, 40), infallibility, and stationary view of society (Ambedkar 1990: 7.14). He challenged the Veda's moral and spiritual value in the past (Ambedkar 1987: 4.41) as well as its authority (4.37, 39) and philosophical worth (4.44) in the present.

Ambedkar began by questionning the Veda's canonicity. Since Rammohan Roy, Hindu reformers had learned a valuable lesson from Christian missionaries. Book religions had definite advantages over bookless religions. They possessed a written constitution or voucher for truth that gave authority and induced obedience (Ambedkar 1989: 5.182). The Veda had the double advantage of being both a book and a revealed religion. Caste, if preached by the Vedas, became both sacred and uncontested (Ambedkar 1989: 5.181); it automatically received the authority of the book and the sanctity of divine word. It had to be accepted as sacred, divine, and

eternal truth; it could not be attacked, lest one risk the guilt of sacrilege
(Ambedkar 1989: 5.183). By giving caste a place in the Vedas, brahmins
ensured their sacredness and invulnerability (Ambedkar 1989: 5.181).

According to Ambedkar, the establishment of Vedic authority and
infallibility (Ambedkar 1987: 4.53) involved a wide-reaching brahmin conspiracy (4.27) to legitimate the *caturvarṇa* system (4.36) and provide it with
an impregnable line of defense (Ambedkar 1989: 5.183). In any other society, the existence of hard and fast classes would have caused embarrassment
and self-recrimination. Hindu society, however, evinced no such concerns.
Thanks to the *Purusha Sūkta* and the authority vested in the greatness of
ancient Aryan civilization, brahmins could steadfastly maintain an iniquitous
class stratification and justify their behavior (Ambedkar 1990: 7.239). Since
they held a monopoly over scholarship, they could safely benefit from a
system that need never undergo scrutiny. No Voltaire had arisen from their
ranks to decry intolerance (Ambedkar 1990: 7.240). Before Ambedkar, no
one had judged the *Purusha Sūkta* immoral, criminal in intent, and antisocial
in its results. By condemning the hymn, Ambedkar also condemned the
Veda and the world of the Aryans. The ultimate goal of his polemic was to
dismantle the caste system they legitimized (Ambedkar 1990: 7.32). Since
the Dāsas were believed to have been conquered by the Aryans, their presumed descendants, the *shūdras*, were seen to inherit their position of sub-
servience legitimately.[18] It was to reject this script of subjugation and to
rehabilitate his own people, the Mahars—the principle and largest
Untouchable community in Mahārāshtra—that Ambedkar sought to rewrite
the Aryan myth. Ambedkar read the *Rig Veda* and constructed an elaborate
portrait of the Aryan people toward this end.

The Aryans were steeped in the worst kind of debauchery of a social,
religious, and spiritual nature. The rampant moral decay (Ambedkar
1979–90: 3.153) of this degraded society manifested itself in their devotion
to human sacrifice and genital worship (Ambedkar 1987: 4.294). They
indulged in high-stakes gambling (Ambedkar 1987: 3.168; 4.108; 4.295) and
were given over to drink and beef-eating (Ambedkar 1987: 3.157; 4.111).
Even their women indulged in drunken excesses (Ambedkar 1987: 3.154;
3.169; 4.109; 4.295). Aryan society was also steeped in sexual immorality
(Ambedkar 1987: 3.171). As there were no rules prohibiting sexual activities
(Ambedkar 1987: 4.109), the Aryans engaged in polyandry, polygamy
(Ambedkar 1987: 4.229), and incest (Ambedkar 1987: 3.155; 3.171; 4.109;
4.298). They routinely performed sexual acts in public (Ambedkar 1987:
3.155; 3.171; 4.109). They shared (Ambedkar 1987: 4.109) and rented out
their women for sex or as breeding stock (Ambedkar 1987: 3.156; 3.172;
4.294; 4.301). Bestiality was prevalent (Ambedkar 1987: 3.157, 173; 4.109).
Aryan society was predicated upon class war and social degradation

(Ambedkar 1987: 3.170). Sacrifice, providing a setting for revelry, drunkenness, gambling, and sexual promiscuity, showcased Aryan carnage and debauchery (Ambedkar 1987: 3.175). When humans were sacrificed, Aryans indulged in cannibalism. When they sacrificed animals, as in the *aśvamedha*, Aryans committed bestiality (Ambedkar 1987: 3.174). Ambedkar claimed that this was the reality of the Aryan world and the ideal toward which high-caste reformers aspired.

Ambedkar judged Aryan religion as a mass of sacrificial, social, political, and sanitary rules possessing no universal value. He deemed that what Hindus called religion was nothing but an iniquitous code of ordinances (Ambedkar 1979: 1.75–76) supporting a class ethic that inspired no loyalty to ideals and deprived its adherents of moral freedom and spontaneity. Moreover, he maintained that Aryan religion was without spiritual content and supported by a canon saturated with wicked thoughts. In the *Rig Veda*, the Aryans did not pray for forgiveness of sins or deliverance from evil. Instead, they praised Indra for killing the pregnant wives of their enemies and otherwise bringing destruction to their foes. Since Aryan religion was never concerned with the righteous life (Ambedkar 1987: 3.175–76), it should be destroyed. It had never even been a religion, but rather a compendium of laws in dire need of amendment or abolition (Ambedkar 1979: 1.76).

Ambedkar also challenged the racial portrayal of the Aryan that presented them as a fair race with sharp noses as compared to the Dāsa/Dasyu who were believed to be dark-complected and flat-nosed. In modern times, the Dāsa has been identified with the *shūdra* and aboriginal tribes. Ambedkar claimed that the philological evidence keeping the racial myth alive was as spurious as the Western equation of *varṇa* with color.[19] Rather than Müller's reading of *anāsa* as *a-nāsa*, without a nose (that is, flat-nosed), Ambedkar sides with Sāyaṇa's reading of *an-āsa*, signifying devoid of good speech (Ambedkar 1990: 7.76). He maintained that the Veda had been consistently misread by brahmin scholars in a racial sense in order to foster a two-nation theory that benefitted their interests. With the brahmins as the representatives of the Aryans and the low castes seen as non-Aryans, brahmins could foster both their hegemonic power over their brethern as well as kinship with Europeans. Ambedkar found no evidence that the term *ārya* was used in the *Rig Veda* in a racial sense. The Dāsas were as civilized and powerful as the Aryans (Ambedkar 1990: 7.105). He did not read any racial distinction between the Aryan and the Dāsa, since there are numerous instances in the *Rig Veda* where Dāsas become Aryans. Similarly, there is no evidence that the Aryans were a different color than the Dāsas (Ambedkar 1990: 7.85).

It was thought that the Aryans invaded India, conquered the Dāsas, and made them slaves. Ambedkar claimed that the Aryan invasion myth was also unfounded (Ambedkar 1987: 3.419). Rather, the evidence shows the contrary, that India is the home of the Aryans. While there does exist in the *Rig Veda* many descriptions of the Dāsa as the enemies of the Aryans, these passages make no reference to their conquest and subjugation, but rather to sporadic fighting. The *Rig Veda* also speaks of the Dāsas and the Aryans standing against a common enemy, suggesting to Ambedkar that their conflict was of a religious rather than a racial nature (Ambedkar 1990: 7.76). The Aryan invasion theory was contrived to support brahmin superiority, justify their overlordship over non-brahmins, and satisfy brahmin arrogance (Ambedkar 1990: 7.80).

Ambedkar read the Veda to suggest that the Aryans were not a single homogeneous people, rather two groups with distinct cultures. One group, the Aryans of the *Rig Veda*, believed in sacrifice, traced their descent through man, and produced the Brāhmaṇas, Sūtras, and Araṇyakas. The other group, the Aryans of *Atharva Veda*, believed in magic, traced their descent through Prajāpati, and produced the Upanishads (Ambedkar 1990: 7.291).[20] These two separate ideologies were fundamentally different and irreconcilable: the former believed in the *caturvarṇa* and the latter did not (Ambedkar 1990: 7.97). The two groups were eventually consolidated with the Rig Vedic ideology prevailing. The term *dāsa*, therefore, denoted persons not observing Aryan forms of religion; they were Aryans of a different sect or class (Ambedkar 1990: 7.107).

According to Ambedkar, the *Rig Veda* (10.49) supports the thesis that the *shūdras* are Aryan (Ambedkar 1990: 7.110) or members of Aryan communities who had been deprived of the title "*Arya*" for opposing belief deemed essential to Aryan culture. Their rights and privileges suggest that they belonged to the *kṣatriya* caste and lived outside the village from the beginning (Ambedkar 1990: 7.278–80). Some *shūdras* were so important a class of *kṣatriyas* that eminent and powerful kings of Aryan communities were *shūdras* (Ambedkar 1990: 7.114). Ambedkar read the *Rig Veda* and the Brāhmaṇas as supporting a three-*varṇa* theory, with the *shūdra* never appearing as the fourth and separate *varṇa* (Ambedkar 1990: 7.132, 139).

It was only the cosmology presented in the *Purusha Sūkta* that justified the creation of the fourth *varṇa*, and Ambedkar denied the authenticity of this fundamental hymn (Ambedkar 1990: 7.134). He claimed that before *Manu*, the *shūdra* was not a non-Aryan (Ambedkar 1987: 3.419). Brahmanic lawgivers, however, selected the *shūdras* as victims of their law-making authority. They devised and imposed disabilities having no parallel anywhere in the world (Ambedkar 1990: 7.56). *Manu*, by positioning the *caturvarṇa* as the essence of Aryanism (Ambedkar 1987: 4.215), silenced once and for all any opposition to the "fictive" ideal set by the *Purusha Sūkta* (Ambedkar 1990: 7.24). The Veda's status as eternal revelation ensured that any rational debate on the justice of the *varṇa* system was foreclosed (Ambedkar 1979: 1.72). *Manu*, by perverting history and defaming respectable and powerful tribes, transformed them into bastards (Ambedkar 1987: 4.224). It completed the task of marginalization begun by the Rig Vedic Aryans.

Thus, the fourth *varṇa* came into existence when the *shūdras* were degraded on account of their violent conflicts with brahmins (Ambedkar 1990: 7.140). Out of jealousy of *shūdra* superiority (Ambedkar 1990: 7.190) and in retaliation for indignities they suffered under certain *shūdra* kings (Ambedkar 1990: 7.186; 7.11–12), brahmins denied them the ritual of the *upanayana* and degraded them from the second to the fourth rank (Ambedkar 1990: 7.156, 186).[21] The *shūdras* were not a vast group as they are in modern times, capable of challenging brahmin abuse. They were then just a single people and unable to fight back effectively. Only in modern Hindu society have they come to represent many uncultured peoples, a heterogeneous collection of tribes with nothing in common except their low cultural standing. In fact, present-day *shūdras* should not even be called "*shūdras*," since they have nothing in common with their namesakes in Aryan culture. Nor should they be made to pay penalties for crimes that they did not commit (Ambedkar 1990: 7.201).

Ambedkar rejected the entire Aryan racial myth (Ambedkar 1990: 7.78). The *varṇa* system cannot stem from Aryan color prejudice, since the Aryans were comprised of different colored peoples (Ambedkar 1990: 7.81). Scientific evidence indicates that the brahmins and Untouchables belong to the same race.[22] If the brahmins are Aryans, then so too are the Untouchables; just as if brahmins are Dravidians, so too are Untouchables (Ambedkar 1990: 7.302). Untouchability has nothing to do with race or with occupation (Ambedkar 1990: 7.305–7). It originated in brahmin antipathy for "broken men."

Ambedkar maintained that the objects of brahmin wrath were actually Buddhists who did not revere or employ them as priests (Ambedkar 1990: 7.315). The brahmins retaliated with such tremendous slander that these Buddhists eventually became regarded as Untouchable. The roots of untouchability are, therefore, to be found in brahmins' hatred and contempt for Buddhism as an assault upon their hegemony (Ambedkar 1990: 7.317). Brahmins hated the Buddhists because they made them look bad. Compared with Buddhist moderation, the brahmins' love of beef concealed in the elaborate pomp of the sacrifice (Ambedkar 1990: 7.334) undermined public esteem. Their constant slaughter of animals produced revulsion for Brahmanism (Ambedkar 1990: 7.346). Realizing how low their stock had fallen, the brahmins sought to recover the ground they had lost to Buddhism. They became vegetarian and made the cow sacred. Since the Buddhists remained meat eaters, they were consequently viewed as sacrilegious (7.350). The brahmins were thus able to marginalize Buddhists and gain ascendancy over them. Ultimately, the brahmins destroyed the Buddhists. They then conspired and succeeded in subjugating their descendants. Ambedkar's rewriting of the Aryan myth was no less fanciful than brahmin-authored versions. It differed, however, in one important respect. It was potent enough to enable him to lead millions of Indians out of the slavery into which they had been born.

CONCLUSION

In India, the Aryans could represent either the true and pure Hindu (Thapar 1992: 81) or the foreign invader. In the former instance such a characterization was achieved through a process wherein the periphery was identified and set apart. In the latter circumstance, the center appears as a construct against which the margin (or in the case of Phule and Ambedkar, the melding of margins) is reshuffled or undergoes reinterpretation. This redefinition of the margin necessarily plays a role in shaping the center.

In the orthodox formulation of the Aryan myth, privileged segments of the Indian population could consider themselves on a par with their conquerers rather than subjects. By framing the myth of an embattled Aryan "We," which purportedly existed before the arrival of the British, the middle-class Indian elite asserted a cohesive social identity and declared their cultural superiority in response to colonial domination. In such instances, the Aryan myth provided a psychological strategy that was instrumental in the eventual expulsion of the colonial authorities.

Outside the elite, groups on the periphery subverted the myth of Aryan hegemony and utilized its deformation as an instrument of unity and social estrangement. Through counter hegemonic inversion, they sought alternative models wherein subordinates and marginals under the present order agitated for the deconstruction of that order and the reconstruction of a novel pattern. Such reform relied upon disruptive discourse gaining a wide audience. It also relied upon the domination of sentiments of estrangement over those of affinity. In the contest for political power between two or more groups, emphasis was thus placed on the cultural separateness of the Aryan and the non-Aryan. Social reformers such as Phule and Ambedkar sought to sharpen separation for each group by identifying their divergent roots. By shifting semantic relations, Phule and Ambedkar called into question the traditional status of the Aryan and the Dāsa, as well as their relationship to each other. They showed that the defining characteristics of Aryanness found their referent in the world of the *shūdra*. They broke with the established definitions by separating the sign from the Aryan ideal as it had been codified in brahmin and Orientalist readings of the Veda.

Their approach was based on faith in the integrity of the outcaste Self and positing it as the norm by which the Aryan Other should be judged deficient. Translated into semantic terms, their position resulted in unifying the *signifié* with its referent. The Aryan was defined by what "one" does, the Dāsa, by what "they" do. They broke this semantic system down further by separating the word "Aryan," the *signifié* of the sign, from its objectification in the outside world. The Aryan and the Dāsa are then both located on the same level and judged in relation to each other. In this manner, the Dāsa/*shūdra* can be assigned to the very place from which it had been excluded. Thus, the discourse of the Aryan Other becomes a discourse of the *shūdra* Self.

The word "Aryan," to paraphrase Michel de Certeau, leaves behind its status as a noun (the Aryan) to take on the value of an adjective (*ārya*, or noble). Phule and Ambedkar's analysis let the word recede to ponder behaviors to which it could apply as a predicate (an adjective). It can do this in three ways: as an ambivalence ("Aryans are superior, *shūdras* are superior"), a comparison ("We *shūdras* are stronger and more powerful than those Aryans"), or as an alternative ("One has to be noble, we *shūdras* or those Aryans, and it's not them!").

As I hope this chapter has shown, there are areas of response in nineteenth-century Indian reform that were hardly touched by relationships of colonial power and significantly address issues of Indian hegemonic abuses. Figures such as Phule and Ambedkar are curiously absent from deconstructions of hegemonic textualities. In those forms of scholarship where truth cannot go beyond deceptive representations of the colonized Other, their voices are absent. The problem, perhaps, is that Phule and, to a far greater degree, Ambedkar were not subalterns in search of a critic to speak on their behalf. They both had rather clear voices. The very fact that significant Indian discourse on the Aryan centered on nativist concerns raises interesting questions concerning the serviceability of postcolonial criticism to a broad spectrum of literary production under colonialism. One might well question whether professional spokespersons for the subaltern are deaf to their voices because they attacked an enemy who was not the colonial power, but an opponent from whose ranks the critics themselves spring and within whose hegemonic structure of knowledge and discourse they continue to operate. In this context, the tendency to demonize all colonial relations as a kind of "original sin" (Rothstein 2001: A17) seems particularly unsupportable. The "original sin" concept has had the effect of whitewashing the checkered past of many colonized and postcolonial elites. Many abuses of power and human rights violations perpetuated by these elites are swept away by the concept of colonialism as *the* hegemonic evil. Are we to read critics' deafness as an oversight (or, as they might say, over-site) or rather as a mask for their own needs to maintain traditional lines of power while restructuring the contemporary image of power?

The oppressor/victim binary of colonial discourse analysis does not fully explain the Indian need to idealize the antiquity of Aryan India and establish culture as diffused from India to the rest of the world. It does not account for the fact that patterns of admiration and positions adopted vary within various groups and from individual to individual in the receiving culture and are rooted in the specific cultural traits of Hindu caste society and its literary tradition. Phule and Ambedkar offered a radical attack on revivalism and challenged the elite myth of the past. They realized that brahmins and upper-caste intellectuals (that is, the new middle class) would always represent the idealized ancient Indian society, since their values could be seen to stem from that past. They also realized that opposition to the colonizing Other could be taken for nationalism, when it merely masked the preservation of traditional lines of power. Students of postcolonial theory should explore such histories and representations because they resonate in our continuing arguments with contemporary racism.

Afterword

The Aryan myth defined both the true Hindu community (Thapar 1992: 81) and the origin of the West. We have investigated how myths regarding the Aryan gave value to ancient Indian history, contributed to the ideological concerns of India during the colonial and nationalist periods, and established a schema of oppositions that continues to resonate in the modern historical and critical context. We also examined how myths concerning the Aryan race and narratives of their migrations served the political and ideological interests of Europe: The history of India could be appropriated as a means of expressing nineteenth-century European theories of origin. An examination of the Aryan myth thus addresses a fundamental concern of postcolonial criticism, namely that the West needed to constitute the Orient as its Other in order to constitute itself and its own subjective position (Ahmad 1993: 182). By idealizing the Indian past, Europe "colonized" the Other in an attempt to define the Self. Finally, we saw how, in both instances, identity came to be defined from the margin. In fact, the logic of the margin contributed significantly to the specific dynamic of the Aryan myth. The Aryan center appears as a construct of the non-Aryan margins and is redefined as those margins are reshuffled or interpreted. By applying concepts such as Deleuze's notion of deterritorialization and Foucault's archaeology to the examination of identity, one can track how margins shape the center and how human subjects relate inside an intersubjective world.

This study also examined how the Indian myth of Aryanhood was utilized to bring about the mobilization of powerful sentiments of affinity and solidarity. Through a transformation of consciousness, segments of the Indian population could consider themselves on a par with their conquerors rather than their subjects. With this myth, privileged segments of Indian society were able to frame an embattled Aryan "We," which purportedly existed before the arrival of the British and could be rallied in the rearticulated tradition. This construct allowed specific groups of Indians to assert a cohesive social identity and declare their cultural superiority in response to colonial domination. The social identity activated by the Aryan myth fostered estrangement from British colonial authorities and thus functioned as an effective instrument of resistance. It was instrumental in the eventual expulsion of the colonial authorities. Outside the brahmin elite, groups on the periphery subverted the Aryan myth for social reform. Thus, the myth was employed both to reassert the social and religious stability of the elite and undermine its hegemony. After independence, reconfigured versions of the Aryan myth became instrumental in destabilizing caste authority and, most recently, fomenting communalism.

As in India, so too in Europe: speculation regarding the Aryan provided essential information concerning the past; it promised to reveal the state of civilization that was closest to the supposed common ancestors of all Indo-European peoples. For those seeking to distance themselves from a Hebrew heritage, Aryan India provided an attractive alternative. Germans, in particular, believed that the study of Vedic mythology could elucidate the history and fate of the Indo-German *Volk*, a national collectivity inspired by a common creative energy, that was promulgated as the unique essence of the German people. German Indology's valorization of the Aryan past and an idealized vision of India further contributed to the identification of this *Volk* with the mythic Aryan. Subsequent racial hygienists would invert this Aryan myth: India became a projection of the German racial situation. Once the metaphorical cradle of German civilization, India now became its symbolic grave. Through the Aryan myth, India functioned both as an example and a warning to the Nazis. Just as the Aryans in India fell, so would those in Europe if racial purity were not recreated. In both the East and the West, the search for the "original" India became bound up with a search for a superior race living in an unchanging utopian past.

The point of departure for our inquiry was the belief that the heterological process is quintessentially hermeneutical. Throughout this volume, we focused on the recuperation of the Aryan past as a heterology unfolding in time and space, as a series of narratives reflecting dialectical processes and as an exemplary story promoting various national identities. Through the rhetoric of a myth of origin, these narratives attempt to bridge the distance between the subjective Self and the objective Other. Part I questioned how versions of the Aryan past articulated an ethical process whereby the European subject defined itself through cultural confrontation. Of particular interest in this discussion was the psychodynamics of appropriation, what Michel de Certeau termed the impossibility of portraying the Other as anything but a translation into a European familiarity of the Self. On a broader level, these chapters called into question the morality of appropriation. Part II examined the internal exoticism involved in Indian recuperations of the Aryan past. We saw how truth is ever elusive and open to reconfiguration. The truth regarding the Aryans was less to be found in their literature than in what it was no longer able to express. Truth was not to be discovered in words, but rather in the lacunae, the message that had been lost through decay, inaccessibility, and the loss of ability to read correctly.

European theories of the Aryan race developed out of scholarly inquiry into the origin of languages, the study of myth, and the historical study of religion. The quest for an original language from which other languages derived involved a search for unity in diversity. The quest for linguistic unity reflected the need for an ultimate textual authority. However, once that authority was identified, something curious occurred. The horizon of the text was virtually swept away; its integrity ignored. The text was treated by interpreters as almost nonexistent; they made it up to suit their needs. In a similar fashion, the horizon of the reader became pure ideology, expressing itself in emotional appeals to return to some golden age or true spirituality of the text.

Western Orientalist scholars focused on the superiority of the Indian Aryans and their legacy of excellence as manifest in their modern European descendants. In the Enlightenment, the Aryans provided an alternative to the Hebrew model. For the Romantics, the Aryan past confirmed those aesthetic and spiritual values that were cherished and promoted in the European present. Among certain nineteenth-century cultural critics, however, an Aryan theory of race inspired counter-hegemonic reveries of degeneration. Gobineau's *Arierdämmerung* heralded the twilight of the gods. It was Nietzsche's task to transform these gods into idols. In the writings of Chamberlain and Rosenberg, notions of who comprised the Aryan race exhibited an endemic feeling that Christianity had empowered a sickly underclass and corrupted German religion. The fall of the Aryan resonated in the "infectous post–World War I story of betrayal by Jewish materialists and the vindictive Allies" (Crews 1996: 39).

In India, theories of Aryan unity ingeniously ignored discrepancies in racial and cultural development. Rammohan Roy and Dayānand focused on the Aryan religious tradition as a basis for Hindu spiritual revival. For Tilak and Ranade, the Aryan's racial superiority could be witnessed in their survival in modern times as caste Hindus. Ranade took a cosmopolitan perspective; he contrasted the Aryan to the Semite and the Dravidian. For Vivekananda, the Aryan was superior both to the Dravidian *and* the West. Tilak valorized the Aryan past to promote the nationalist cause. Vivekananda held expansionist designs: he saw itinerant Indian preachers setting forth to perfect (Aryanize) the world. Phule and Ambedkar challenged the myth of the Aryan, bringing back into discussion what nationalist discourse had excluded. Discussions of Aryanhood were thus either system-maintaining or counter-systemic. The system in question was the caste system, and specifically the role of brahmins as the disseminators of the Veda, its legitimate readers, and (ab)users of secular and religious power. There was some suggestion that the Veda had been corrupted by barbarian influences and the intolerance of ruthless conquerors. It was also believed that the process of textual degradation could be reversed. In those cases where the discourse was systems-maintaining, brahmins jealously guarded their access to the text and their right to interpret it. In those instances where Aryan discourse was counter-systemic, reformers desperately sought to wrest the texts away from their brahmin custodians.

These nineteenth-century quests for the Aryan past can be viewed as forms of popular culture, susceptible to the political and institutional forces that inform cultural criticism. They collaborate in the political structure that they inhabit and in their position and complicity within the power structure. Popular culture, even when Marxist in inspiration and populist in spirit, is defined by the mechanisms of exclusion. Like all quests for origin, it expresses moments in time when elites feel themselves threatened. When a culture has lost its means of self-defense, it turns to the ethnologist and the archaeologist (Certeau 1986: 123). Nineteenth- and twentieth-century German and Indian history bear out this maxim. The myths of the Aryan articulate this fear of impotence and present what Certeau in another context has termed a "geography of the eliminated" or "a negative silhouette" formed from the political and symbolic distributions of power. The larger question addressed by the authors we have examined in this volume is central to all critical endeavors: Who should read or interpret texts of authority? Who is the legitimate reader? It is with this fundamental concern that we conclude our discussion of the Aryan myth. Let us take this question even further. Are those "legitimate" readers of the Veda in the nineteenth century so unlike the modern critics? Both claim positional knowledge. Both, laboring notions of voicelessness and absence, can license the neglect of texts that contradict their master narratives. Both claim privilege to speak for the Other. The brahmin custodian of the Veda received his hermeneutical mandate from God. Critics are self-anointed and legitimized by their peers. The nationalist reformer defined the Aryan in order to reassert sociopolitical power and retain traditional lines of control. The critic, impotent through alienation from real political action, compensates by a posture of powerlessness vis à vis representation. Political parallels may well be drawn between extravagant claims in the mythology of the Aryan race and the more sober evocations of colonial discourse analysis. We have seen how the problem of identity finds no clear resolution. Identity, both individual and national, continues to be problematic into the new millennium. What I hope this volume has shown is that games of identity never really change. In fact, the politics of identity determines in many ways the theoretical and critical discourse of the present moment. The refusal to acknowledge operant codes of power limits our ability to recognize the shared culture of oppression that does not end with the colonialists' departure, but lives on in critical categories and methodology.

Aryan warlords still wander the earth. They have abandoned the plains of Kurukshetra to settle in the groves of academe. The brahminization of theory is complete.

Notes

INTRODUCTION

1. In the Brahmanical age, when the chief philosophical schools developed, the use of the Saṃhitās (or hymn portions) were limited to the ritual context. In the medieval period, *bhakti* (or devotional) texts gained prominence. Some of these affirm explicitly that Vedic religion was no longer appropriate to the present degenerate age (Llewellyn 1993: 95).

2. The term "Veda" is often used in a metaphorical sense to refer to the "end of the Veda," namely the Vedānta, most often the Upanishads.

3. The Aryans are often conceived of as having been ruled by a moral ethos that is chronologically much later encapsulated in the *Mānava Dharma Shāstra*, hereafter *The Laws of Manu*.

4. The primary level of textual retrieval necessary is of the original semantic denotations and connotations. The second necessary step involves the restoration of the extralinguistic context, which includes the retrieving of allusions to sociocultural references and an understanding of the literary tradition in which the activity of the writer and the comprehension of his audience took place.

5. A comparatist is not limited to a particular literature or set of literatures as the exclusive source of standards on which to base truth claims. In fact, comparative literature scholars legitimately situate literary works in relation to significant movements of elements in the repertory of any literature (Remak 1960: 20–22). Each literature offers internal traditions of hermeneutic guidance, and the general systems approach recognizes these hermeneutic principles as cultural facts in specific historical flows. The juxtaposition of phenomena in which cultural interferences play a prominent part can be realized without the necessity of presuming the superiority of either the nature or the initially foreign repertorial elements as a basis for formulating truth-claims. Comparative Literature views ideational contents as repertorial facts (Gillespie 1997: 5–6).

6. I do not offer anything close to the orthodox reading that these authors customarily experience from scholars of philosophy, history of religions, Indology, *Germanistik*, or French literature.

7. Similarly, the authors treated in this study are not usually subjected to comparative or literary analysis. A general systems approach justifies what may appear to some readers as rather *insolites* juxtapositions. Some readers may be shocked by the juxtaposition of the Indian nationalist articulation of the Aryan myth with that of Germany. I justify the appearance of individuals whom many Indians today revere as national heroes alongside individuals whom most Europeans revile on the grounds that both groups, by identifying the Aryan, designated a non-Aryan Other and sought to challenge its secular power. The European binary between the Aryan and Semite parallelled the Indian binary that was established between the Aryan and the non-Aryan or Aryan and Dravidian. Both India and Germany have sought authenticity in non-scholarly interpretations of history and prehistory (Hock 1996: 3). In this analysis, I deal with European (colonialist and non-colonialist) as well as Indian authors. The decision to read Orientalists does not make me an accomplice in some "diabolically clever cultural imperialism" (Gillespie 1997: 6). I believe that even Orientalists can exist as agents. Their relationship to India and the knowledge that they derived from the power situation by which they were authorized was produced; it was not the product of their interventions (Clark 1996: 27). Another critical stance bears mentioning, since a central concern of this volume deals with who is conceived as the appropriate reader or, in some cases, who is even allowed to read the texts in question. This author does not ascribe to the belief that critics either through race or gender possess some "intuitive or existential positional knowledge" (Clark 1996: 31). If such were the case, this reader could not/should not read Indian pundits or nineteenth-century German males.

8. Others championed the fundamental unity of ancient Aryan culture in India and beyond. In 1936, the Mahasabhā proclaimed that non-Hindus must be made to understand that Hinduism is primarily for the Hindus and that the Hindus live for the preservation and development of the Aryan culture and the Hindu *dharma*, which are bound to prove beneficial for all. This trajectory has enabled the Aryan past to be presently used to legitimate Hindu communal ideology. The fluidity of Hinduism has allowed thinkers to draw on a supposed religious identity and use it as a basis of ideology. In Savarkar's terms, one becomes Aryan (Savarkar 1923: 38–39). The constructed identity of the Aryan seeks to neutralize diversity. If conformity can be achieved, this identity can be used for political ends, specifically domination over other groups through an emphasis on racial or religious superiority.

PART I. THE AUTHORITY OF THE ABSENT TEXT

1. THE ENLIGHTENMENT AND ORIENTALIST
DISCOURSE ON THE ARYAN

1. The *Bedang* (Vedānta) was accompanied by two other "authentic" texts, the *Dirm Shaster* (*Dharmashāstra*) and the *Neadirzen Shaster de Goutam* (*Nyāyashāstra of Gautama*).

2. Elsewhere Voltaire dates it as exactly 4,866 years old (Voltaire 1885: 26.325).

3. According to Voltaire, Plato wrote two thousand years after the Indian author of the *Shasta* (Voltaire 1885: 29.479, 481).

4. Sir Alexander Johnston (1775–1849) found a copy of the *Ezour Vedam* in Pondicherry along with other manuscripts similar in format. Guided by Johnston's discovery, Francis Whyte Ellis wrote an important analysis of this trove in an article entitled "Account of a Discovery of a Modern Imitation of the Vedas with Remarks on the Genuine Works," *Asiatick Researches* 14 (1822): 1–59). Ellis identified these manuscripts as imitations (written in Sanskrit with Roman characters and in French) of the three other "Vedas" and concluded that the *Ezour Vedam* was authored by the Italian Jesuit Roberto de Nobili. Ellis did not charge de Nobili as the perpetrator of the forgery; he attributed that act to another who must have edited, transcribed, and translated the Sanskrit text into French. Ellis agrees with Sonnerat's contention that the *Ezour Vedam* was written for converting idolators.

Ellis had made several significant comments concerning the style of the *Ezour Vedam*. He noted that the French was loose, defective, and not at all stylistically consistent with what he learned about the Vedas from Colebrooke's article on the style and contents of the Vedas that appeared in the *Asiatick Researches* (Colebrooke 1805: 369–476). Ellis judged its style to be rather *purāṇic* or similar to the dialogue of the *Bhagavad Gītā*, texts with which the Jesuits were familiar. Most importantly, Ellis noted the existence of marginal notes that did not correspond to the text in the original or in the translation. This seemingly minor point, disregarded in all subsequent discussions on the *Ezour Vedam*, proves pivotal to Ludo Rocher's monograph, which, to my mind, lays to rest the mystery surrounding the *Ezour Vedam* fraud.

Rocher examines the manner in which the manuscript came to Europe, possibilities as to its authorship, and the reason for which it was composed. Rocher rejects de Nobili as the author of the work (Rocher 1983: 30–42). Since the *Ezour Vedam* was written entirely in French without the facing Sanskrit translation found in the other Pondicherry manuscripts, Rocher concludes that the French text constitutes the original. Due to certain idiomatic French expressions, concepts which were totally European in nature, the consistent lack of orthographic unity, and transliterations typical to the French language, Rocher speculates that its author was a Frenchman who had learned Sanskrit from various people in different regions of India.

5. The *Shaster Bedang* was, according to Voltaire's chronology, 1,500 years younger than the *Ezour Vedam*.

6. The allusion here is to the *Ezour Vedam* version of Hindu creation myths involving the birth of Adimo and Prokriti that are related in the course of a debate between Biache, a proponent of idolatry, and Chumontou, who combats *purāṇic* polytheism with the monotheism of the Vedas.

7. Sonnerat (*Voyage aux Indes orientales* 1782: 1.7) and Paulinus a Sancto Bartolomeo (*Systema Brachmanicum* 1791: 315–17) had attacked its authenticity.

8. The *Ezour Vedam* identified the four Vedas with the following nomenclature: the Rik, Chama, Zozur, and Adorbo, Adarvan or Obartah-Bah, each with a supplement (*oupa bedam*) and summary (*sanitah-vedam*).

9. Sainte Croix claimed that Vedic fragments were also extant in the Purāṇas and that these communicated the substance of the Veda better than the "tiring and nauseating extravagances" of the *Ezour Vedam* (Sainte Croix 1778: 126).

10. Its original title (*Zozur Bedo*) was not included as one of the original Vedas identified by Ellis. In his article, Ellis identified the third manuscript of the Pondicherry corpus as the *Yajur Veda*, precluding any possibility that the *Ezour Vedam* was a misnomer for the *Yajur Veda*.

11. In Sanskrit, rules determining the changes that vowels and consonants undergo in certain combinations.

12. Even Diderot (under the rubric "*vedam*") joined in such brahmin-bashing, when he asserted that the Fourth Veda had been lost for a long time, to the regret of brahmins who would have gained tremendous power, had it still existed. Diderot further noted that the Vedas were held in such great respect by brahmins that they did not wish to share copies of them with anyone, especially the Jesuits who had made great efforts to obtain them.

13. For India as the site of the Garden of Eden, see Voltaire (1885: 13. 432–33).

14. Colebrooke cites others in the West who doubted their existence or pronounced the Vedas to be forgeries (Colebrooke 1805: 479).

15. The Veda was revealed by Brahma and compiled by Vyasa. It was divided in four parts: the Rich, Yajush, Saman, and the Atharvana (Colebrooke 1805: 429–30). Colebrooke noted that *itihāsa* and the Purāṇas comprise a fifth Veda.

16. Colebrooke used fragments from Uvata's gloss and the commentaries of Sāyaṇa, Mahādhara, and Gauḍapāda.

17. Colebrooke claimed that a more manageable rendition of Aryan theology (Colebrooke 1805: 473) could be found in the Upanishads, mantra portions of the Brāhmaṇas (Colebrooke 1805: 388), or supplements of the Veda (Colebrooke 1805: 441).

18. In addition to Rosen's *Rigvedae Specimen* (1838), a Latin translation of the first *aṣṭaka* of the *Rig Veda* that put 121 hymns at the disposal of future scholars, other translations of Vedic excerpts appeared roughly simultaneously with Müller's edition: the Stevenson edition of the *Sāma Veda* was brought to press by Wilson in 1843; Roth's *Contributions to the History and Literature of the Veda* (1846); Weber's *Vajasaneyi-Sanhitae Specimen* (1848), followed by the beginning of an edition of the White Yajur text (1852), its brāhmaṇa (1855), and sūtras (1859); Benfey's *Sāma Veda* text with a translation and glossary (1848); Whitney's and Roth's *Atharva Veda* (1856). The competition was fierce. When Whitney (1987: 1.3) noted in *Oriental and Linguistic Studies* the various translations and editions of the Vedas, he relegated Müller's edition of the *Rig Veda* to a footnote and totally omitted Müller's name from the citation.

2. THE ROMANTIC ARYANS

1. His terms for Aryan were *Arier* and *Indo-Germanen* (Müller 1895: 1.65).

2. They traveled along two possible paths, through Russia to the shores of the Black Sea and Thrace, and from Armenia across the Caucasus or across the Black Sea to northern Greece and along the Danube (Müller 1899: 298).

3. He placed considerable emphasis on the "childish"; it was alternately "childish and absurd" (Müller 1909: 282) or "childish and foolish" (Müller 1895: 1.37).

4. "The only real Veda is the *Rig Veda*. The other so-called Vedas which deserve the name of Veda no more than the Talmud deserves the name of Bible, contain chiefly extracts from the *Rig Veda* together with sacrificial formulas, charms and incantations" (Müller 1895: 1.8).

5. The Brāhmaṇas, for example, consist of "twaddle, and what is worse, theological twaddle" (Müller 1895: 1.113). "They deserve to be studied as a physician studies the twaddle of idiots and the ravings of mad men" (Müller 1978: 389; see also 1895: 1.85–89; 1.67).

6. "The Hindu mind, however, was like the lotus leaf after a shower of rain has passed over it; his character remained the same—passive, meditative, quiet and thoughtful. A people of this peculiar stamp was never destined to act out a prominent part in the history of the world . . . it is with the Hindu mind as if a seed were placed in a hot-house. It will grow rapidly, its colors will be gorgeous, its perfume rich, its fruits precocious and abundant. But never will it be like the oak growing in wind and weather, and striking its roots into real earth, and stretching its branches into real air beneath the stars and the sun of heaven" (Müller 1895: 1.65).

7. In Henotheism, each god is as good as another: they are not ranked hierarchically (Müller 1895: 1.28, see also 1891: 180; 1879: 251).

8. See also Müller 1892: 112: "I maintain that to everybody who cares for himself, for his ancestors, for his history, or for his intellectual development, a study of Vedic literature is indispensible; and that, as an element of liberal education, it is far more important and far more improving than the reigns of Babylonian and Persian kings, yea even, than the dates and deeds of many of the kings of Judah and Israel."

9. The fact that we cannot explain how so many dialects could be traced back to Hebrew (although many have tried) suggested to Müller that the problem had been misformulated (Müller 1899: 147).

10. After qualifying his position as longstanding, Müller offers Risley his advice: "If you were to issue an interdict against any of your collaborateurs using linguistic terms in an ethnological sense, I believe that your Ethnological Survey of India would inaugurate a new and most important era both in the science of language and in the science of man" (Müller 1888: 247).

3. NIETZSCHE'S ARYAN *ÜBERMENSCH*

1. In particular, see Conway 1997; Santaniello 1997; Santaniello 1994; Parkes 1991; Mistry 1981; Stambaugh 1972; Rollman 1978; von Glasenapp 1960; Alsdorf 1944.

2. On the title page to *Daybreak*, he purportedly cites the *Rig Veda*: "There are so many days that have not yet broken" ["Es giebt so viele Morgenröthen die noch nicht geleuchtet haben"] (Nietzsche 1986: 9.413). As Sprung has noted (Parkes 1991: 78–79), Nietzsche here freely adapted this quote from a Vedic passage (*Rig Veda* 7.76) that both German and English translations of the time read in a contrary sense. Both Griffith and Geldner translate the passage as: "There are so many dawns that have already dawned."

3. Sprung maintains that the connection between Nietzsche and India rests to a great degree on the philosopher's long-standing friendship with Paul Deussen, the prominent nineteenth-century Vedānta scholar. But, this critic's analysis of Nietzsche's library and correspondence, and that of his friends suggests that Nietzsche did not read much regarding Indian philosophy and did not discuss it at all with his acquaintances.

4. German Sanskrit dictionaries of the time (Böhtlingk, Cappeller) define *ārya* in concordance with the standard English dictionaries. It is, indeed, ironic that a philologist of Nietzsche's caliber should base his understanding of the Aryan on a faulty definition.

5. For the codification of Nietzsche by the Nazis, see the work of Alfred Bäumler (*Nietzsche der Philosophe*, 1931); Heinrich Römer ("Nietzsche und das Rasseproblem," 1940, 61): and Richard Oehler (*Nietzsche und die deutschen Zukunft*, 1935).

6. It is not the place here to categorize the Nietzsche-Nazi relationship or demonstrate the transmission of influence and causal relationships or assess their overall historical significance.

7. I am thinking primarily of Milan Kundera's remarks in *Testaments Betrayed* (Kundera 1996: 150), but the same can be said of a number of poststructuralist readings.

8. In this regard, Richard Schacht has written: "They [rhetorical excesses] blemish and mar its surface; but one must school oneself to look past them, filtering them out as so much unfortunate static" (Schacht 1983: xv).

9. Translations that were available for Nietzsche's use include: Sir William Jones, *Institutes of Hindu Law: or the Ordinances of Meno, according to the gloss of Cullúca* (1776); J.C. Hüttner's translation of Jones's translation entitled *Hindu-Gesetzbuch oder Manu's Verordnungen nach Cullucas Erläuterungen* (1797); the French translation of Auguste Loiseleur Deslongchamps, *Manava Dharma Śāstra* (1833); and George Bühler, *The Laws of Manu, Sacred Books of the East*, vol. 25 (1886).

10. A copy of Jacolliot's book was listed in the inventory of Nietzsche's Weimar library (Etter 1987: 345).

11. *Manu* is believed to date between the first century B.C. and the first century A.D.

12. There are four aims of Hindu life: *dharma* (duty), *artha* (worldly gain), *kāma* (erotic love) and *moksha* (liberation).

13. Some historians have claimed that before British colonial rule, *Manu* had been used by jurists (Manu 1992: ix).

14. See letter to Peter Gast of May 31, 1888.

15. In the next sentence, Nietzsche claimed that no one epitomized his point as much as the Jews, who exacted satisfaction on their enemies through the radical and vengeful transvaluation of their values.

16. The German translation of the term that Nietzsche uses is *Tschandala*.

17. The term *caṇḍāla* denotes "outcaste," "man of the lowest stratum of society," "extremely despised and shunned," "a mixed caste born of a brahmin mother and a *shūdra* father" (Monier Williams 1990: 383).

18. Elsewhere, I have discussed the symbolic use of the outcaste in European thought and artistic representation and have touched upon the importance of this metaphor in Nietzsche's writing (Figueira 1994: 29–45).

19. It is important to note that Nietzsche's references to the *caṇḍāla* are not found in *Manu*, but were inventions of Jacolliot.

20. Nietzsche, *Will to Power* 854: "In the age of universal suffrage (i.e., when everyone may sit in judgment of everyone and everything), I feel impelled to reestablish order of rank." Nietzsche, *Genealogy of Morals*, sec. 2; *Beyond Good and Evil*, sec. 257.

21. The order of rank provides "that tremendous energy of greatness in order to shape the man of the future through breeding" (*Will to Power* 964).

22. In contrast, the Jews had an order of rank that allowed them to avoid decadence even after they had become enslaved (*Will to Power* 427).

23. Without a firmly established order of rank, spiritual strength is worthless (*Will to Power* 53).

24. *Will to Power* 398: "What I want to make clear by all the means in my power: a. that there is no worse confusion than the confusion of breeding with taming; which is what has been done—Breeding, as I understand it, is a means of storing up the tremendous forces of mankind so that the generations can build upon the work of their forefathers—not only outwardly, but inwardly, organically growing out of them and becoming something stronger."

25. Nietzsche seems to use the term "race" interchangably with "caste." Therefore, the "races" to which Nietzsche refers consist of the brahmins (priests), *kṣatriyas* (warriors), *vaishyas* (merchants), and *shūdras* (outcastes).

26. This notion was an invention of Jacolliot, who traced the Jews' subject status as *caṇḍālas* to their Chaldean past.

27. Nietzsche claimed that the Chinese also seemed to have learned much from *Manu*, as seen in the teachings of Confucius and Laotse.

28. As a *caṇḍāla* religion, Judaism early on lost two of their castes, the warriors and the peasant (*Will to Power* 184).

29. A case can be made for Nietzsche's "splendid blond beast" not being a German. This term occurs five times (three times in the first section of the *Genealogy of Morals*, one time in the second section, and one time in the *Twilight of the Idols*). With the first reference in the *Genealogy*, Nietzsche states that the beast is at the bottom of all noble races including the Romans, Homeric Greeks, Arabs, Japanese and Vikings (*Genealogy of Morals*, pt. 1, sec. 2). When reference is made to Teutons, they are Teutons of old, distinct from Germans of today (Santaniello 1994: 106). Kaufmann conjectured that Nietzsche might have meant by the term, "the noble lion" (Kaufmann 1974: 225). However, since Nietzsche discussed the blondness of the ancient Aryans a few pages before his first reference to the blond beast (*Genealogy of Morals*, pt. 1, sec. 2, cited in Detweiler 1990: 110), it is safe to assume that this pregnant symbol represented the values that Nietzsche read into the ancient Aryan (via *Manu*), projected onto the presumed descendants (the brahmin caste) and envisioned for the *Übermensch*. We should remember that in the *Genealogy of Morals* (I.5) he refers to the Aryans as blond.

30. Nietzsche, *Beyond Good and Evil* 251.

31. For a discussion of Nietzsche's categorizing of different groups of Jews, see Santaniello 1994; Santaniello 1997: 31; Gilman 1997: 76.

32. In a letter to Köselitz (cited in Cancik 1997: 64), Nietzsche claimed that even Jewish laws were derived from the Aryan law as codified in *Manu*.

33. Nietzsche, *Will to Power* 164, 954; *Beyond Good and Evil* 251.

34. For a discussion of Nietzsche's admiration for Indian asceticism, see Hulin's essay in Parkes 1991: 69–70.

35. *Antichrist* 57: "Gentle, frugal, self effacing, he voluntarily lets the *shūdra* wallow in vulgar pleasures, the *vaishya* parade his opulence, and the *kṣatriya* strut upon the political stage while his preoccupation is getting others to affirm cosmic order."

36. Nietzsche drew no distinctions between brahmin behavior codified in *Manu* and the present-day brahmin. Both embodied those values that Nietzsche sought in the higher aristocracy he envisioned for the future (*Will to Power* 752, 866).

37. Nietzsche use the term *caṇḍāla* (translated as "chandala") frequently, a more exotic equivalent for another favorite term, *canaille*. He defined *caṇḍāla*s as *mischmasch-Menschen* or *Nicht-Zucht Menschen*. *Caṇḍāla*s are not to be confused with *shūdra*s, whom Nietzsche defined as a service race, a lower kind of people whom the Aryans discovered in situ when they landed in India. For Nietzsche, the *caṇḍāla* represents the degenerated of all castes, permanent phlegm (*Auswurfstoffe*) (Nietzsche 1986: 13.396–97).

38. Kaufmann supports Nietzsche's supposed rejection of *Manu* with the following quote from the *Twilight of the Idols* 4: "These regularities are instructive enough: in them we find for once Aryan humanity, quite pure, quite primordial—we learn that the concept "pure blood" is the opposite of a harmless concept. It becomes clear, on the other hand, in which people the hatred, the Chandala hatred for this "humanity" has become immortalized, where it has become religious, where it has become genius."

39. I would assume Kaufmann is referring to *The Republic* 5.459, where Plato has Socrates note:

It follows from what we have just said that, if we are to keep our flock at the highest pitch of excellence, there should be as many unions of the best of both sexes, and as few of the inferior, as possible, and that only the offspring of the better unions should be kept. And again, no one but the Rulers must know how all this is being effected; otherwise our herd of Guardians may become rebellious.

Attributing Nietzsche's discussions on race and breeding to Greek sources continues in recent scholarship (Cancik 1997: 65, 67; Conway 1997: 35).

40. Golomb (1997:40) claims that Nietzsche was also well acquainted with Gobineau's work. However, he offers no references to substantiate this claim. Whether Nietzsche was directly influenced by the Frenchman or Gobineau's citations of *Manu* further popularized the lawgiver whom Nietzsche had read and, thus, stimulated independent reflections is a matter open to discussion.

41. Kaufmann claimed that Nietzsche only considered using the terms *Zucht* and *Züchtung* once as the title of the fourth and last part of *The Will to Power*. Förster-Nietzsche later chose this draft when she edited this volume because they fit her and Förster's interests (Kaufmann 1968: 304). According to Kaufmann, Nietzsche abandoned the title "Zucht und Züchtung" as soon as he had written it down. It was his sister who chose to perpetuate it (Kaufmann 1968: 306). Kaufmann claimed that Nietzsche's strong concern with breeding derived from Plato (Kaufmann 1968: 305).

4. LOOSE CAN[N]ONS

1. See in this regard, Alexander von Humboldt (1849).

2. The effort to make the Aryans our primeval neighbors reached its acme in the work of Hans F.K. Günther, who from the early 1930s onward, developed elaborate proofs that Germany was the seat of Aryan origins. Günther (1891–1968), a social anthropologist and spokesman of Nazi race ideology, was Professor of Racial Science at Jena. A prolific author whose work portrayed the Nordic as an ideal racial type in contrast to the Jew, who was a product of racial mixing and responsible for the disintegrating movements such as democracy and liberalism. Although influenced by Gobineau, Günther heralded the age when the Nordic will will halt bastardization

and eugenically purge the ranks of disintegrative elements. Up to his death in Freiburg in 1968, Günther was still publishing toned-down variations of his racial theories.

3. Even Nietzsche, who reviled Treitschke, shared the historian's view of history as a battle between two races for mastery. He disagreed only with Treitschke's portrayal of modern types as exemplars of true noble characters. Instead, Nietzsche posited the ancient Aryan as the alternative model for future nobility.

4. Gobineau's *Essai sur l'inégalité des races humaines* received a cold reception in France when published. The author's friend De Tocqueville opposed its thesis regarding the inevitable decadence of race. Renan refused to review it for the *Revue des Deux Mondes*.

5. Among the female nations, he classified the Egyptians, the Assyrians, and the Hindus. Among the male, he designated the Chinese, primitive Romans, and Germans.

6. In Gobineau's dedication to the king of Hanover, he spoke of the Vedas wherein events described are "bien proches du lendemain de la création" (Gobineau 1983: 136).

7. Gobineau's *Histoire des Perses*, written a few years after the *Essai*, traced the rise and decay of the Iranian Aryans.

8. In the *Essai* and the *Histoire des Perses*, Gobineau wisely did not focus much on the anthropological characteristics of the Germanic type when he described the Aryans. Nor did the German type figure prominently among his fictional visions of Aryans as heroes (*L'Abbaye de Typhaines, Nouvelles asiatiques*). Harriett and Amado in the *Pleiades* provide the ideal type of German, all brunettes and black-eyed, like Gobineau. However, the physical takes a backseat to the moral and ethnic side. Gobineau's Aryans did not achieve the racial ideal he had established. They tended to look like him, a strategy that Nazi leaders should have emulated.

9. As understood by Théodore Pavie in *L'Inde ancienne et moderne*.

10. The first theory was supplied to him by Lassen (1847–61: 1.391).

11. Gobineau (1983: 500) cites *Manu*, paragraphs 88, 90.

12. Gobineau (1983: 504) reads *Manu* in light of Lassen (1847–61: 1.817), who consistently downplays the lawgiver's harsh injunctions. Lassen reads a kinder, gentler *Manu* that forbids mistreatment of *shūdras* and speaks of their gentle tutelage and protection from famine and misery at the hands of the high castes.

13. The term *boue* appears throughout Gobineau's works; see *Amadis*, bk. 3, chap. 3.

14. See for example Gustav Klemm's *Allgemeine Kulturgeschichte der Menschheit* (1843–52) that explained history of the breeding of active and passive races.

15. Buddha was for Chamberlain the antithesis to Christ. He represented the senile decay of a culture which had reached the limits of its possibilities, where everything

was directed to thought, where a religious symbolism had gone amok, and where philosophy resulted in the deep silence of the primeval forest (Chamberlain 1968: 1.184–85).

16. Although the concept of the "Aryan" had become an ever more dispensible idea for anthropologists, ethnographers, historians, theologians, philologists, and legal authorities, many denied that the the Aryan race had ever existed (Chamberlain 1968: 1.266). Nevertheless, those who dared to still speak of it used it as a working hypothesis.

17. When Chamberlain used the term "Aryan," he took it in what he thought to be its original Sanskrit sense, "belonging to the friends." In other words, he took its meaning to signify homogeneity (Chamberlain 1968: 1.265).

18. Chamberlain 1968: 2.206.

19. Chamberlain cites the case of the Jews, as an example of this organic potential, since they developed along a path different from that of other Semitic groups (Chamberlain 1968: 1.262–63).

20. See also Chamberlain 1968: 1.18, 258–61, 343, 544–46, 561–63, 588, 590, 596–601.

21. As in the case of Gobineau, Chamberlain cites Lassen (1847–61: 414–16) in support of his thesis.

22. In Chamberlain as well as in Rosenberg, Eckhart's mysticism is associated with that of the great Aryan philosophers. In the *Foundations* (Chamberlain 1968: 2.411), Chamberlain wrote: "Scarcely a hair's breadth separates our great Teutonic mystics from their Aryan predecessors."

23. Chamberlain did not, however, reject the Old Testament outright. He felt that some Protestant scholars of his time had made it possible to sift out the Indo-Aryan myths that had been engulfed by Semitic concepts.

24. I have not included in this number those who were tried in absentia, received lesser sentences of imprisonment, or were acquited.

25. Outside the scope of this study is the role played by popular Eastern European anti-Semitism. Rosenberg was greatly influenced by a stint in Russia and his experiences in Munich, a haven for anti-Semitic White Russians who had escaped the Bolshevik Revolution. His rabid anti-Semitism found expression in such works as *Die Spur der Juden im Wandel der Zeiten* and *Pest in Russland.*

26. The *Mythus*, second only to *Mein Kampf* as a Nazi bestseller, was acknowledged by Hitler as an unreadable text.

27. According to Rosenberg, the Aryans, like their German descendants, were white, blond, and blue-eyed.

28. Rosenberg also blamed Buddhism's passivity and call to alleviate suffering for the deteriorization of Aryan values.

29. It was the same individuality that had been present in Homer's heroes and Tacitus's Germans (Rosenberg 1937: 71).

30. Hitler left it to Rosenberg to launch the attack on Catholicism. Rosenberg hated the "black, international" Roman Catholic Church as much as he hated Judaism. It had corrupted the Germans from the start.

31. Rosenberg defines this period as the time when the *Ātman/Brahman* teaching had moved them away from the importance of action (Rosenberg 1937: 229–30).

32. F.L. Jahn's gymnastic societies had the object of building up a strong race and surmounting class barriers.

33. Nietzsche's antinationalism and his preference for the Asiatic Dionysus over the Hellenic Apollo were consistently deemphasized. It should be noted that when Rosenberg composed the *Mythus*, Nietzsche had already been successfully "packaged" by Elisabeth Förster-Nietzsche and the Nietzsche Archive for consumption by the fledgling movement.

34. Gobineau's reception in Germany dates from 1894 with the dissemination of his work by Ludwig Schemann and the Gobineau Society. Gobineau was also popularized by the Richard Wagner Circle and the Pan-German League.

35. However, Gobineau's conclusions regarding the inevitability of racial bastardizaion, while acknowledged by Rosenberg (Rosenberg 1937: 115), were singularly ignored by National Socialism.

36. This theory would animate German anthropology and Nazi eugenics.

PART II. WHO SPEAKS FOR THE SUBALTERN?

5. RAMMOHAN ROY

1. Other late eighteenth- and early nineteenth-century sects openly abjured polytheism and idol worship, and renounced caste such as the Karta Bhajas, Spashtadayakas, Bālarāmis, Sahebdhanis, Khusi Viśvasis, and Rāmvallabhis. Their leaders were non-Brahmins and did not cash in on the prestige of an original faith.

2. Just as their low-caste origin places them outside the colonial power struggle, so too, perhaps, does this lack of status place them at one remove or "translated into" postcolonial criticism. One wonders whether the moniker "subaltern" points more often to the self-conscious self-definition of the critic than to the objects of inquiry.

3. The widow is nowhere seen as subject (Mani 1988: 97). Official discourse forecloses any possibility of women's agency (Mani 1988: 98). "It is difficult to know how to interpret these accounts, for we have no independent access to the mental or subjective status of widows outside of these overdetermined colonial representations of them" (Mani 1988: 97). "Superslave or superhuman, women in this discourse remain

eternal victims" (Ibid.). Now this is patently not true. The research of Anne B. Waters in the Pune Daftar shows that there are countless instances where the women "find a voice" and challenge both the strictures of Peshwa society and interact with colonial administrators (dissertation, University of Michigan 1997). The victim/oppressor binary is not a universally applicable construct.

4. The Raja did not develop any clear-cut program of reform, except perhaps his anti-*satī* agitation, before he departed for England in 1831, where he died two years later. His organization was later transformed by Dwarkanath Tagore and Keshab Chandra Sen, undergoing several subsequent incarnations.

5. This attempt at unity of cult through diversity did not ultimately succeed and, as Kopf (1969: 202) has noted, brought about its eventual schism. Keshub Sen and Dwarkanath Tagore represented this polarization. The Sabhā was virtually moribund until Dwarkanath Tagore resuscitated it as the Ādi Brāhmo Samāj.

6. Kopf correctly problematizes the extent to which the Raja borrowed contextually and methodologically from both the British Orientalists and other Bengalis. He has shown that Roy's arguments were also derivative of the polemic of the missionaries themselves. An early tract of the Serampore Mission, the *Jñānoday* (*The Dawn of Knowledge*) by Ramram Basu, attacked the twin evils of moral laxity and idolatry. Basu described the Vedic Brahmā with attributes which are common to Jehovah. Kopf suggests that it was Ramram Basu and not Roy who was the inventor of monotheism in Hinduism and that the Raja was his successor (Kopf 1969: 125).

7. In the introduction to a recent translation, Doniger and Smith claim that *Manu* did not deserve the priority status that the British accorded it; a number of other *dharmashāstras* as well as *Manu*'s own commentaries debate almost every point that *Manu* makes. There were other contending voices within and without Hinduism (Manu 1992: vi).

8. The cornerstone of Rammohan's reformation movement was the idea of a theistic Brahmo (Kopf 1969: 198).

9. The sole regulator of the universe is one (Roy 1906: 63). Vedas, Purāṇas, Tantras, and so forth reveal a single attributeless godhead, and the worship of figured beings is applicable to those who are incapable of elevating the mind to the idea of an invisible supreme being. Moreover "those passages referring to a multiplicity of gods are to be taken in a figurative sense" (Roy 1906: 64–65). The individual believer chooses the form of worship which best suits his capacities.

10. "[T]hose texts which seem to command the worship persons or things are only directed to those who are incapable of adoring the invisible supreme being" (Roy 1906: 13). Roy championed individual responsibility in matters religious. He also advocated equal rights. The householder's right to worship god is as legitimate as that of the *yati* (Roy 1906: 65).

11. Thus Roy's interpretation of "Vedic" texts centers on their purported ethical concerns. He made a concerted effort to show how faith in the Supreme Being can only lead to eternal happiness when it is united with moral works. Whereas action entails

moral merit for the Christian, for the Hindu, religious rites and ceremonies are "often irreconcilable with the commonly received maxims of moral duty" (Roy 1906: 106). Good works are not an indispensable accompaniment to holy knowledge in the Hindu context. Rammohan Roy highlighted and allowed how ethics is often ignored in the texts in question. He stopped short of imposing ethical values on them directly or overtly reading such values into them.

12. The Sanskrit is as follows:
asuryā nāma te lokā tamasāvrtāḥ
tām ste pretyabhigacchanti ye ke cātmahano janāḥ

13. Roy 1906: 120: "It is, however remarkable that, although the learned Brahmin and his Brethern frequently quote the name of the Vedas and other shāstras, both in writing and in verbal discussion, they pay little or no attention in practice to their precepts."

14. Fifty years later, Max Müller would also stress the importance of liberating the text. He noted that Westerners could hardly grasp the idea of the brahmins' absolute power as the only repository of the Vedas.

15. Elsewhere, he questioned the need for separate paths, noting that virtually all were as capable of worshipping God in the same manner as the renunciant. He thus challenged the need for grosser forms of worship and upheld human equality before God (Roy 1906: 15).

16. See Chris Bongie, *Islands and Exile*; Christopher Miller, *Nationalists and Nomads*; and Susanne Zantop, *Colonial Fantasies*, to name a recent few examples.

6. TEXT-BASED IDENTITY: DAYĀNAND SARASWATĪ'S RECONSTRUCTION OF THE ARYAN SELF

1. The sixth *niyam* calls for doing good in the world as the chief goal of society. The ninth *niyam* calls for attention to be paid to the wider world. The tenth *niyam* stipulates that all people should be bound in maintaining social principles which affect the welfare of the community and that everyone should be free in these principles that affect the welfare of the individual.

2. It may be remembered that in his own writings, Rammohan Roy made little reference to caste and that the schism of 1866 within the Brāhmo Samāj centered on this very issue of caste. The older group under D. Tagore took the name Ādi Brāhmo Samāj, "First" Brāhmo Samāj. The subsequent new organization, the Brāhmo Samāj of India under Keshab Chandra Sen, completely disavowed caste.

3. He introduced the innovation of *shuddhi* (purification and readmission of Hindus to the fold). *Shuddhi* served as a response to present fears that Islam and Christianity aggressively proselytized by conversion (K. Jones 1976: 276). It was a method that

had proved successful to foreigners in the past and could be appropriated by Dayānand to combat present foreign domination.

4. This eclecticism was carried to the extreme by the Ādi Brāhmos under the leadership of Keshab Chandra Sen.

5. In this sense, Dayānand was not unique in his thinking. Jordens claims that he got the notion that an understanding of pure Hinduism was to be found in ancient sources from his guru Virjananda. Dayānand's guru, however, had never defined which sources these might include. Dayānand, therefore, studied the Tantras, Purāṇas, *Mahābhārata*, the Upanishads, *Manu*, and the Brāhmaṇas, gradually eliminating all except the four saṃhitās (Jordens 1978: 278).

6. The *Bhūmikā* is a four-hundred-page commentary written around themes such as the origin and nature of the Vedas, their science and technology, mathematics, astrology, telegraphy, and medicine. Written in the customary form for Sanskrit commentaries, it presents the grammatical analysis of the terms followed by the *padārtha* that explains the components for meaning and function in a sentence. Finally, there is the *bhāvārtha*, a sentence giving the meaning of the text, whether it is an injunction, statement of principle, or comparison. The *padārtha* and *bhāvārtha* are in Sanskrit with Hindi translations.

7. In the first edition of the *Satyārth Prakāsh*, Dayānand followed the traditional view of Hindu orthodoxy in precluding the *shūdras* from access to the Vedas. In the second edition, all Hindus were allowed this access.

8. Dayānand's commentary of the *Rig Veda* (*Rgvedādibhāshyabhūmikā* or *Introduction to the Commentary of the Rig Veda and other Vedas*) was completed up to 7.4.60. He also completed a commentary of the *Yajur Veda* in four volumes.

9. In Sanskrit, literally "the meanings of the scriptures." In the course of his public career of two decades, Dayānand participated in at least thirty-nine disputations.

10. For a complete discussion of the book disputations, see Llewellyn 1993.

11. Although Dayānand did not share Rammohan Roy's admiration for Christian social values, he did rely on one important Christian tenet: the sanctity of the book. To a much greater extent than the Brāhmo Samāj, the Ārya Samāj endowed the physical manifestation of the word of God with as much significance as Christianity endowed the Bible. He fully accepted the premise that God revealed himself in a book (Jordens 1978: 273).

12. After the initial free-for-all debates with brahmins, Dayānand demanded more formalized structures, with official transcripts signed by the participants and a preliminary list of authoritative books to be considered. J.T.F. Jordens has suggested that for Dayānand, the canon became narrower with time. The public lecture later became his major means of propaganda (Jordens 1978: 95); most dealt with subjects such as creation, the nature of God, the Vedas and India in Vedic times.

13. It is to be remembered that Max Müller limited his Veda to the mantra portions of the *Ṛg Veda Saṃhitā* alone. Unlike Dayānand, he disregarded the saṃhitās of the other three Vedas.

14. It is important to note that Dayānand's definition of the Vedic canon differed from that of traditional Indian usage, where the Veda is comprised of a vast body of texts including Brāhmaṇas, Āraṇyakas, Upanishads, and other literature related to the application of hymns in ritual, texts such as the Gṛhya, Kalpa, Śrauta, and Dharma Sūtras (Llewellyn 1993: 162). As Llewellyn has noted, limiting the Vedic canon to include only the saṃhitās was a radical move on Dayānand's part since, compared to the Upanishads, they historically were subject to little philosophical inquiry. In recent centuries, the Upanishads, considered to contain the best and most exalted of Vedic teaching, had been read to the exclusion of other Vedic literature (Llewellyn 1993: 179). The saṃhitās were not read closely and were distrusted as part of an outmoded ritual system (Llewellyn 1993: 230–31).

15. The Mahābhārata War was the key event of Aryan decline. Dayānand maintained that after the war the Jains took advantage of Aryan disarray to propagate their own religion by building temples and encouraging idol worship. Shaṅkarāchārya had tried to defeat the process of decline by reviving Vedic wisdom, as did Vikramāditya and Bhoja. All these attempts failed. Further damage was wrought when Muslims destroyed the country and persecuted Hindus.

16. The Advaitic influence present in the first edition is tempered in the second edition (Jordens 1978: 25).

17. Llewellyn further notes that when he did use a Vedic text to support some reading, it was often from the *Yajur Veda* and, unlike his use of *ārsha* texts, he did not apply to it a customary interpretation.

18. For data, I rely on Llewellyn's statistical analysis: Of the 342 mantras quoted in the *Ṛgvedādibhāṣya*, 91 are not commented upon, 179 are commented upon without any citation from a secondary source, and a mere 72 are commented upon with the help of some authority.

19. Llewellyn, upon examining how these texts offer a range of hermenuetic options, found that the *ārsha* books cited with the most frequency in the *Satyārth Prakāsh* include the *Śatapatha Brāhmaṇa*, the *Nighaṇṭu*, and the *Aṣṭadhyāyi*. The *Ṛgvedādibhāṣya* makes ample use of the *Yoga Sūtra* and the *Aṣṭadhyāyi*.

20. He demonstrated knowledge of telegraphy by translating *tarataram* (derived from *tṛ* meaning "to cross") as "it crosses inaccessible places and takes the message easily or it has its expansion everywhere." He then rendered it: "you make the instrument named telegraph." Dayānand interpreted the Rig Vedic (1.2.7) invocation to Mitra and Varuna as signifying that the Aryans knew that water is generated by the combination of hydrogen and oxygen.

21. Dayānand supported his condemnation of idol worship, for example, by citing the *Yajur Veda* (40–48). A literal reading of this passage makes no allusion to idol worship.

22. Dayānand ascribed ten separate meanings to the term *deva*: "play, desire to conquer, general activity, glory, praise, delight, rapture, sleep, beauty, and progressiveness."

23. In the context of ritualism (*karmakāṇḍa*), *devatā* refers to a Vedic mantra in that function of expounding the various "methods of performing a ritual act."

24. Dayānand did not view the Veda as books in the sense that the Bible and the Qur'an are books (Dayānand 1915: 237). While the Vedas are eternal, the books called "Veda" are not; merely the words and ideas are eternal. The four Vedas were handed down by God to four rishis (Dayānand 1915: 236). However, this is not the form by which humanity experiences them. They were initially revealed to other peoples (Dayānand 1915: 272). They were disseminated in Sanskrit for the purpose of impartiality, so as not to favor any particular group. For, as Dayānand held, Sanskrit is a language which belongs to no country and is the mother of all other languages. Just as the earth and other material creations benefit all, so should the language of Divine Revelation be accessible to all countries (Dayānand 1915: 237), as all men and women have a right to study it (Dayānand 1915: 78).

25. Proper nouns, such as Jamadagni and Kaśyapa, he claimed, do not refer to embodied humans. For example, Kaśyapa is the linguistic equivalent to *karma* which, in turn, signifies *prāna*.

26. In general, Dayānand was critical of Western incursions into the field of interpreting Hinduism. In particular, he singled out Max Müller and blamed him (along with others) for fostering the "delusion" that the Veda was of human origin (Dayānand 1981: 38). He was well aware of Müller's thesis that the Veda presented simple, natural, and even commonplace religious ideas of a "primitive" people, which rendered them valuable for the comparative study of religion and linguistics. Dayānand had even had Müller's writings translated for his use. He countered Müller's generally accepted view with the claim that the Vedas were sophisticated rather than primitive, certainly more so than the sacred writings of Christianity and Islam.

27. Jordens shows how Dayānand's movement from Advaita Vedānta to a rejection of monism is reflected in the different versions of the *Satyārth Prakāsh*.

28. He felt that such conjectures concerning the Aryans' movements were "imaginary tales attributable to foreigners" (Dayānand 1981: 266).

29. Dayānand situated Āryavarta as bordering the Himalayas to the north, the Vindhyachal Mountains to the south, and the sea on both the east and west.

30. Foreign faiths such as Jainism, Islam, and Christianity also contributed to the gradual loss of Vedic truth (Dayānand 1915: 320–27).

31. The *Purusha Sūkta* of the *Rig Veda* explains creation as a result of the dismember-ment of Primeval Man into the physical elements of the world, the social order, and the seasons. The brahmin (priest) arose from the head; the *kṣatriya* (warrior) from the arms; the *vaishya* (merchant or general people) from the thighs; the *shūdra* (servant) from the feet and nether parts.

32. "He who is head, that is, a leader of men, is called a brahmin. He in whom power and strength (*bahu*) reside is the *kṣatriya*. He who travels from place to place and obtains things on the strength of his thighs is called a *vaishya*. He who is ignorant is called a *shūdra*. . . ."

33. Real brahmins can never falsely teach and lead selfish, hypocritical lives, or can never live on alms—all of which tend to make them prejudiced and partial in religious and scientific matters (Dayānand 1915: 51). Dayānand defines the brahmin as some-one who "studies the true sciences, practices *brahmacārya*, accepts truth, rejects untruth, disseminates true knowledge by leading a virtuous life, and, enjoined by the Veda, performs the *homa* sacrifice, reproduces good children, discharges the five great daily duties, and performs good works beneficial to the community (Dayānand 1915: 96).

34. This rule held for the censuses of 1891, 1911, and 1921, whereupon it was altered against Dayānand's directives (*Swami Dayānand-ka-Patravyawahar*, letters # 206, 8245).

35. *Updesh Manjiri*, Poona, Lecture No. 4. Delhi, Dayānand Sanstha 1976: 26.

36. *Updesh Manjiri*: Poona, Lecture No. 8. Delhi, Dayānand Sanstha 1976: 84.

37. Jordens has noted that the chapter dealing with the *sannyāsī* was rewritten in the second edition of the *Satyārth Prakāsh*. Dayānand omitted highlighting privileges tra-ditionally accorded to the *sannyāsī* and drastically reduced references to their status in society (Jordens 1978: 263).

38. Jordens shows that the portrayal of the *sannyāsī*'s being-in-the-world only appears in the second edition of the *Satyārth Prakāsh*, suggesting that in the period between the first edition (1875) and the second edition (1883), Dayānand's vision of man became increasingly cosmic and active. Activity implied lasting involvement in the world.

39. As Jordens has shown, Dayānand's emphasis on action and worldly involvement is also reflected in his treatment of the themes of *pralaya* and *moksha*. In the first edi-tion of the *Satyārth Prakāsh*, Dayānand affirmed an absolute beginning (*ādisrishti*) and absolute end to the universe (*atyant pralaya*) with liberation (*moksha*) as irre-versible. Once the soul reaches *moksha*, it never again returns to *saṃsāra*. The second edition of the *Satyārth Prakāsh* claims that all three events are reversible (Jordens 1972: 373–73). Man remains an active cosmic force beyond *moksha*, a concept unique to Dayānand's thought and not expounded elsewhere in Indian philosophy (Jordens 1972: 375). It was clearly Dayānand's intention to define the soul in life and in *moksha* as connected to action.

40. Among revolt traditions, Dayānand was not unique. The Sādhs did not observe caste and rejected brahmin authority, monotheism, idol worship, pilgrimages, the *shraddha* ritual, and most other Hindu ceremonies. Their text, the *Pothī*, was a collection of sermons and songs, and extracts from the *Ādi Granth* of the Sikhs.

7. ARYAN IDENTITY AND NATIONAL SELF-ESTEEM

1. For a discussion of the role of the Chitpavan brahmins in Mahārāshtra, see Wolpert 1962: 1–4.

2. The Chapekars were the assassins of Walter Charles Rand, appointed by Governor Sandhurst in 1897 as chairman of Poona's Plague Committee. Rand angered both secular and orthodox Hindus with the measures he took in his failed attempt to contain the plague. His methods were felt to be assaultive and insensitive to religious sensibilities.

3. The eminent Sanskrit scholar Ramkrishna Gopal Bhandarkar drew attention to the similarity between Chitpavan names and the names of geographical sites in Palestine (Enthoven 1975: 242).

4. Reform efforts were also directed at prohibitions against foreign travel and the readmission of converts into the Hindu fold.

5. The Shaṅkarāchārya of Sankeshwar was the religious head of the majority of the Deccani brahmins.

6. Alongside passages from the Vedas, Ranade relied also on *smṛti* literature (especially *Manu*) in favor of widow remarriage.

7. Remarriage is allowed if the husband is abroad and no news has been heard, he is dead, he has become a *sannyāsī*, he is impotent, or he has been found guilty of the five great unatonable sins.

8. He found this ruling particularly important since the lawmaker had expressly intended it for the Kali Yuga (one of the four ages of man, akin to the Greek mythological notion of the age of iron) in which the *smṛti* has precedence over all others. The letter of the text itself was subject to the historical position of the reader. The new texts had been introduced to condemn the old approved Aryan institutions as unsuited to men in the Kali Yuga. Even though practiced in old times, they were now forbidden (Ranade 1902: 192). Ranade rejected this argument with the assertion that Indians had not yet attained the Kali Yuga age and could not be held to its degenerate laws. Ranade borrowed this line of thought from Vyaṅkata Shāstrī's argument at the Poona disputation. This reformer had first noted that even if widow remarriage were applicable in the Kali Yuga, its time of application had not yet arrived. In the late nineteenth century, we were still in the *saṃdhya* period of the Dvāpara Yuga, so texts prohibiting late marriages were not then applicable nor would they be for another 31,000 years.

9. The chronology here is significant. The Scoble Bill (1891) sought to raise the marriageable age of consent from ten to twelve years of age. Below this age, intercourse with or without consent would constitute rape. Reformist opposition to infant marriage predated the Scoble Bill by a decade.

10. This commentary was entitled "State Legislation in Social Matters."

11. The texts of various *smṛti* writers fixed the minimum age for men at twenty-five and the maximum at fifty.

12. For a summary of the defamation suit against Tilak by the Diwan of Kolhapur, M.V. Barve (1882), and the Rakhamabai case of marital litigation (1887), see Wolpert 1962: 20–21, 37.

13. He cites Posche and Penka, who saw the tall, dolichocephalic race, the ancestors of present-day Germans, as primitive Aryans. He also cites the Frenchmen Chavée and Mortillet, who viewed the bracycephalic (represented by the Gauls) as Aryans. The Swiss German Schräder placed (*Antiquities of Aryan Peoples*) their original home somewhere in the Swiss lake district (Tilak 1971: 14).

14. By examining the astronomical phenomena in the region around the North Pole, Tilak had noticed two sets of characters—one for the observer stationed exactly at the terrestrial North Pole and the other for an observer located in the circumpolar regions (that is, tracts between the North Pole and the Arctic Circle). In the polar zone (terrestrial North Pole), the sun rises. The stars do not rise or set, but revolve in horizontal planes, one long day of six months and one long night of six months. In the polar zone, twilight lasts for two months. In the circumpolar zone, however, the sun is always found to the south of the zenith of the observer. The year is one long night, lasting more than twenty-four hours and less than six months according to the latitude. The dawn following this long continuous night lasts several days. He recognized a similarity between this astronomical data and descriptions found in the *Rig Veda*. From this similarity, Tilak concluded that the Vedic Aryans must have had an Arctic home (Tilak 1971: 64). The *Rig Veda* descriptions of the dawn moving like a wheel neatly described the condition of the polar dawn (Tilak 1971: 88). Similarly, the polar calendar, characterized by half-year-long days and nights, finds parallels in the Rig Vedic descriptions of long dawns with revolving splendors and continuous nights matched by corresponding long days. In their poetry, the Vedic rishis must have been describing physical phenomena that could only be witnessed in arctic regions.

15. Specifically, Tilak pinpoints the primeval home to be north of Siberia, rather than north of Russia or Scandinavia (Tilak 1971: 388).

16. This negative assessment of the Semitic God was fairly common among Hindu reformers. Ranade, in discussing the Aryan gods as gods of love and brightness, of sweetness and light, compared them to the Semite who dwelt on a terrific manifestation of a distant God whose "glory could not be seen save through a cloud, a severe chastiser of human frailties, and a judge who punished more frequently than He rewarded and even when He rewarded, kept the worshipper always in awe and trembling—such a God was not to be found in the Aryan religions of Greece, Rome, or

India, where God always is a father, mother, brother, and friend more than a judge and chastiser" (Ranade 1902: 222–23).

17. Vivekananda cited the following proverb concerning the all-inclusiveness of the Vedas: "If a man loses his cow, he goes to look for her in the Vedas" (Vivekananda 7:41).

18. Vivekananda did not ascribe to the belief, championed by Dayānand, that only the Saṃhitās comprise the Veda. He judged that Dayānand devised this interpretation so that he could find a consistent theory in the Vedas based on a new interpretation of the Saṃhitās. Vivekananda notes that this was impossible; difficulties of interpretation remain and are attributed to the Brāhmaṇas. He was of the belief that building a consistent religion is more reasonable, if one based an understanding on the Upanishads (Vivekananda 5:130).

19. Vivekananda tells his reader that Aryans are the best dressers, a fact that even Europeans have to admit (Vivekananda 5:374).

20. Vivekananda claimed that India was a nation peopled with Negrito-Kolarians, Dravidians, Aryans, Mongoloids, Mongols, Tartars, Persians, Yunchi, Huns, Scythians, Jews, Parsees, Arabs, and descendents of the Vikings.

21. Vivekananda did not claim that the Aryans migrated to India from elsewhere; he soundly rejected the Aryan invasion theory as a foolish lie foisted upon the Indians by the West (Vivekananda 5:534).

22. Vivekananda admitted that some brahmins had immorally abused their custodianship (Vivekananda 7:17). Selfish brahmins had also introduced a large number of strange, non-Vedic, and immoral doctrines to bolster their prestige.

8. THE ANTI-MYTH

1. The Sanskrit term *varṇa* signifies both "caste" and "color." Today such linguistic suppositions concerning the Aryans carry little weight. Furthermore, the idea that Vedic texts present an unproblematized vision of the Indo-Aryan has been seriously questioned. In fact, Vedic texts are presently seen to register the presence of non-Aryan speakers, and linguists now view the Aryan and non-Aryan as living in a symbiotic relationship of mutual adoption in vocabulary and linguistic structures. Nevertheless, the myth of Aryan cultural identity resists all attempts to reduce it to history and deprive it of its capacity to reconstruct social forms.

2. *Rig Veda* 2.20.8; 2.12.4; 3.34.9; 1.33.4; 4.16.3; 5.29.10; 10.22.8.

3. As scholars have noted, the Vedic passages are ambiguous. For a discussion, see Muir (1873: 2.374-75). Sanskritists such as Hans Hock still hold to the belief that those passages offer alternative readings (personal discussion).

4. Hock also finds that other racial descriptions customarily cited are equally dubious. The term *anās* has been broken down into components *a*-negative + *nās* (nose)

and read as "noseless." But, the term equally can be read as *an*-negative + *ās* (mouth), with the meaning "mouthless" or "speechless" barbarian. Likewise, in the term *vṛṣaśiprā*, racially translated "bull-lipped," *śiprā* could have the meaning of lip, jaw, or cheek and *vṛṣa* could mean bull in the figurative sense of male strength. These terms also need not be read racially.

5. Hock cites literature to this effect. This point was brought home to me constantly in India as a white mother of a black child. On a supposedly more intellectual level, the topic of color was perceived as intrinsic to the topic of this book. After describing to a Sanskrit professor in Poona recently my interest in the manner in which identity is constructed from readings of canonical sources, I was surprised when this learned scholar responded with the non sequitur of whether I really did not find black Indians physically repulsive.

6. Āryavarta was determined by sources to correspond to the cultural source. In late Vedic sources, it represented the Ganga, Yamuna, Doab area and its fringe as opposed to the *mleccha-deśa* such as Magadha and Anga (i.e., Patna, Gaya, Monghyr, and Bhagalpur districts of Bihar where there are mixed castes and thus unfit to the Aryan. In Jain sources, these regions are Āryavarta. In Buddhist sources, Āryavarta is thought to be to the east of Doab (modern Rajmahal area). In *Manu*, Āryavarta is northern Indian, north of the Vindhyas (Thapar 1992: 6).

7. This situation has, of course, changed since Independence. Nevertheless, notions of racial inferiority do not disappear overnight. Nor are holy men immune to their allure. Aurobindo Ghose provided a clear example of this racialist script. Aurobindo characterized the Dasyu as someone who robs and withholds wealth from the Aryan. The Dasyu is a thief, enemy, wolf, devourer, and divider. He represents also the power of darkness and ignorance. Aurobindo identified this Dasyu with the dark-skinned Southern Dravidians whom he deemed as culturally and spiritually distinct from the Aryans (Aurobindo 1964: 39–41). They were never to be confused with the Aryans, whom the goddess Lakshmi prophesized would rise again to conquer, rule (Aurobindo 1942: 1.77–80), and Aryanize the world (Aurobindo 1960: 94).

8. Alongside the suppressed *shūdras* lived the *kṣatriyas*, who originated from a pre-Aryan society of flourishing peasants. The *kṣatriyas* were ancestors of the Marathas and, like the Aryans, originally emigrated from Iran. As opposed to the brahmins, however, they lived in harmony with the *shūdras* and helped them fend off Aryan attacks (Phule 1991a: 2.21).

9. The great king Bali, who serves as a symbol of the peasant, is cheated out of his kingdom by the treacherous brahmin boy Waman. Phule intentionally set Bali up as a model in response to the elite's and orthodoxy's use of Ram, Ganpati (in Tilak), and Kali.

10. Phule interpreted the nine avatars of Vishnu as an allegorical representations of the various stages of Aryan conquest. *Matsya* (fish) and *Kaccha* (tortoise) represent invasion by sea. *Varah* (boar) symbolized the Aryan barbarian in conflict with the more civilized native population. *Narasinh* and *Prahlad* represent conquest by treachery.

11. Phule succinctly described the Aryan invasion in the "First Ballad of Priestcraft Exposed":

The circles of rishis, the strength of dharma and the power of the Vedas
A great shower of curses
A kick in the chest of God.

12. "Jotirao: After the death of Brahma, the venerable sages divided the compositions of Brahma into three divisions or Vedas. Some equally celebrated sages changed and chopped these compositions. They put together some legends that they happened to remember along with some similar compositions, and created a fourth Veda. The minds of all the existing Kṣatriya Satraps were greatly impressed and awed by the power of the magic incantations of the Brahmins when (they saw for themselves how) Parashuram vanquished and totally routed the subjects of Banasura. The effeminate (eunuch) Narada paid frequent visits to the royal residences of devout and superstitious Satraps . . . He used to regale the queens and their children by playing upon his Veena . . . but in reality he sowed seeds of dissension in their minds and succeeded in poisoning their minds against one another by spreading palpably false tales and reports about them. Thus he weakened the Satraps and by the same ruse, consolidated the ascendancy of the Brahmins. During that period the Brahmin authors put together their magical sacred incantations and the palpably absurd legends relating thereto, stealthily produced heaps of new scriptures designating them as smritis, Saṃhitās, Purāṇas, etc. with the sole object of establishing their permanent domination over the (luckless) *shūdras*. They also succeeded in brain-washing the *shūdras* to stick to their ancestral (traditional) vocation of serving the Aryans as menials as it was the 'truly religious' path. They also enjoined upon the Aryans not to allow the *shūdras*, condemned to the Hell of ignorance, any access to knowledge, and incorporated strict instructions to that effect in their unholy books like the Manu Smriti with the sole intention that the *shūdras* should never get even an inkling into the fraud practiced by the Aryans upon them and also intending to retain the liberty to change and chop these so-called scriptures, even in future, as the need arose."

13. Phule made a good joke for anyone who has tried to read Sanskrit. Phule claimed that the fact that the Vedas were written in Sanskrit was proof that God did not compose them. If they were meant for all mankind, a beneficient God would certainly not have written them in that idiom.

14. Phule 1991a: 2.37: "Firstly, the Aryans presumed to be Vedantic experts on the authority of their wholly illogical, philosophical arrogance (deceitfulness), rendered our Creator redundant, and subsequently supplanted Him. They further grew all-powerful and have become the 'earth-gods' of the ignorant, defeated folk. . . ."

15. Phule 1991b: 33: "they would utter nonsensical and incoherent words and would claim that they were in communion with God Himself. They used this subterfuge only to dupe the ignorant masses. This is corroborated by (many references in) the Vedas themselves. Many European authors also have expressed a similar opinion. Taking a cue from this vicious practice some Bhats/Brahmins of today dupe poor ignorant gardeners and farmers by indulging in practices such as recitations, esoteric

practices, magic incantations, etc. to earn their livelihood by unholy means. What a pity it is that these poor, ignorant, unfortunate victims of the guiles of the hypocritical (cunning) brahmins cannot fathom the depth of their tricks and guiles so shamelessly practiced upon them." Phule 1991b: 85: "The English scholars churned (the ocean of) the Vedas and revealed to us all, the esoteric secret contained in them. They exposed the erroneous philosophy of the Vedas (Scriptures), expounded the eternal truth, and thus established the reign of righteousness. The Brahmins were at their wit's end (were confused), and hence some of them embraced Christianity, pretending all the while to profess Truth. The Machiavellian Brahmins often found (establish) "People's Organisations" in diverse places and try to enlist members by holding out a false promise (subterfuge) of promoting unity (among the people). (The *shūdras* should) realise the crafty nature of the Aryans, and try to search for the eternal Truth." Phule 1991b: 73: "The Brahmins forbade the *shūdras* even to hear (the recitation of) the Vedas but (they did not think it a pollution) and they taught (Sanskrit and vernacular languages to) the Englishmen readily."

16. Upon his return to India, his opportunities in law were extremely limited due to prevailing prejudice. He did, however, eventually teach at the Government Law College in Bombay.

17. Ambedkar dedicated "Who are the Shūdras" to the memory of Phule, whom he esteemed "as the greatest *shūdra* of Modern India who made the lower classes of Hindus conscious of their slavery to the higher classes and who preached the gospel that for India social democracy was more vital than independence from foreign rule."

18. See A.C. Das, *Rig Vedic Culture*, 133 and most importantly, P.V. Kane, *Dharmashāstra* II (I), p. 33 (7.101).

19. By comparing the term *varṇa* with its *Zend Avesta* equivalent *varana* or *varena* (meaning faith, religious doctrine, or creed), Ambedkar concludes that *varṇa* must have originally meant a class holding to a particular faith (Ambedkar 1990: 7.85).

20. He breaks down the Vedas into the Rig and the Atharva, with brahmins viewing the Sama and the Yajur as different forms of the Rig and the Rig regarded as far more sacred than the Atharva (7.87).

21. The *upanayana* is the sacred thread ceremony administered by brahmins to brahmins.

22. Ambedkar cites the cephalic index of Risley's survey of 1901 showing four different races and the migration theories of Guha (1936) delineating two racial stocks in India (Ambedkar 1990: 7.78).

Bibliography

Aherne, Daniel P. 1995. *Nietzsche as Cultural Physician*. University Park: Pennsylvania State University Press.

Aherne, Jeremy. 1995. *Michel de Certeau: Interpretation and Its Other*. Stanford, Ca.: Stanford University Press.

Ahmad, Aijaz. 1993. *In Theory: Classes, Nations, Literatures*. Bombay: Oxford University Press.

Alsdorf, Ludwig. 1944. *Deutsch-Indische Geistesbeziehungen*. Heidelberg: K. Vowinckel.

Ambedkar, B.D. 1979–90. *Writings and Speeches*. 9 vols. Bombay: Education Department, Government of Maharashtra.

Anderson, Benedict. 1983. *Imagined Communities: Reflections on the Origin and Spread of Nationalism*. London: Verso.

Appiah, Kwame Anthony. 1992. "The Postcolonial and the Postmodern." In *My Father's House: Africa in the Philosophy of Culture*. London: Methuen.

Ashcroft, Bill, Gareth Griffiths, and Helen Tiffin. 1989. *The Empire Writes Back: Theory and Practice in Post-Colonial Literatures*. London: Routledge.

———. 1995. *The Post-Colonial Studies Reader*. London and New York: Routledge.

Bahri, Deepika. "Once More with Feeling: What is Postcolonialism?" *Ariel* 26 (1995): 51–82.

Bäumler, Alfred. 1931. *Nietzsche der Philosoph und Politiker*. Leipzig: Reclam.

Bhabha, Homi K. 1990. "DissemiNation: Time, Narrative and the Margins of the Modern Nation." In *Nation and Narration*, 291–322. London: Routledge.

189

Bhandarkar, R.G. 1891. "A Note on the Age of Marriage and Its Consumation according to Hindu Religious Law." Poona.

Cancik, Hubert. 1997. "Mongols, Semites and the Pure-Bred Greeks: Nietzsche's Handling of the Racial Doctrines of his Time." In *Nietzsche and Jewish Culture*, edited by Jacob Golomb, 55–75. London: Routledge.

Cassirer, Ernst. 1944. *An Essay on Man: An Introduction to a Philosophy of Human Culture*. New Haven, Conn.: Yale University Press.

———. 1946. *Language and Myth*. Trans. Susanne K. Langer. New York: Harper and Brothers.

Certeau, Michel de. 1986. *Heterologies: the Discourse on the Other*. Minneapolis: University of Minnesota Press.

———. 1988. *The Writing of History*. Trans. Tom Conley. New York: Columbia University Press.

Chamberlain, Houston Stewart. 1902. *Dilettantismus, Rasse, Monotheismus*. Munich: Bruckmann.

———. 1903. *Die Grundlagen des neunzehnten Jahrhunderts*. Munich: Bruckmann.

———. 1925. *Rasse und Persönlichkeit*. Munich: Bruckmann.

———. 1928. *Briefe*. Munich: Bruckmann.

———. 1968. *Foundations of the Nineteenth Century*. 2 vols. New York: Howard Fertig.

Chatterjee, Partha. 1986. *Nationalist Thought and the Colonial World: A Derivative Discourse*. London: Zed Books.

Chow, Rey. 1993. *Writing Diaspora: Tactics of Intervention in Contemporary Cultural Studies*. Bloomington: Indiana University Press.

———. 1995. "The Fascist Longings in our Midst." *Ariel* 26: 23–50.

Clark, John. 1996. "On Two Books by Edward W. Said." *Jurnal Bicara Seni*, Universiti Sains Malaysia. June: 20–47.

Colebrooke, H.T. 1795. "On the Duties of a Faithful Hindu Widow." *Asiatick Researches* 4: 109–19.

———. 1798. "Enumeration of Indian Classes." *Asiatick Researches* 5: 53–67.

———. 1802. "On the Religious Ceremonies of the Hindus." *Asiatick Researches* 7: 199–231.

———. 1805. "On the Vedas or the Sacred Writings of the Hindus." *Asiatick Researches* 8: 369–476.

Collet, S.D. 1962. *The Life and Letters of Raja Rammohun Roy.* Edited by D.K. Biswas and P.C. Ganguli. Calcutta: Sadharan Brahmo Samaj.

Conway, Daniel W. 1997. *Nietzsche and the Political.* New York: Routledge.

Creuzer, Georg Frederick. 1819–23. *Symbolik und Mythologie der alten Völker, besonders der Griechen.* 6 vols. Leipzig and Darmstadt.

———. 1840. *Aus dem Leben eines alten Professors.* Heidelberg, Leipzig, and Darmstadt: Heyer and Leske.

Crews, Frederick. 1996. "The Consolation of Theosophy, II." *The New York Review of Books,* October 3.

Dayānand, Saraswatī. 1915. *Satyārth Prakāsh.* Trans. Chiranjiva Bharadwaja. Agra and Oudh: Arya Pratinidhi Sabha.

——— 1981. *Rgvedādibhāshya-Bhūmikā.* Trans. Parmanand. Delhi: Mehardhand Lachmandas.

de Bary, William Theodore, Stephen Hay, and S.H. Qureshi. 1988. *Sources of Indian Tradition.* New York: Columbia University Press.

Dirlik, Arif. 1997. *Third World Criticism in the Age of Global Capitalism.* New York: Westview.

Deo, S.B. and Suryanath Kamath. 1993. *The Aryan Problem.* Pune: Bharatiya Itihasa Sankalana Samiti.

Deshpande, Madhav M. "Aryans, Non-Aryans, and Brâhmanas: Processes of Indigenization." *Journal of Indo-European Studies* 21: 215–35.

Detweiler, Bruce. 1990. *Nietzsche and the Politics of Aristocratic Radicalism.* Chicago: University of Chicago Press.

Dow, Alexander. 1772. *The History of Hindustan from the earliest account of time to the death of Akbar (. . .) with a dissertation concerning the Religion and Philosophy of the Brahmans.* London: Vernor and Hood.

Duffy, Michael, and Willard Mittleman. 1988. "Nietzsche's Attitudes toward the Jews." *Journal of the History of Ideas* 49: 301–17.

Ellis, Francis Whyte. 1822. "An Account of a Discovery of a Modern Imitation of the Vedas with Remarks on the Genuine Works." *Asiatick Researches* 14: 1–59.

Enthoven, R.E. 1975. *The Tribes and Castes of Bombay.* Delhi: Cosmo Publications.

Erdosy, George. 1995. *The Indo-Aryans of Ancient South Asia: Language, Material Culture and Ethnicity.* Berlin and New York: de Gruyter.

Etter, Annemarie. 1987. "Nietzsche und das Gesetzbuch des Manu." *Nietzsche Studien* 16: 340–52.

L'Ezour Vedam ou ancien commentaire de Veidam contenant l'exposition des opinions religieuses et philosophiques. 1778. Traduit du Samscretam par un Brame. Edited by Guillaume Emmanuel Joseph Guilhem de Clermont Lodève, Baron de Sainte-Croix. Revu et avec des observations préliminaires des notes et des éclaircissements. 2 vols. Yverdon: De Felice.

Feuerstein, George, Subash Kak, and David Frawley. 1995. *In Search of the Cradle of Civilization.* Wheaton, Ill.: Quest Books.

Field, Geoffrey G. 1981. *Evangelist of Race: The Germanic Vision of Houston Stewart Chamberlain.* New York: Columbia University Press.

Figueira, Dorothy. 1991. *Translating the Orient.* Albany: State University of New York Press.

———. 1993. "Myth, Ideology and the Authority of an Absent Text." *Yearbook of Comparative and General Literature:* 53–61.

———. 1994. *The Exotic: A Decadent Quest.* Albany: State University of New York Press.

Fluck, Winfried. 1990. "The Americanization of Literary Studies." *American Studies International* 128, no. 2: 9–22.

———. 1992. "The Americanization of History in New Historicism." *Monatshefte* 82, no. 2: 220–28.

———. 1996. "Literature, Liberalism and the Current Cultural Radicalism." In *Why Literature Matters; Themes and Functions of Literature,* edited by Rüdiger Ahrens and Laurenz Volkmann, Heidelberg: C. Winter.

Foucault, Michel. 1988. *Technologies of the Self.* Edited by H. Gutman et al. London: Tavistock.

Frawley, David. 1994. *The Myth of the Aryan Invasion of India*. New Delhi: Voice of India.

Gérard, René. 1963. *L'Orient et la pensée romantique allemande*. Paris: Didier.

Ghose, Aurobindo. 1942. *Collected Poems and Plays*. 2 vols. Pondichery: Sri Aurobindo Ashram.

———. 1960. *Bhawani Mandir*. Reprinted in *The Life of Sri Aurobindo*, by B.A. Purani. Pondichery: Sri Aurobindo Ashram.

———. 1964. *On the Veda*. Pondichery: Sri Aurobindo Ashram.

Gillespie, Gerald. 1997. "The Significance of Limits of Cultural Relativism." In *Cultural Dialogue and Misreading*, edited by Mabel Lee and Meng Hua. Sidney, Australia: Wild Peonie.

Gilman, Sander. 1997. "Heine, Nietzsche and the Idea of the Jew." In *Nietzsche and Jewish Culture*, edited by Jacob Golomb, 76–100. London: Routledge.

Glasenapp, H. von. 1960. *Das Indienbild Deutscher Denker*. Stuttgart: K.F. Koehler.

Gobineau, Arthur de. 1983. *Oeuvres*. Paris: Gallimard.

Golomb, Jacob. 1997. *Nietzsche and Jewish Culture*. London: Routledge.

Görres, Joseph. 1810. *Mythengeschichte der asiatischen Welt*. Heidelberg: Mohr and Zimmer.

Gozzano, Guido. 1996. *Journey toward the Cradle of Mankind*. Trans. David Marinelli. Evanston, Ill.: Northwestern University Press.

Guha, Ranajit, editor. 1982-90. *Subaltern Studies*. 4 vols. Delhi: Oxford University Press.

———. 1997. "Not at Home in Empire." *Critical Inquiry* 20: 482–93.

Günther, Hans F.K. 1923. *Rassenkunde des deutschen Volkes*. Munich: J.F. Lehmann.

———. 1934. *Die Nordische Rasse bei den Indogermanen Asiens*. Munich: J.F. Lehmann.

Halbfass, Wilhelm. 1988. *India and Europe*. Albany: State University of New York Press.

————. 1991. *Tradition and Reflection: Explorations in Indian Thought.* Albany: State University of New York Press.

Hannaford, Ivan. 1996. Race: *A History of an Idea in the West.* Baltimore, Md.: Johns Hopkins University Press.

Hawley, Daniel S. 1974. "L'Inde de Voltaire." *Studies on Voltaire and the Eighteenth Century.* Vol. 120. Edited by Theodore Besterman, 139–77. Oxfordshire: Therpe Mandeville.

Heimsath, Charles Herman. 1964. *Indian Nationalism and Hindu Social Reform.* Princeton, N.J.: Princeton University Press.

Herder, J.G. 1786–92. *Zerstreute Blätter.* Gotha: C.W. Ettinger.

————. 1877–1913. *Sämtliche Werke.* 33 vols. Edited by B. Suphan. Berlin: Weidmannsche Buchhandlung.

Hock, Hans Henrich. 1999. "Through a Glass Darkly: Modern 'Racial' Interpretations vs. Textual and General Prehistoric Evidence on ārya and dāsa/dasyu in Vedic Society." In *Aryan and Non-Aryan in South Asia: Evidence, Interpretation and Ideology,* edited by Johannes Bronkhorst and Madhav Deshpande. Cambridge, Mass.: Harvard University Press.

Holwell, John Zephaniah. 1765-71. *Interesting historical events relative to the Provinces of Bengal and the Empire of Indostan . . . As also the Mythology and Cosmogony, fasts and festivals of the Gentoos, followers of the Shastah, and a Dissertation on the Metamorphoses commonly thought erroneously called the Pythagorean doctrine.* London: n.p.

Hulin, Michel. 1991. "Nietzsche and the Suffering of the Indian Ascetic." In *Nietzsche and Asian Thought,* edited by Graham Parkes, 64–75. Chicago: University of Chicago Press.

Jacolliot, Louis. 1896. *Les Législateurs religieux, Manou-Moïse-Mahomet.* Paris: A. LaCroix et Cie.

Jaffrelot, Christophe. 1993. *Les nationalistes hindoues.* Paris: Presses de la Fondation Nationale des Sciences Politques.

Jameson, Fredric. 1986. "Third World Literature in the Age of Multi-national Capitalism." *Social Text* 5, no. 15: 66–88.

Jones, Kenneth W. 1976. *Arya Dharm: Hindu Consciousness in Nineteenth-Century Punjab.* Berkeley and Los Angeles: University of California Press.

———. 1992. *Religious Controversy in British India.* Albany: State University of New York Press.

Jones, Sir William. 1788. "Third Anniversary Discourse." *Asiatick Researches* 1: 415–31.

Jordens, J.T.F. 1972. "Dayananda Saraswati and Vedanta: A Comparison of the First and the Second Editions of his *Satyârth Prakâsh.*" *Indian Economic and Social History Review* 9: 367–79.

———. 1978. *Dayananda Saraswati: His Life and Ideas.* Delhi: Oxford University Press.

Joshi, V.C. 1975. *Rammohun Roy and the Process of Modernization in India.* Delhi: Vikas.

Kaufmann, Walter. 1974. *Nietzsche: Philosopher, Psychologist, Antichrist.* 4th ed. New York: Vintage.

Kerler, Dietrich Heinrich. 1910. *Nietzsche und die Vergeltungsidee.* Ulm: Heinrich Kerler.

Kirchner, E. 1925–26. "Nietzsches Lehren im Lichte des Rassenhygiene." *Archiv für Rassen- und Gesellschaftsbiologie* 17: 279–96.

Kohler, Josef. 1907/1908. "Nietzsche und die Rechtsphilosophie." *Archiv für Rechts- und Wirtschaftsphilosophie* 1: 355–60.

Kopf, David. 1969. *British Orientalism and the Bengal Renaissance.* Berkeley: University of California Press.

Krishmaswamy, Revathi. 1995. "Mythologies of Migrancy: Postcolonialism, Postmodernism, and the Politics of (Dis)Location." *Ariel* 26: 125–46.

Kuenzli, Rudolf E. 1983. "The Nazi Appropriation of Nietzsche." *Nietzsche-Studien* 12: 428–35.

Kundera, Milan. 1996. *Testaments Betrayed.* Trans. Linda Asher. New York: Harper.

Lassen, Christian. 1847–61. *Indische Altertumskunde.* Bonn: B. Koenig.

Leopold, Joan. 1970. "The Aryan Theory of Race." *The Indian Economic and Social History Review* 7: 271–97.

Lettres edifiantes et curieuses . . . par quelques missions de la Compagnie de Jésus. Paris: Bibliothèque des Amis de la Religion, 1706–76.

Lincoln, Bruce. 1989. *Discourse and the Construction of Society.* Oxford: Oxford University Press.

Llewellyn, J.E. 1993. *The Arya Samaj as a Fundamentalist Movement.* Delhi: Manohar.

McClintock, Anne. 1992. "The Angel of Progress." *Social Text* 31/32: 84–97.

Mani, Lata. 1988. "Contentious Traditions: The Debate on Sati in Colonial India." In *Recasting Women: Essays in Colonial History,* edited by K. Sangari and S. Vaid, 88–126. New Delhi: Kali for Women.

Manu. *Manusmṛtiḥ.* 1969. Mathura: Pustaka Mandra.

———. 1992. *The Laws of Manu.* Trans. Wendy Doniger and Brian K. Smith. New York: Penguin.

Michel, Martina. 1995. "Positioning the Subject: Locating Postcolonialism." *Ariel* 26: 83–101.

Mishra, Vijay, and Bob Hodge. 1991. "What is Post(-)colonialism." *Textual Practice* 5: 399–414.

Mistry, Freny. 1981. *Nietzsche and Buddhism.* Berlin: de Gruyter.

Monier-Williams, Monier. 1990. *A Sanskrit-English Dictionary.* Delhi: Motilal Banarsidass.

Muir, J. 1873. *Original Sanskrit Texts on the Origin and History of the People of India.* London: Trübner and Co.

Müller, Friedrich Max. 1837. "Discourse at the Royal Asiatick Society of Great Britain and Ireland." *Miscellaneous Essays.* 2 vols. London: William H. Allen and Co.

———. 1849–74. *Ṛg Veda Samhitâ: The Sacred Hymns of the Brahmins.* 6 vols. London: William H. Allen.

———. 1869–76. *Essays.* 4 vols. Leipzig: W. Englemann.

———. 1872. *Lectures on the Science of Religion.* New York: Scribners.

———. 1872. *Über die Resultate der Sprachwissenschaft. Vorlesungen gehalten der Kaiserlichen Universität zu Strassburg am xxiii anni MDCCCLXXII.* Strassburg: K.J. Trübner.

———. 1874. *Einleitung in die vergleichende Religionswissenschaft.* Strassburg: Karl J. Trübner.

———. 1879. *Lectures on the Origin and Growth of Religion as illustrated by the Religions of India.* London: Longmans, Green and Co.

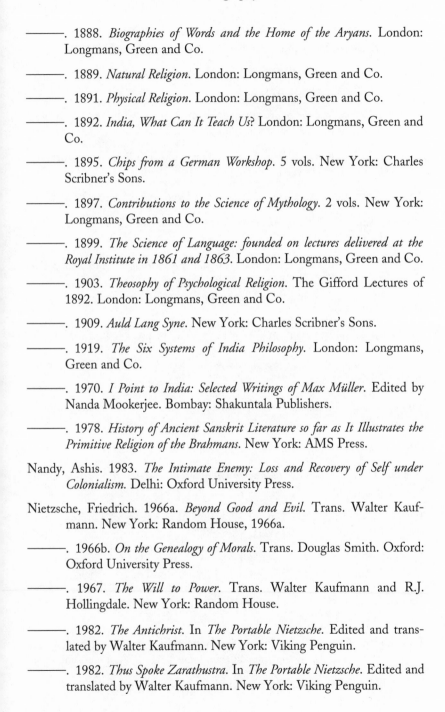

————. 1888. *Biographies of Words and the Home of the Aryans*. London: Longmans, Green and Co.

————. 1889. *Natural Religion*. London: Longmans, Green and Co.

————. 1891. *Physical Religion*. London: Longmans, Green and Co.

————. 1892. *India, What Can It Teach Us?* London: Longmans, Green and Co.

————. 1895. *Chips from a German Workshop*. 5 vols. New York: Charles Scribner's Sons.

————. 1897. *Contributions to the Science of Mythology*. 2 vols. New York: Longmans, Green and Co.

————. 1899. *The Science of Language: founded on lectures delivered at the Royal Institute in 1861 and 1863*. London: Longmans, Green and Co.

————. 1903. *Theosophy of Psychological Religion*. The Gifford Lectures of 1892. London: Longmans, Green and Co.

————. 1909. *Auld Lang Syne*. New York: Charles Scribner's Sons.

————. 1919. *The Six Systems of India Philosophy*. London: Longmans, Green and Co.

————. 1970. *I Point to India: Selected Writings of Max Müller*. Edited by Nanda Mookerjee. Bombay: Shakuntala Publishers.

————. 1978. *History of Ancient Sanskrit Literature so far as It Illustrates the Primitive Religion of the Brahmans*. New York: AMS Press.

Nandy, Ashis. 1983. *The Intimate Enemy: Loss and Recovery of Self under Colonialism*. Delhi: Oxford University Press.

Nietzsche, Friedrich. 1966a. *Beyond Good and Evil*. Trans. Walter Kaufmann. New York: Random House, 1966a.

————. 1966b. *On the Genealogy of Morals*. Trans. Douglas Smith. Oxford: Oxford University Press.

————. 1967. *The Will to Power*. Trans. Walter Kaufmann and R.J. Hollingdale. New York: Random House.

————. 1982. *The Antichrist*. In *The Portable Nietzsche*. Edited and translated by Walter Kaufmann. New York: Viking Penguin.

————. 1982. *Thus Spoke Zarathustra*. In *The Portable Nietzsche*. Edited and translated by Walter Kaufmann. New York: Viking Penguin.

——. 1982. *Twilight of the Idols*. In *The Portable Nietzsche*. Edited and translated by Walter Kaufmann. New York: Viking Penguin.

——. 1984. *Briefe, Kritische Studienausgabe*. Edited by G. Colli and M. Montinari. Berlin: de Gruyter.

——. 1986. *Kritische Studienausgabe*. Edited by G. Colli and M. Montinari. Berlin: de Gruyter.

——. 1996. *Human, All too Human*. Trans. R.J. Hollingdale. Cambridge: Cambridge University Press.

Nolte, Ernst. 1990. *Nietzsche und der Nietzscheanismus*. Munich: Propyläen.

Oehler, Richard. 1935. *Friedrich Nietzsche und die Deutschen Zukunft*. Leipzig: Armanen.

O'Hanlon, Rosalind. 1985. *Caste, Conflict and Ideology: Mahatma Jotirao Phule and Low-Caste Protest in Nineteenth-Century Western India*. Cambridge: Cambridge University Press.

Pankratz, James W. 1998. "Rammohun Roy." In *Religion in Modern India*, edited by Robert D. Baird, 335–49. New Delhi: Manohar.

Parkes, Graham. 1991. *Nietzsche and Asian Thought*. Chicago: University of Chicago Press.

Phule, Jotirao. 1991a. *Collected Works of Mahatma Jotirao Phule*. Bombay: Education Department, Government of Maharashtra.

——. 1991b. *Gulamgiri*. Nagapura: Diragatavad Prokasam.

Possehl, Gregory L. 1982. *Harappan Civilization: A Recent Perspective*. Delhi: AIIS.

Prasad, Madhava. 1992. "On the Question of a Theory of (Third World) Literature." *Social Text* 31/32: 57–83.

Radhakrishnan, Sarvapalli, and Charles A. Moore. 1957. *A Sourcebook in Indian Philosophy*. Princeton, N.J.: Princeton University Press.

Radhakrishnan, R. 1993. "Postcoloniality and the Boundaries of Identity." *Callaloo* 16: 750–75.

Rai, Lajpat. 1916. *Young India: An Interpretation and a History of the Nationalist Movement from Within*. New York: B.W. Huebsch.

Rajan, Balchandra. 1998. "Excess of India." *Modern Philology* 171: 490–500.

————. 1998. "Hegel's India and the Surprise of Sin." *Indian Literature*: 168–87.

Rajaram, Navaratna. 1995. *The Politics of History; Aryan Invasion Theory and the Subversion of Scholarship*. New Delhi: Voice of India.

Ranade, Mahadev Govind. 1902. *Religious and Social Reform*. Edited by M.B. Kolaskar. Bombay; Gopal Narayan and Co.

————. 1915. *Miscellaneous Writings*. Bombay: Manoranjan Press.

Raychaudhuri, Tapan. 1988. *Europe Reconsidered: Perceptions of the West in Nineteenth Century Bengal*. Delhi: Oxford University Press.

Remak, H.H. 1960. "Comparative Literature at the Crossroads: Diagnosis, Therapy and Prognosis." *Yearbook of Comparative and General Literature*. Vol. 9. Chicago: 1–29.

Renou, Louis. 1960. "Le destin du Veda in India." *Etudes védiques et paninéennes*. Vol. 6. Paris: De Boccard.

————. 1965. *The Destiny of the Veda in India*. Edited and translated by Dev Raj Channa. Delhi: Motilal Banarsidass.

Richter, Raoul. 1909. *Friedrich Nietzsche: Sein Leben und sein Werk*. Leipzig: Verlag des Durr'schen Buchhandlung.

Ritter, Carl. 1820. *Die Vorhalle der Europäischen Völkergeschichte vor Herodots, um den Kaukasus und an den Gestaden des Pontus. Eine Abhandlung zur Alterthumskunde*. Berlin: G. Reimer.

Robb, Peter. 1995. *The Concept of Race in South Asia*. Delhi: Oxford University Press.

Rocher, Ludo. 1978. "Max Müller and the Veda." *Mélanges Armand Abel*, Edited by A Destrée. Vol. 3. Leiden: Brill.

————. 1983. *Ezourvedam: A French Veda of the Eighteenth Century*. Amsterdam/Philadelphia: John Benjamins.

Rollman, Hans. 1978. "Deussen, Nietzsche and the Vedanta." *Journal of the History of Ideas* 39, no. 1: 125–32.

Römer, Heinrich. 1921. *Nietzsche*. 2 vols. Leipzig: Klinkhardt and Biermann.

————. 1949. "Nietzsche und das Rasseproblem." In *Rasse, Monatsheft für der nordischen Gedenken* 7: 56–68.

Römer, Ruth. 1985. *Sprachwissenschaft und Rassenideologie in Deutschland*. Munich: Wilhelm Fink.

Rosenberg, Alfred. 1937. *Der Mythus des Zwangzigsten Jahrhunderts.* Munich: Hoheneichen.

———. 1970. *Race and Race History and Other Essays.* Edited by and translated by Robert Pois. New York: Harper and Row.

Rothstein, Edward. 2001. "Attacks on U.S. Challenge the Perspectives of Postmodern True Believers." *New York Times,* September 22, 2001, A17.

Roy, Rammohun. 1906. *The English Works of Rammohun Roy.* 2 vols.. Edited by Jogendra Chunder Ghose. Calcutta: Cosmo Publications.

Said, Edward W. 1978. *Orientalism.* New York: Pantheon.

———. 1990. "Third World Intellectuals and Metropolitan Culture." *Raritan Quarterly* 9, no. 3 (Winter): 27–50.

Santaniello, Weaver. 1994. *Nietzsche, God, and the Jews.* Albany: State University of New York Press.

———. 1997. "A Post-Holocaust Re-examination of Nietzsche and the Jews: Vis à vis Christendom and Nazism." In *Nietzsche and Jewish Culture,* edited by Jacob Golomb, 21–54. London: Routledge.

Savarkar, Vinayak Damodar. 1923. *Hindutva.* Bombay: Veer Savarkar Prakashan.

Schacht, Richard. 1983. *Nietzsche.* London: Routledge.

Schlegel, Friedrich. 1846. *Sämtliche Werke.* 15 vols. Vienna: I Klang.

———. 1906. *Seine prosaische Jugendschriften 1792–1802.* 2 vols. Edited by Jakob Minor. 2nd edition. Vienna: C. Konegan.

———. 1966. *Kritische-Friedrich-Schlegel-Ausgabe.* 24 vols. Edited by Ernst Behler. Munich: Ferdinand Schöningh.

———. 1977. *Über die Sprache und Weisheit der Indier.* Edited by S. Timparero. Amsterdam: John Benjamins.

Schwab, Raymond. 1950. *La Renaissance orientale.* Paris: Payot.

Seillière, Ernest. 1903. *Le Comte de Gobineau et l'Aryanisme historique.* Paris: Plon-Nourrit.

Sen, S.P. 1978. *Social Contents of Indian Religious Reform Movements.* Calcutta: Institute of Historical Studies.

————. 1979. *Social and Religious Reform Movements in the Nineteenth and Twentieth Centuries*. Calcutta: Institute of Historical Studies.

Sharma, Arvind. 1995. "The Aryan Question: Some General Considerations." In *The Indo-Aryans of Ancient South Asia: Language, Material Culture and Ethnicity*, edited by George Erdosy, 177–91. Berlin and New York: de Gruyter.

Shohat, Ella. 1992. "Notes on the Post-Colonial." *Social Text* 31/32: 99–113.

Slemon, Stephen. 1995. "Introductory Notes: Postcolonialism and its Discontents." *Ariel* 26: 7–23.

Smith, Brian K. 1989. *Reflections on Resemblance, Ritual and Religion*. New York: Oxford University Press.

Sonnerat, Pierre. 1782. *Voyage aux Indes orientales et à la Chine*. 2 vols. Paris: The author.

Spivak, Gayatri Chakravorty. 1988. "Can the Subaltern Speak." In *Marxism and the Interpretation of Culture*, edited by Cary Nelson and Lawrence Grossberg, Urbana: University of Illinois Press.

Sprung, Mervyn. 1991. "Nietzsche's Trans-European Eye." In *Nietzsche and Asian Thought*, edited by Graham Parkes, 76–90. Chicago: University of Chicago Press.

Stambaugh, Joan. 1972. *Nietzsche's Thought of the Eternal Return*. Baltimore, Md.: Johns Hopkins University Press.

Sunder Rajan, Rajeswari. 1997. "The Third World Academic in Other Places or, the Postcolonial Intellectual Revisited." *Critical Inquiry* 23: 596–616.

Thapar, Romila. 1966. *A History of India*. Vol. 1. London: Penguin.

————. 1990. *From Lineage to State: Social Formation in the Mid-First Millenium B.C. in the Gangetic Valley*. Delhi: Oxford University Press.

————. 1992. *Interpreting Early India*. Delhi: Oxford University Press.

Thomas, R. Hinton. 1983. *Nietzsche in German Politics and Society 1890–1918*. Manchester, U.K.: Manchester University Press.

Tilak, B.G. 1966. *Letters of Lokamanya Tilak*. Edited by M.D. Vidwans. Poona: Kesari Prakashan.

————. 1971. *The Arctic Home of the Vedas*. Poona: Tilak Brothers.

————. 1992. *Selected Documents of Lokamanya Bal Gangadhar Tilak.* Vol. 1. Edited by Ravindra Kumar. New Delhi: Anmol Publishers.

Tilak, B.G., and G.K. Gokhale. 1991. *Legislative Council: Compilations of Questions asked and Speeches Delivered.* Bombay: Bombay Legislative Council Government Publications.

Tull, Herman W. 1991. "F. Max Müller and A.B. Keith—Orientalism versus Indology—Twaddle, the Stupid Myth and the Disease of Indology." *Numen* 38, no. 1: 27–58.

Updesh Manjiri. 1976. Delhi: Dayānand Sanstha.

Van der Veer, Peter. 1995. "The Politics of Devotion to Râma." In *Bhakti Religion in North India,* edited by David N. Lorenzen, Albany.: State University of New York Press.

————. 1998. *Religious Nationalism: Hindus and Muslims in India.* Delhi: Oxford Univesity Press.

Vivekananda. 1991. *The Complete Works of Swami Vivekananda.* Calcutta: Advaita Ashram.

Voltaire. 1885. *Oeuvres complètes.* Paris: Garnier Frères.

————. 1953–65. *Correspondence.* Edited by Theodore Bestermann. Geneva: Institut et Musée Voltaire.

————. 1963. *Essai sur les moeurs et l'esprit des nations.* 2 vols. Paris: Garnier Frères.

Whisker, James Biser 1982. *The Social, Political and Religious Thought of Alfred Rosenberg: An Interpretive Essay.* Washington: University Press of America.

Whitney, W.D. 1987. *Oriental and Linguistic Studies.* 2 vols. Delhi: Sri Satguru.

Wolpert, Stanley A. 1962. *Tilak and Gokhale: Revolution and Reform in the Making of Modern India.* Berkeley: University of California Press.

Index